From Lynch Mobs to the Killing State

THE CHARLES HAMILTON HOUSTON INSTITUTE SERIES
ON RACE AND JUSTICE

The Charles Hamilton Houston Institute for Race and Justice
at Harvard Law School seeks to further the vision
of racial justice and equality through research,
policy analysis, litigation,
and scholarship,
and will place a special emphasis on the issues of voting rights,
the future of affirmative action,
the criminal justice system,
and related areas.

From Lynch Mobs to the Killing State

Race and the Death Penalty in America

EDITED BY

Charles J. Ogletree, Jr., and Austin Sarat

New York University Press

NEW YORK AND LONDON

NEW YORK UNIVERSITY PRESS
New York and London
www.nyupress.org

Library of Congress Cataloging-in-Publication Data
From lynch mobs to the killing state :
race and the death penalty in America /
edited by Charles J. Ogletree, Jr., and Austin Sarat.
p. cm.
(The Charles Hamilton Houston Institute series on race and justice)
Includes bibliographical references and index.
ISBN–13: 978–0–8147–4021–7 (cloth : alk. paper)
ISBN–10: 0–8147–4021–9 (cloth : alk. paper)
ISBN–13: 978–0–8147–4022–4 (pbk. : alk. paper)
ISBN–10: 0–8147–4022–7 (pbk. : alk. paper)
1. Discrimination in capital punishment—United States.
2. African American criminals—Civil rights. 3. Lynching—
United States. 4. Criminal justice, Administration of—United States.
I. Ogletree, Charles J. II. Sarat, Austin. III. Series.
KF9227.C2F76 2006
364.66089'96073—dc22 2005035414

New York University Press books are printed on acid-free paper,
and their binding materials are chosen for strength and durability.

Manufactured in the United States of America

c 10 9 8 7 6 5 4 3 2 1
p 10 9 8 7 6 5 4 3 2 1

To my son Mr. B.,
with the hope that someday he will live in a world
in which justice is truly blind to race.
(AS)

This book is dedicated to my granddaughters, Marquelle and Nia Mae,
two young African-American children who, it is hoped,
will live in a society where the matters raised in this book
are part of a distant past, and the burden of race
in the criminal justice system will be eliminated.
(CO)

Contents

Acknowledgments

This has been a genuinely collaborative effort, and we would like to say what a pleasure it has been for us to have this chance to work together and to work with the distinguished scholars who have contributed their work to help clarify the relationship of race and state killing. We would like to thank Colin Ovitsky for his stellar efforts in helping put this book together, as well as Alex Ewing, Chris Grohman, Adam Hardy, Lisa Willis, Anika Simmons, and Lauren Sudeall for their meticulous work in finding useful information for this book. We also would like to acknowledge the generous financial support provided by the Axel Shupf Fund for Intellectual Life at Amherst College.

Introduction

Charles J. Ogletree, Jr., and Austin Sarat

By now the connection between race and the killings of African-Americans, in particular through lynchings and the death penalty, is widely recognized among scholars, activists, and legal officials. As a result, saying that there is a long and deep connection between this country's racial politics and its uses of the killings of African-Americans through lynchings and the death penalty will come as a surprise to few. Indeed, one way to track this connection is by examining the recent history of the United States Senate's response to the history of lynching and the United States Supreme Court's death penalty jurisprudence. Prior to the summer of 2005, there had been palpable silence concerning this country's history of lynching. The House of Representatives had passed four antilynching bills and seven presidents, Republicans and Democrats, had repeatedly urged Congress to pass legislation making lynching a federal crime. These measures were consistently rebuffed by powerful southern senators who used the filibuster (ironically, the same way it was employed to prevent the desegregation of public schools) to prevent this legislation from ever receiving a formal vote.[1] Fortunately, in June 2005, the Senate voted to apologize formally for its failure to pass anti-lynching legislation. The Senate's recent apology is both admirable and regrettable. It is admirable in that there is finally a public acknowledgement of our history of lynching. It is regrettable in that occurred only after nearly five thousand reported lynchings, many of whom were African-American.

Starting with *Furman v. Georgia*, decided in 1972, the Court has confronted a series of cases in which petitioners have asserted that decisions throughout the system of capital punishment are illegitimately influenced by race. Sometimes the Court has acknowledged those claims; sometimes it has not. In the late 1970s, in *Maxwell v. Bishop* and *Coker v. Georgia*, statistical evidence was presented to the Court that showed that African-American defendants were being sentenced to death for the crime of rape as part of a racially discriminatory pattern.[2] The Court did not include this racial dynamic in its reasoning, but it did find that applying the death penalty for the crime of rape was grossly disproportionate and therefore unconstitutional.[3]

A decade later, in *McCleskey v. Kemp*, the Court held that statistics showing racial disparity in the imposition of the death penalty were "insufficient to demonstrate discriminatory intent or unconstitutional discrimination in the Fourteenth Amendment context, [and] insufficient to show irrationality, arbitrariness and capriciousness under any kind of Eighth Amendment analysis."[4] It is important to note, however, that the Court did not dispute the validity of the petitioner's statistical findings; instead, it said that the findings did not show with clear enough proof that the statistical anomaly was caused by racial discrimination within the system. Simply put, the Court held that although there appears to be a strong correlation between race and the death penalty, statistics alone cannot prove causation.[5]

For several decades social science studies of capital punishment have focused on the connection of race and capital punishment. Those studies, including the one that provided the basis for the *McCleskey* litigation, have documented a rather consistent pattern of racialization, showing, for example, powerful race-of-the-victim effects in the decisions about who will receive a death sentence. Furthermore, we know that of all the executions that have taken place in the United States since 1976, nearly 43% have been of defendants that were either black or Hispanic. Of current death row inmates, approximately 55% are either black or Hispanic.[6] Of all defendants sentenced to death since 1976, 81% of the victims in their cases have been white.[7] As a recent report by the Sentencing Project suggests, "[W]hile racial dynamics have changed over time, race still exerts an undeniable presence in the sentencing process."[8]

The legitimacy, if any, of the state's ultimate sanction depends on its fairness, its consistency with our deepest commitments to due process and equal treatment under law. Indeed over time, the trend in arguments about the death penalty has shifted from arguments about whether the death penalty can be justified on retributive or deterrence grounds to arguments about whether the accused in all cases has been adequately represented by counsel and other process-oriented arguments. At the same time, this shift has been accompanied by a general truncation of appellate review in capital cases, thereby making it all the more important to bring to light any potential biases in the administration of the death penalty. In this context, our book is an effort not so much to describe the fact of the race-capital punishment nexus but to show the ways that the death penalty is racialized, the places in the death penalty process where race makes a difference, and the ways the very meanings of race in the United States are constituted in and through our practices of capital punishment.

In addition to our effort to examine the ways race influences capital punishment, this book also attempts to situate the linkage between race and the death penalty in the history of this country.[9] Doing so reveals that the death penalty is, and has always been, rarely a punishment used objectively against those deserving of it; it has been instead a tool that has been used, throughout history, to oppress racial minorities, and specifically, African-Americans.[10] Today, the connection of race and the death penalty has become a substantial issue of national debate following former Illinois Governor George Ryan's decision to put a moratorium on the death penalty in that state and commute the sentences of all current death row inmates.[11] Governor Ryan explicitly questioned the effect race might be having in sentencing decisions when he discussed his reasons for stopping capital punishment in Illinois.[12] Since this decision, several other states have begun to examine the impact that race may have on local administration of the death penalty. For example, Pennsylvania has considered and Kentucky has enacted legislation that allows defendants to use statistical data to prove that race was a factor in the decision either to seek the death penalty in their cases or to ultimately impose a capital sentence.[13] Moreover, the former governor of Maryland placed a moratorium on the death penalty pending the outcome of a study by the University of Maryland on the fairness of the state's death penalty administration.[14]

The connection of race and the death penalty has been further thrust into the limelight by the recent proliferation of DNA testing. Spearheaded largely by Barry Scheck's Innocence Project, progressive groups in nearly every state have used DNA testing to exonerate death row inmates. Over the past five years, more than one hundred death row inmates have not only been removed from death row but freed from prison altogether due to the DNA testing of evidence stored from the original crime scenes proving conclusively that they were not the perpetrators.[15] Most of those who have been exonerated have been members of racial minorities. As they have left death row, they have provided the nation a vivid portrait of the racial composition of those given capital sentences. Also in recent years, courts have been taking race into consideration when reviewing sentencing decisions. Thus, Wilbert Rideau, a famed prison journalist, was granted a new trial when the Supreme Court overturned his conviction after nearly forty-two years on the grounds that blacks were completely excluded from his jury.[16]

In Congress, attention is now being given to the impact of race on capital punishment. Thus the Racial Justice Act (RJA) has twice passed the United States House of Representatives. That act would allow capital defendants to do what *McCleskey* forbids, namely, to challenge their death sentences by using statistical evidence of discriminatory impact and thereby raising an equal protection claim. In making such an "impact" claim under the RJA, defendants may demonstrate that within "the state in which they were convicted, a disproportionately higher number of one particular race is given the death penalty."[17]

This book appears at an important time in our national conversation about capital punishment. Indeed, it seems fair to say that we are now in a period of national reconsideration of the issue. This period has been marked by dramatic declines in the number of people receiving death sentences and the number of people being executed.[18] In addition, the Supreme Court has demonstrated increasing skepticism about the death penalty and its constitutionality in different contexts; as a result, the Court has begun to narrow its application. Thus, in 2002, it held that execution of the mentally retarded constitutes cruel and unusual punishment and is therefore prohibited by the Eighth Amendment.[19] Just a few years later, in *Roper v. Simmons*,[20] the Court narrowed the scope of the death penalty even further, declaring that the execution of juveniles who have committed a capital crime before the age of 18 is unconstitutional under the Eighth and Fourteenth Amendments.[21] In that holding, the Court relied on "the evolving standards of decency that mark the progress of a maturing society."[22] In both *Atkins* and *Roper*, the Court also referred to a "national consensus"[23] that has arisen against the death penalty in those two contexts. It is not a far leap for one to assume if a similar "national consensus" forms around the connection of race and the death penalty, that the Court might be willing to further scrutinize capital sentencing decisions where race can be shown to be a substantial contributing factor.

Three cases decided during the Supreme Court's 2004 term, *Miller-El v. Dretke*,[24] *Johnson v. California*,[25] and *Roper v. Simmons*[26] indicate that the

Supreme Court has begun to reevaluate the way the death penalty is applied and at the same time reexamine the process that has operated to produce all-white juries and sentence a disproportionate number of blacks to death. *Miller-El* and *Johnson* marked a revival of *Batson v. Kentucky*,[27] the case holding that excluding blacks because of their race denied both the defendant and the excluded jurors of equal protection of the laws.[28] Together, these cases suggest that race is once again at the forefront of the Court's thinking about the death penalty.

International law played a significant role in narrowing the scope of the death penalty. In *Roper v. Simmons,* which held the juvenile death penalty unconstitutional, the Court "referred to the laws of other countries and to international authorities as instructive for its interpretation of the Eighth Amendment's prohibition of 'cruel and unusual punishments.' "[30] Justice Kennedy, writing for the Court, noted "the overwhelming weight of international opinion against the juvenile death penalty."[31] He cited Article 37 of the United Nations Convention on the Rights of the Child, the laws of the United Kingdom, and the fact that only seven other countries in the world—Iran, Pakistan, Saudi Arabia, Yemen, Nigeria, the Democratic Republic of Congo, and China—had executed juvenile offenders since 1990.[32]

Combined with the Court's increasing willingness to refer to international norms, *Roper, Miller-El,* and *Johnson,* three cases from the Court's 2004–05 term, highlight what may be a progressive trend in the Court's death penalty jurisprudence. *Roper, Miller-El,* and *Johnson,* taken together, suggest that the Court has begun to rethink the groups to whom the death penalty is applied, as well as the role of race in the process by which it is applied. Because Justice O'Connor and the Chief Justice were not members of the *Roper* majority, even if Chief Justice Roberts and Justice O'Connor's replacement share Justice Scalia's views, both the holding and the Court's more expansive vision of rights informed by international norms should remain intact. While there is little evidence to indicate that the Court would reconsider the constitutionality of the death penalty, *Roper, Johnson,* and *Miller-El,* and the concept of rights prompting the Court's references to international law may serve as basis for a serious reexamination of race and the death penalty.

The Supreme Court also has demonstrated increasing frustration with lower courts, such as the Texas Court of Criminal Appeals, which stridently refuses to follow Supreme Court precedents in the death penalty context.[33] On June 13, 2005, a divided Supreme Court issued two surprising decisions.[34] Both involved African-American defendants convicted of crimes against white victims. Both were convicted of murder and in one case the defendant was sentenced to death. In an extraordinary rebuke of prosecutors, and to some extent of the judges who presided over these cases, the Court found that prosecutors had removed black jurors who were otherwise competent to serve on the juries. A largely conservative Court, seven of whose members had been appointed by Republican presidents, drew a line in the sand: race still matters in insuring that persons tried in America's courts receive a fair trial. Even in cases where the evidence against the defendant may be overwhelming, the government can't enhance its ability to obtain a conviction by denying qualified African-Americans the opportunity to serve on juries in cases where African-Americans are the defendants.

In addition, the Texas Court of Criminal Appeals and the United States Court of Appeals for the Fifth Circuit have both been targets of criticism in recent years "for denying appeals from prisoners seeking to overturn their death sentences" as well as their insistence on "going to great lengths to justify their decisions, even in the face of overwhelming evidence or contrary rulings from the Supreme Court."[35] Making the connection between this resistance and race explicit, a scholar likened the behavior of the Texas judges to that witnessed during "desegregation days."[36]

Individual Justices have also spoken publicly about their doubts about capital punishment. For example, Justice Sandra Day O'Connor was quoted in 2001 as noting that "[s]erious questions are being raised about whether the death penalty is being fairly administrated in this country."[37] She also expressed some concern about the system's potential for error, as indicated in our prior discussion of DNA testing: "If statistics are any indication, the system may well be allowing some innocent defendants to be executed."[38] Additionally, in recent years, Justice Stephen Breyer and Justice O'Connor have emphasized the importance of considering international legal standards in the area of capital punishment.[39] This trend in relying on international law was apparent in Justice Anthony Kennedy's opinion in *Roper* as well.[40] In conjunction with doubts about the death penalty's capability for fair and just administration expressed by state officials like Governor Ryan, such sentiments about the penalty's operation in the United States may signal its troubled and uncertain future.

The essays in this book speak to these doubts and this future, focusing in particular on the question of how and why the connection between race and the death penalty has been so strong throughout American history.

We do not believe that the connection can be explained through the examination of just one aspect of race or just one aspect of the death penalty system; rather, each aspect, from the jury's decision to invoke the death penalty, to the historical underpinnings of the death penalty itself, must be examined in order to understand the statistics that show such a strong link between race and the death penalty. Thus Part I, entitled "The Meaning and Significance of Race in the Culture of Capital Punishment," assesses the proposition that the death penalty has its historical origins in lynching and that the impetus behind mob-style justice persists in today's capital punishment system. Part II, "Race and the Death Penalty Process," focuses on how race and racial politics influence the decisions of actors in the death penalty process, especially juries, to apply the death penalty in particular cases. Part III, "Race, Politics, and the Death Penalty," seeks to move the discussion of race and the death penalty outside the purely legal context. It features essays that take a broader look at that relationship and concludes with an assessment of the significance of race in today's national reconsideration of capital punishment.

Part I, "The Meaning and Significance of Race in the Culture of Capital Punishment," begins with "Capital Punishment as Legal Lynching," by Timothy Kaufman-Osborn, who discusses how the death penalty developed from southern lynchings of suspected black criminals. Courts began to sentence defendants to death because they knew that angry mobs would try to achieve such results unlawfully if the courts did not do so. He contends that although the death penalty is a secret, ostensibly race-neutral process, it has served to perpetuate racial categories. Yet he contends that although some aspects of current execution may mirror lynchings of the past, it is important not to let this analogy obscure more pointed analysis. He argues that even though both acts, execution and lynching, help to solidify the racial subordination of African-Americans, the techniques used to accomplish the result are very different. The author concludes that the practices of due process do not make lynching and capital punishment identical but "mask the continued articulation of the racial contract within a polity that no longer openly espouses the rhetoric of white supremacy."

In the next essay, Charles Ogletree discusses the historical use of the death penalty as a discriminatory mechanism and, like Kaufman-Osborn, argues that racism still exists throughout our capital punishment system. Courts and legislatures have long tolerated the disparate impact of the death penalty, despite the obvious questions it raises regarding justice and fairness within our legal system. The impact exists based on the race of the victim as well as on the race of the defendant. However, the courts have rejected numerous statistical accounts of the disparity (as seen in *McCleskey v. Kemp*).

The death penalty in our country is historically and inextricably tied to race. Under slavery, the harsh penalties meted out to slaves reflected "white supremacy and fear, and allowed slaves to be put to death for transgressions ranging from helping a fellow slave escape to destroying property." These punishments were determined solely on the whim of the master. Postslavery, lynching became the new method for whites to quite literally control the lives of blacks. The next phase in American death penalty history moved to the courtrooms, where "legal lynchings" occurred. These proceedings had all the accessories of a fair trial—the courtroom, the judge, the jury. However, there was little fairness to be had for black defendants because "whites deferred to the courts, but remained ready to return to mob justice if the results were not favorable to them."

Like Kaufman-Osborn, Ogletree argues that although we may have more sophisticated accessories, our current death penalty system does little to counteract the old discriminatory impulses exemplified during the lynching phase of American history. *McCleskey* clearly invited the legislature to determine the issue of discrimination, but efforts to implement remedies have met with opposition. The proposed Racial Justice Act, which would allow defendants to seek judicial relief if their states administered the death penalty disproportionately, has not yet been enacted into law. Finally, citing declining international support for the death penalty (including its abolition in South Africa), Ogletree ends by noting that "the time has come to finally embrace the moral courage to reject the tolerance of racial discrimination in the application of capital punishment, and also to follow the lead of progressive nations throughout the world in shutting down the state-operated machinery of death."

Part I concludes with Stuart Banner's "Traces of Slavery: Race and the Death Penalty in Historical Perspective." Banner suggests that the death penalty is haunted by the continuing specter of racial subordination in the United States—"of black victims lynched by white mobs, of black defendants condemned by white juries, of slave codes and public hangings." Understanding the racial history of capital punishment may help to elucidate the continuing importance of these images. Banner asserts that "for most of American history, capital crimes were defined unequally divided by race." This practice of discrimination, as well as the ceremonial and public nature of the executions helped to "reinforce the racial hierarchy."

Early in our history, state governments instituted separate punishments for blacks and whites, with blacks being subjected much more often to the capital penalty. Banner notes that there were two other methods for eliminating convicted blacks from society, lynching or deportation. After the Civil War, though, these methods were outlawed, as were unequal sentencing statutes. However, instead of creating true reform, this simply led to an effort to mask racial disparities and create a façade of a race-neutral justice. In such a system, one method of ensuring racially unequal sentences was "by vesting capital sentencing discretion in all-white juries," guaranteeing harsher sentences for black defendants. Capital sentencing became a useful tool to maintain racial subordination under the guise of formal equality.

Banner concludes by noting an interesting shift in the race-death penalty nexus. In the 1960s and '70s, opposition to capital punishment was used in the battle against racial disparities in general. Today, in contrast, racial disparities are used to condemn the capital punishment system as a whole.

Part II, "Race and the Death Penalty Process," examines the effect of race in today's death penalty process, focusing in particular on the role of the capital jury. The beginning essay takes a broad view of one death penalty system. Glenn L. Pierce and Michael L. Radelet analyze legal and extralegal factors in the death penalty system of Illinois, using statistical data they gathered from various criminal agencies. The extralegal factors include sex of offender and victim, race of offender and victim, and geographic region.

Pierce and Radelet found that cross-regional differences, sex of murder victim, and race of victim were all statistically significant. The authors also note that although it first appears that black offenders are less likely to receive a death sentence, "it is important to also control for the race of the victim." Seeing the data in this light shows that "blacks are most likely to be convicted for killing other blacks, and the murders of black victims are the least likely to receive a death sentence."

In "Death in 'Whiteface': Modern Race Minstrels, Death Penalty Judgments, and the Culture of American Apartheid," Benjamin Fleury-Steiner grapples with how racial prejudice enters the jury room. He examines stories told by capital jurors in an effort to analyze the effect on death penalty sentencing of the "ideology or broad belief system grounded in the idea that the poor nonwhite or 'white trash' others are innately prone to irresponsibility and immorality." He asserts that in order to fulfill jury expectations, jurors must don a "white face," identifying themselves with the class of privilege and solidifying their own identity by defining the "other" as their polar opposite. Juries, behind closed doors, are able to "keep the nefarious tradition of minstrelizing the other *alive*."

The minstrel shows of the nineteenth century were as much about "communicating stories of dominant-subordinate racial *identities*" as they were tools for demeaning blacks. Today, however, overt acts of racism are no longer as commonplace in the justice system. Instead, Fleury-Steiner asserts, the racism that is unseen or unsaid is "driven by *implied* ideological representations minus the blatantly racist, cork-painted face that was synonymous with Jim Crow–era black face minstrel performances."

The criminal black minstrel narrative is an often-relied-upon stereotype in jury sentencing decisions, and just as during the pre-civil-rights era, this narrative tells the story that "whites are law-abiding and blacks are lawless." Creating and heeding this narrative of black lawlessness "serves to legitimize America's excessively punitive war on economically and racially marginalized outsiders." Specifying blacks as inherently criminal "has been an indispensable way for political elites to justify the 'dangers' of black crime as it simultaneously reinvests . . . in white suburban privilege."

The juror stories collected by Fleury-Steiner exhibit the tenacity of these images in current American thought. The racialization of the defendant is a way for the juror to help identify and assimilate the defendant's identity into the juror's schema. Mitigating factors, such as a language barrier or a history of abuse, are not significant to the white-faced juror and can be seen as threatening to his sense of the defendant's individual responsibility. The death penalty provides an arena within which these minstrelized narratives operate in our criminal justice system. Fleury-Steiner concludes that "[t]he death penalty forces jurors into an endless and, indeed, arbitrary game of privileging one life over another."

Mona Lynch concludes Part II by trying to understand further the dynamics of racialization in death penalty juries. Lynch notes that stereotyping of the kind described by Fleury-Steiner operates below the level of consciousness, a circumstance that renders impossible its removal from the jury sentencing process. Modern prejudice is especially insidious in that it veils itself with the formalities of the law, masking its previously overt nature.

Lynch lists four elements of the capital system that leave room for the articulation of subconscious racism. First, the capital jury selection process allows for a demographically skewed group of people more likely to "hold racial stereotypes and biased attitudes about people of color." Second, the nature of capital trials "involves violence and often other forms of serious criminal behavior [and] feeds into cultural stereotypes about several ethnic groups." While some stereotypes of blacks have faded, their purported "inherently violent nature" is one that has held strong over time. Third, the ambiguous nature of death-sentencing allows room for aversive racism to flourish (aversive racism espouses egalitarian beliefs but engages in racism under "nonracial" auspices). Fourth, because empathy plays a large role in sentencing, generalized racism will prevent jurors from empathizing with the defendant, and will affect the way jurors view mitigating evidence.

To test these hypotheses, Lynch reports the results of an experiment whereby laypersons were shown footage of a simulated capital trial but were told was a real trial. Investigators manipulated the footage to vary the race of the defendant and the victim, and then asked the test subjects to render their decisions based on the evidence of the crime, as well as the aggravating and mitigating evidence presented. Some were asked to give an individual judgment; others were grouped into "juries." The test was designed to determine if, "in this complex, yet ambiguous, decision-making task, race of defendant and race of victim would have an impact on penalty decision."

Lynch asserts that these findings show the "pervasive influence of cultural stereotypes about race." Even more, with the pretense of "guided discretion," jurors are able to "rationalize that the law and the guidelines have led them to the outcome they have chosen." She concludes that the law clings to the traditional model of overt racism and continues to ignore the very different and subtle modern racism that pervades our capital system today.

Part III, "Race, Politics, and the Death Penalty," moves beyond the legal process to broaden our understanding of ways to think about and combat the racialization of capital punishment. It begins with Stephen Bright's "Discrimination, Death, and Denial: The Tolerance of Racial Discrimination in Infliction of the Death Penalty." Bright argues that the legal safeguards in our capital punishment system, "are either nonexistent or inadequate." To combat racism, *McCleskey* relied upon the right to a representative jury, prohibition of peremptory challenges on the basis of race, and the right to question jurors regarding potential bias in interracial crimes. However, as Bright asserts, these rights are not being enforced, and even when they are, are not strict enough to combat the kind of racism described by Fleury-Steiner, Lynch, and others. Moreover, the historical racism of the death penalty cannot be ignored because it is one of America's "most prominent vestiges of slavery and racial violence."

Bright outlines many studies as well as specific cases that show the racism faced by black defendants. Within the death penalty system, blacks are present often only as defendants because "even in many areas with substantial minority populations, all of the judges and prosecutors are white." Voting jurisdictions are drawn to dilute minority votes; juror commissions help keep blacks out of the jury pools; and minorities are excluded from top positions in law enforcement. Unconscious racism is extremely dangerous to the capital system in that it is very hard to detect. A juror may have a latent fear of blacks, thus making conviction or a death sentence a more likely outcome.

Although there is popular support for the death penalty, Bright argues that we must not expedite executions lest we undermine the foundations of our entire legal system. "Courts cannot deliver justice when they tolerate prejudice and racial exclusion." He says that courts must officially recognize the discrimination because "[s]ilence about racial discrimination in capital cases will only allow it to continue to fester." Once it is acknowledged, we can begin to consider the rearrangements in our society and politics that will be necessary to begin to come to terms with it.

We conclude this book by considering the place of race in today's abolitionist politics. In "The Rhetoric of Race in the 'New Abolitionism,' " Austin Sarat declares that traditional abolitionists opposed the death penalty on three principles closely associated with humanist liberalism or political radicalism: (1) the sanctity of life (all humans are to be treated with dignity, even criminals); (2) "the moral horror, the 'evil,' of the state willfully taking the lives of any of its citizens"; and (3) death is always a cruel punishment. Today's abolitionism, instead, turns on the legal precepts of due process and equal protection. Central to both forms of abolitionism has been the question of racial inequalities in death sentencing.

After *Furman,* which halted all executions, an intense pro-capital-punishment backlash occurred, and the Supreme Court reversed its position in *Gregg,* allowing executions to continue with certain procedural safeguards. Pro-capital-punishment sentiment, until recently, has been on the rise, making the work of abolitionists extremely difficult. Procedural safeguards have been stripped as the public grew impatient with the small number of executions and the slow pace of the appeals system. On all this, the new abolitionist seeks to "change the subject from the legitimacy of execution to the imperatives of due process."

Long after *Furman*, Justice Harry Blackmun became a leading voice for the new abolitionism, declaring boldly that he would "no longer tinker with the machinery of death."[41] He had determined that the goals of consistency and individuality could not be attained simultaneously. Race was the center of his attention. He noted that the guided discretion formula provided for in *Gregg* allowed the racial prejudices in society to infect the justice system.

The American Bar Association embraced the principles of new abolitionism when it "called for a complete moratorium on executions in the United States." Taking a somewhat optimistic approach, like Blackmun, the ABA implied that the death penalty, as *currently administered*, is unconstitutional—apparently leaving open the possibility of a reformed, constitutional death penalty scheme at some future time. However, Sarat asserts that this is effectively "a call for the abolition, not merely the cessation, of capital punishment." The reforms for which the ABA holds out hope for are simply impossible in light of the "pervasiveness of racial prejudice throughout the society combined with the wide degree of discretion necessary to afford individualized justice." The ABA's action lends "legitimation to the new abolitionism, and the basis for a nationwide moratorium movement."

Sarat views the actions of Illinois Governor George Ryan as a "powerful expression of the new abolitionism." In January 2000, Ryan declared a moratorium on all executions and then subsequently commuted all death row sentences. He remarked upon the pervasiveness of race in the death penalty system but leaned most heavily on the notion of condemning innocent men and women. His attention to the subject has helped provide "new abolitionists with their most powerful rhetorical weapon and a springboard to other issues." The moratorium announcement helped fuel the debate about race and capital punishment, but Sarat contends that with it, "wrongful conviction, not race, became the central element" of new abolitionism.

The place of race in death penalty debate has shifted since the times of *Furman*. Governor Ryan's reliance on innocence has "diminished the importance of race in new abolitionist rhetoric." The shift is necessary, according to Sarat, in order to "transcend the usual political and ideological divides" that the issue of race tends to create. He cautions, however, that new abolitionists "must resist the temptation to further marginalize the discourse of race in their rhetoric and politics," and must also use "the practices of capital punishment to highlight the role that the state has played, and continues to play, in the constitution of race relations."

Today the death penalty is the new "peculiar institution" of American society. Its advocates proclaim that it is doled out only to the guilty. However, statistics illuminate an abyss between the number of minority executions relative to the minority population as a whole; the fact that the vast majority of capital defendants are charged with crimes against whites; and the overwhelming numbers of innocent men freed from death row in recent years who were from minority groups. Race and the death penalty have been, and continue to be, deeply entangled. When these facts are looked at in light of the amount of discretion that is involved in the capital sentencing process from the time of arrest through the time of sentencing, it is hard not to conclude that in the future race will continue to pervade the process. From the racial profiling that occurs before an arrest, to the prosecutorial decision of whether to seek the death penalty, to the peremptory challenges of jurors, to the final decision of whether to impose the death penalty, there are many opportunities for prejudice to infect the system.

The chapters in this book illustrate the various ways that the death penalty is racialized, address the reasons for the profound impact of race on the death penalty, and highlight the blight that the racially discriminatory application of the death penalty has placed on the United States. Together, they invite and foster discussion of a persistent problem that we no longer have the luxury of ignoring.

NOTES

1. Sheryl Gay Stolberg, *Senate Issues Apology Over Failure on Antilynching Law*, N.Y. TIMES, June 14, 2005.

2. *See Maxwell v. Bishop*, 398 U.S. 262 (1971) and *Coker v. Georgia*, 433 U.S. 584 (1977).

3. *See id.*

4. *Id.* at 289 (quoting *McCleskey v. Kemp*, 753 F.2d 877, 891 (11th Cir. 1985)) (alteration in original). As an example of the drastic claims of disproportionality that were nonetheless found unacceptable under *McCleskey*, see *Stephens v. State*, 456 S.E.2d

560, 561 (Ga. 1995) (finding insufficient for federal and state due process and equal protection challenges Stephens's evidence that "[i]n Hall County, where Stephens was convicted, the trial court found that one hundred percent of the persons serving a life sentence [were] African-American, although African-Americans make up less than ten percent of the county population and approximately fifty to sixty percent of the persons arrested in drug investigations. Relying on evidence provided by the State Board of Pardons and Paroles, the trial court also found that 98.4 percent of the persons serving life sentences for drug offenses were African-American, although African-Americans comprise only 27 percent of the state's population.").

5. *McCleskey*, 481 U.S. at 297 n.7.

6. http://www.aclu.org/DeathPenalty/DeathPenalty.cfm?ID=9312&c=62 and http://www.deathpenaltyinfo.org/article.php?scid=5&did=184.

7. *Id.* at 7.

8. The Sentencing Project, Racial Disparity in Sentencing: A Review of the Literature 1 (Mark Mauer, ed., 2005).

9. *See, e.g.*, Jesse Jackson et al., Legal Lynching: The Death Penalty and America's Future 72 (2001) ("[T]here is a special relationship between the death penalty and African-Americans, a relationship going back to antebellum days, when the gallows was a means of punishing slaves, and on through the worst years of Jim Crow.").

10. "The death penalty is a direct descendant of lynching and other forms of racial violence and racial oppression in America." Stephen B. Bright, *Discrimination, Death, and Denial: Race and the Death Penalty, in* Machinery of Death: The Reality of America's Death Penalty Regime 45 (David R. Dow & Mark Dow, eds., 2002).

11. For an analysis of Ryan's decision, see Austin Sarat, Mercy on Trial: What It Means to Stop an Execution (2005). *See* Jeffrey L. Kirchmeier, *Another Place Beyond Here: The Death Penalty Moratorium Movement in the United States,* 73 U. Colo. L. Rev. 1 (2002) (maintaining that Governor Ryan's decision was not based on a moral opposition to the death penalty but, rather, on concerns about systemic problems, and that 66 percent of Illinois residents approved of the governor's moratorium).

12. *See* Amnesty International, *United States of America: Death by Discrimination—The Continuing Role of Race in Capital Cases* (April 2003).

13. For example, a Pennsylvania committee recommended that the state legislature pass a racial justice act and commission studies to scrutinize the impact that a victim's race may have on a jury's decision to put a defendant to death. Kentucky has also enacted its own version of the Racial Justice Act, which allows defendants in capital cases to use statistical evidence of racial discrimination to demonstrate that race influenced the decision to seek the death penalty. Amnesty International USA, Death Penalty Facts: Racial Prejudices, available at http://www.amnestyusa.org/abolish/racialprejudices.html.

14. Maggie Mulvihill & Franci Richardson, *It's Time for Age of Innocence: A Call for Commission on Wrongful Convictions*, BOSTON HERALD, May 7, 2004, available at http://news.bostonherald.com/localRegional/view.bg?articleid=22001.

15. http://www.innocenceproject.org/.

16. http://www.deathpenaltyinfo.org/newsanddev.php?scid=5.

17. In Senate hearings, the proposed bill was referred to as the so-called Racial Justice Act: opponents of the bill said that "the racial quota death penalty provision—the so-called Racial Justice Act is really a death penalty abolition act." 140 Cong. Rec. S-12269, 103rd Cong., 2d Sess. (1994).

18. Data available from the Death Penalty Information Center, http://www .deathpenaltyinfo.org.

19. *Atkins v. Virginia*, 536 U.S. 304 (2002).

20. 125 S. Ct. 1183 (2005).

21. *Id.* at 1200.

22. *Trop v. Dulles*, 356 U.S. 86, 100–01 (1958).

23. *Roper*, 125 S. Ct. at 1191–92.

24. 125 S. Ct. 2317 (2005).

25. 125 S. Ct. 2410 (2005).

26. 125 S. Ct. 1183 (2005).

27. 106 S. Ct. 1712 (1986).

28. *Id.* at 1716.

29. *Roper*, 125 S. Ct. at 1200.

30. *Id.* at 1198.

31. *Id.*

32. *Id.* at 1199.

33. *See* Linda Greenhouse, *Justices Give Second Hearing in a Texas Death Row Case*, N.Y. TIMES, Dec. 7, 2004 ("In the intervening two years [before the Miller-El case], the Supreme Court has made clear its growing unease with the administration of the death penalty in Texas and its exasperation with the state and federal courts that hear appeals from the state's death row.").

34. *Johnson v. California* (125 S. Ct. 2410); *Miller-El v. Dretke* (125 S. Ct. 2317)

35. *Id.*

36. Cragg Hines, *Supremes to Texas Appeals Court: You Still Don't Get It*, HOUSE CHRON., Nov. 21, 2004.

37. *See* http://www.cbsnews.com/stories/2001/07/03/supremecourt/main299592 .shtml.

38. *Id.*

39. *See, e.g.,* O'Connor Speech Puts Foreign Law Center Stage, Jonathan Ringel, *Fulton County Daily Report* 10-31-2003, available at http://www.law.com/ jsp/newswire_article.jsp?id=1067350962318 (maintaining that international decisions should be persuasive authority in American courts). Justice Breyer has repeatedly demonstrated a reliance on international law in such contexts. *See, e.g.,*

Knight v. Florida, 528 U.S. 990 (1999) (Breyer, J. dissenting from the denial of certorari) ("A growing number of courts outside the United States—*courts that accept or assume the lawfulness of the death penalty*—have held that lengthy delay in administering a *lawful* death penalty renders ultimate execution inhuman, degrading, or unusually cruel.").

40. See *Roper*, 125 S. Ct at 1198 ("Our determination that the death penalty is disproportionate punishment for offenders under 18 finds confirmation in the stark reality that the United States is the only country in the world that continues to give official sanction to the juvenile death penalty.").

41. See *Callins v. Collins*, 510 U.S. 1141, 1145 (1994).

Part I

The Meaning and Significance of Race in the Culture of Capital Punishment

Lynching of Thomas Shipp and Abram Smith. August 7, 1930, Marion, Indiana.
Without Sanctuary plate 31. *Courtesy of the Allen-Littlefield Collection.*

Chapter 1

Capital Punishment as Legal Lynching?

Timothy V. Kaufman-Osborn

I. Introduction

In the early morning hours of August 7, 1930, three African-American men, Tom Shipp, Abe Smith, and James Cameron, confessed to the murder of Claude Deeter, a 24-year-old white factory worker, and to the rape of his 18-year-old companion, Mary Ball. That evening, enraged by the sight of Deeter's bloody shirt, which police had hung from a window in city hall, a band of local residents broke into the Grant County jail, overwhelmed Sheriff Jake Campbell and his deputies, and removed the three teenagers from their cells. After hanging Shipp from the window bars of his cell, they forced Smith to run through a gauntlet whose members tore off most of his clothing and then hanged him from the limb of a maple tree at the northeast corner of Courthouse Square. Returning to the jail, several men cut down Shipp's body, carried it to the square, and, after hoisting his corpse alongside that of his friend, attempted but failed to light a fire aimed at incinerating both. James Cameron was spared only because someone, possibly Mary Ball's uncle, or perhaps the head of the local American Legion, climbed atop a car parked on the square and insisted that he was innocent, thereby affording Sheriff Campbell an opportunity to return Cameron to his cell. Sometime after midnight, but before daybreak, on Friday, August 8, when the bodies of Shipp and Smith were cut down, local photographer Lawrence Beitler captured the scene in the heart of downtown Marion, Indiana.[1]

Sixty-four years later, on December 5, 1994, local members of Amnesty International organized a protest against the imminent execution of Gregory Resnover, an African-American convicted of conspiring to murder and then murdering a white Indianapolis police officer in 1980. Standing on the steps of the Indiana Statehouse, Resnover's attorney, Robert Hammerle, noted that even the former chief deputy prosecutor for Marion County now agreed that the trial record reviewed by the state Supreme Court contained numerous factual errors, including the statement that Resnover's fingerprints had been found on two weapons fired at the officer. Moreover, Hammerle proceeded, Resnover's original attorney had failed to introduce any witnesses during the sentencing phase of the trial, and had later been found incompetent by the state's highest court after it reversed the conviction of the one other individual he had represented in a capital case: "In the old South," Hammerle concluded, "they didn't pretend to give you due process. We're pretending to give Gregory Resnover due process and that makes this death more diabolical." Resnover's three brothers then read from a letter recently sent by Gregory to several state officials: "Society as a whole needs to be certain that you are convinced beyond doubt that racism played no role in my case. Show them that you are certain." Finally, to drive home their brother's point, Kevin, Steve, and Dwight held aloft an enlarged version of the photograph taken by Lawrence Beitler in 1930.[2] Four days later, Gregory Resnover was executed by means of electrocution at the Indiana state prison in Michigan City.

The purpose of this essay is to explore the sense and adequacy of the charge that was implicitly leveled when Gregory Resnover's brothers displayed the photograph of Tom Shipp and Abe Smith. As I understand it, that accusation contends that because racism continues to taint the criminal justice system, the contemporary execution of African-Americans and, more particularly, African-American men is akin to the lynchings that occurred throughout the United States, but especially in the South, in the era roughly delimited by the end of Reconstruction and the onset of World War II. As Stephen Bright, director of the Southern Center for Human Rights, puts the point: "The death penalty is a direct descendant of lynching and other forms of racial violence and racial oppression in America."[3] To the extent that this indictment is accurate, it renders problematic the tale many of us would like to be able to tell ourselves about America's consolidation of the due process protections that are said to secure a categorical distinction between the extralegal violence of lynching and the legal violence of capital punishment.[4] There is, I grant, good reason to reject this Whiggish tale, and I will indicate why that is so in what follows. Yet, it is equally true that appropriation of the category of lynching to make sense of the contemporary practice of capital punishment, as with all categories, conceals as much as it reveals. Specifically, identification of these two practices draws attention away from the ways that capital punishment, as now conducted in the United States, occludes what lynching accomplished all too well. Whereas lynchings visibly marked the bodies of its victims as black and so reconsolidated the color line that was indispensable to the reproduction of racial subordination, key elements of the contemporary practice of capital punishment veil that line and so render its contribution to racial subordination more difficult to apprehend and so to contest.

In section II, I establish a theoretical context for my analysis by appropriating an argument advanced by Charles Mills. That argument suggests that the liberal social contract of the United States has always been underwritten by what Mills calls "the racial contract," and hence racist practices, including lynching, are not aberrations from this nation's true principles but, rather, manifestations of its abiding commitment to sustain the conditions of racial exploitation. In section III, I advance a very selective history of lynching following Reconstruction. Here, my inquiry is confined to two aspects of this practice: first, in part A, the character of many lynchings during this era as highly ritualized public spectacles, which, I argue, transformed formally emancipated African-American men into racially marked and hence resubordinated subjects of white power; and, second, in part B, the permeability of the boundary between, on the one hand, the bands of white citizens who typically instigated such lynchings and duly authorized agents of law enforcement, on the other. In the penultimate section (IV), I inquire into the usefulness of the category of lynching as a way of articulating the contemporary relationship between race and capital punishment. In the first part of that section, corresponding to part A of section III, I ask how capital punishment, now conducted not as a public ritual but as a rationalized administrative procedure hidden from view, constructs a body that better coheres with the imperatives of the liberal social contract, but in doing so masks its participation in the replication of racial subordination. In the second part of that section, corresponding to part B of section III, I suggest that capital punishment, as practiced today, better meets liberalism's requirement that the official realm be neatly segregated from the unofficial, but in doing so once again obscures the state's complicity in the constitution of racial power. Finally, and very briefly, in the conclusion (V), I explain why my argument suggests the problematic character of any effort to remedy the racist character of capital punishment from within the confines of liberal political doctrine.

II. The Racial Polity

To establish a theoretical context for this inquiry, I begin with a schematic account of an argument advanced by Charles Mills in *The Racial Contract* and subsequently elaborated in *Blackness Visible*. The central premise of Mills's argument is that "the United States has historically been, and in some ways continues to be, a racial polity, a political system predicated on nonwhite subordination."[5] On this account, the liberal social contract implicit in the Declaration of Independence, the Constitution, and elsewhere has been and still is underwritten by a racial contract whose general terms can be read off legally codified institutions (e.g., slavery), formal government acts (e.g., Jim Crow laws), unofficial modes of official conduct (e.g., racial profiling by law enforcement officers), informal practices in the private sphere (e.g., patterns of residential segregation), theoretical discourses (e.g., biologistic accounts of racial inferiority), pernicious stereotypes (e.g., regarding the criminal propensities of young black men), and so on. The central purpose of the racial contract is to secure and ratify limitations on the freedoms, rights, and privileges of those whose exploitation is a condition of the freedoms, rights, and privileges of the superordinate group. Racial domination, on this account, cannot be understood as an unfortunate departure from a norm of universal equalitarianism, for, from its very inception, the United States has been "a system for which racially determined structural advantage and handicap are foundational."[6]

Within a liberal political order formally committed to an ideal of equal citizenship, ratification of such subordination has been accomplished, Mills argues, through generation and ongoing activation of a distinction between "persons" and "subpersons." In the United States, perhaps the most obdurate materialization of this distinction has been that between white and black, where racial identity is understood "as a *politically constructed categorization*," "the marker of locations of privilege and disadvantage in a set of power relationships."[7] The racialized category of subperson, Mills continues, has been differently defined at different moments in American history, depending on whether its members have been identified with the nonhuman (e.g., the animal); the innately inferior but human (e.g., the "colored," who, by nature, are lazy and shiftless); the permanently immature but human (e.g., the Negro as child); the formally equal but nonwhite human (e.g., the "persons of color" through reference to which whiteness is known as such); and so forth. No matter what its exact formulation, however, members of the category of persons are considered full citizens, and, as such, deemed eligible for uncircumscribed participation in the mythic contract that founds a liberal political order, and so full civil status in that order once created. Subpersons, in contrast, are either excluded altogether from participation in that contract, as under slavery, or relegated to an inferior, marginalized, or suspect status that compromises their standing as members fully eligible for the freedoms, rights, and privileges enjoyed by persons.

On Mills's account, the disposition of American history may be understood, at least in part, as a product of the relationship assumed between the social and racial contracts at any given moment in time. As I have already indicated, the wrong way to construe this relationship is to think of racial subordination as a regrettable deviation from the universalistic principles of the social contract, and to conclude that, as such, this form of oppression is destined to disappear as liberalism progresses toward complete realization of its essential ideals. That noted, to the extent that the category of subpersons has sometimes been subject to challenge by its members and their allies, to the extent that the boundary dividing this group from that of persons has sometimes proven permeable, to the extent that the liberal state has sometimes been compelled to acknowledge and respond to the tension between the formal equality mandated by the terms of the social contract and its complicity in maintaining the conditions of the racial polity, to that extent has the relationship between these two contracts, and so between black and white, proven susceptible to rearticulation. "The Racial Contract," Mills writes, "is *continuously being rewritten* to create different forms of the racial polity," which means in turn that "the effective force of the social contract itself changes, and the kind of cognitive dissonance between the two alters."[8]

To illustrate, in the South prior to the Civil War, so long as the enslavement of blacks was codified in law, so long as white supremacy was openly proclaimed, there was little reason to doubt that the social contract applied to whites only, and so the relationship between it and its racial counterpart proved relatively unproblematic. However, as I shall explain in greater detail in the following section, when that structure of domination lost its de jure character, when political and civil rights were formally extended to emancipated male slaves, the category of persons was no longer officially coextensive with that of whites. Consequently, obfuscation of the tension between an abstract, i.e., formally color-blind, conception of citizenship and various institutions that actively participated in the construction of "colored" individuals required a different and less transparent set of practices, legal and otherwise. Barely less transparent than slavery, for example, were those post-Reconstruction laws, which, dispensing with any façade of statutory neutrality, expressly excluded blacks from participation in certain practices definitive of citizenship (e.g., jury duty). Somewhat less transparent were the various mechanisms devised in the post-Reconstruction South to disenfranchise blacks without technically violating the Fourteenth and Fifteenth Amendments, including poll taxes, grandfather clauses, and literacy tests. Through these means, the neutrality of the liberal state was formally upheld, as demanded by the social contract, without in any significant way challenging the racial polity.

Today, re-creation of the racial contract in the United States requires ongoing negotiation of the tension between the social contract's formally color-blind principles and the color-coded practices, which, although necessary to white superordination, must now do their work in a state of relative (but not complete) invisibility. The capacity of such invisibility to veil the workings of the racial contract is enhanced, Mills argues, by the "epistemology of ignorance"[9] that is often evinced by those who benefit from the racial contract but whose self-conception renders them unable to recognize, let alone to acknowledge, that they do so. This epistemology can assume many forms, including racially coded language (e.g., talk of "welfare queens"), statutory proxies for more direct forms of racial oppression (e.g., longer sentences for crack as opposed to powder cocaine users), hostility to government policies on the grounds that they are harmful to their intended beneficiaries (e.g., neoconservative opposition to affirmative action), and, perhaps most significantly, obfuscation of the distinctive history of African-Americans by formally assimilating them to the general category of persons and so denying that the category of subperson, no matter how unlike the form it assumed under slavery or following Reconstruction, remains a living reality: "The danger of the universalist and colorless language of personhood is that it too easily slips over from the normative to the descriptive, thus covertly representing as an already achieved reality what is at present only an ideal, and failing to register the embedded structures of differentiated treatment and dichotomized moral psychology that 'subpersonhood' captures."[10] The epistemology of ignorance is most effective and, as Gregory Resnover's attorney put it, most "diabolical" when it either elides altogether the history of racial domination in the United States, or, alternatively, when it concedes that history but denies it any role in the constitution of the present. It is this latter contention that is challenged by those who, joining Resnover's brothers, insist that the contemporary practice of capital punishment, when directed against African-American men, is lynching conducted under the guise of law.

III. Spectacle Lynchings

In this section, I explore the post-Reconstruction articulation of the relationship between social and racial contracts, as that articulation was manifest in the conduct of lynchings. The first of the two parts in this section asks how what came to be known as "spectacle lynchings" participated in the generation of the class of subpersons (and, reciprocally, the class of persons as well). The second asks how the conduct of lynchings, spectacle and otherwise, often affirmed the racial contract by violating or, perhaps better, by paying no heed to the distinction drawn by the social contract between the law's official violence and its unofficial counterpart.

A. Making Bodies Black

Prior to the Civil War, only rarely were the punishments imposed under what had come to be known as "Lynch's Law" specifically capital.[11] The most commonly inflicted extralegal penalties during the later decades of the eighteenth and the first half of the nineteenth century included whipping, tarring and feathering, beating, and sometimes expulsion from the community. This was true in the North (although, with increasing frequency, after 1850, vigilante groups adopted hanging as a method of punishment in the territories of the West); and it was equally true in the South, where, except for the crime of murder, slaves were often whipped but only occasionally executed, whether legally or extralegally, for the obvious reason that they were highly valued commodities.

Only during and after Reconstruction did the term "lynching" come to acquire its contemporary connotations, which characteristically include the punishment of death, the targeting of African-Americans, and, more specifically, African-American men, chiefly in the South, and absent due process of law.[12] Whether explained as a response to increased economic competition experienced by lower-class whites, or as retaliation for efforts at black political organization, or as punishment for the real or alleged crime of rape, or as a symptom of a premodern culture predicated on a chivalrous code of honor, or as a misdirected reprisal against Northern intervention, or as sacrificial atonement for the collective guilt incurred through loss of the Civil War, or as a means of reaffirming an endangered form of white masculine identity,[13] during the half century following the withdrawal of Federal troops in 1877, lynching became a lethal means of regenerating the racial contract once the racial polity could no longer be secured through the institution of chattel slavery. As such, it was part and parcel of a more comprehensive set of practices, including denial of access to education, race-specific codes of etiquette, systems of economic marginalization, especially debt peonage, and methods of political disenfranchisement, including denial of the right to vote and to serve on juries, that re-created the category of subpersons, but absent the legally codified construction of blacks as private property.

Although lynching, like slavery, helped to secure the racial polity, the differences between these two practices (like that between lynching and contemporary capital punishment) should not be elided. As I noted in the preceding section, so long as blacks remained slaves, so long as white supremacy remained the law of the land, membership in the racial and social contracts remained fully coextensive. That equation was disrupted, however, by Emancipation and, more particularly, by the Civil Rights Act of 1866, which conferred the rights of citizenship on freed male slaves, thereby removing them from the status of property and formally including them within the social contract.

Lynching responded to this rearticulation of the relationship between the racial and social contracts, and it did so by imposing on its victims a stark and all-consuming corporeal identity. That identity reduced lynching's targets, as well as the race they mimetically represented, to the status of mute black bodies, which, as such, were available for discursive construction in terms that reconsolidated the racial polity. By effectively equating the meaning of blackness with the predatory, the savage, the animalistic, the hypersexualized, lynchings demonstrated the patent ineligibility of those so marked to inhabit the category of citizen, while it simultaneously recertified the identity of those defined not by their degraded corporeality but by their white personhood and so their exclusive occupation of that same category.[14] As Mills puts the point, although not expressly in reference to lynching, "if the Racial Contract creates its signatories, those party to the Contract, by constructing them as 'white persons,' it also tries to make its victims, the objects of the Contract, *into* the 'nonwhite subpersons' it specifies."[15]

Just how post-Reconstruction lynchings marked the objects of the racial contract is perhaps best illustrated by what came to be known as "spectacle lynchings," which garnered far more publicity than did any other sort during the decades between 1880 and 1930.[16] Consider the following incident, one of many that might be cited:

> Accused of raping and killing Myrtle Vance, the three year old daughter of the local sheriff, seventeen year old Henry Smith was seized near Hope, Arkansas in February, 1893, and then returned by train to the scene of his alleged crime in Paris, Texas. After hundreds of spectators arrived from the countryside, along with those who had boarded special excursion trains in Dallas, Smith was driven from the depot, through the center of town, and then to an open prairie, strapped to a chair fixed atop an open cart drawn by four white horses and decorated to resemble a parade float. Upon arriving at a makeshift elevated platform, upon which the word "JUSTICE" had been painted in large white letters and to which the young man was secured, the sheriff was given the first opportunity to sear his flesh to the bone, using irons heated in a small furnace. After silencing Smith by burning his tongue and blinding him by putting out his eyes, the participants soaked the entire platform in oil and set it ablaze, as those with cameras, including the local press, snapped away. When the fire had cooled sufficiently, spectators began scouring the area for souvenirs, including buttons, teeth, and segments of the charred platform.[17]

As this account makes clear, spectacle lynchings are not well understood in strictly instrumental terms, i.e., as simple auxiliaries aimed at remedying the occasional failure of the official criminal justice system to accomplish expeditiously the ends of retribution and deterrence. Instead, they were highly ritualized expressive performances aimed at communicating the terms of the racial contract to blacks and whites alike, and the medium of that message was the (sub)human body.

Unlike the very rare white targets of spectacle lynchings, whose bodies were almost never tortured or mutilated, black victims of this form of communal justice were routinely riddled with gunfire and, as the example of Henry Smith indicates, often tortured and burned. The deployment of torture, aimed at inflicting unbearable pain, destroyed its victim's capacity to do other than cry out in anguish, and so transformed what might otherwise menace the regime of white supremacy into an inarticulate black body, denied its capacity for any sort of agency, political or otherwise: Smith's "tongue was silenced by fire," a local newspaper reported, "and henceforth he only moaned, or gave a cry that echoed over the prairie like the wail of a wild animal."[18] To burn and then display the corpse of a black man reduced to the status of a nonhuman creature, or to hang a sign on that corpse in order to warn others about the boundaries of acceptable race-specific conduct, or to photograph that corpse and then circulate its image in the form of a postcard, as was often done,[19] is to compel that body to continue to signify long after its capacity to speak has been destroyed. To blacks, and especially black men, the lynched body communicated their vulnerability, their debasement, their exclusion from the community to which, by federal law, they now uneasily belonged. To whites, that same body reaffirmed the racial contract and, more particularly, the collective integrity of the master race at a time when its exclusive title to the rights and privileges afforded by the social contract was no longer altogether secure.

Relegation of black men to the status of subhuman things was additionally confirmed, as the example of Henry Smith once again suggests, by the common practice of dismembering the corpse of a lynching victim and then distributing its parts, whether finger, ear, or toe, as souvenirs. Such mutilation, which was reminiscent of the nonlethal punishments often meted out to slaves prior to the Civil War, also ensured that the lynched body serve as a sort of text, relaying to all the differential meanings essential to the reproduction of racial subordination. Indeed, in a sense, reduction of black bodies to their constituent parts, which were then bought, sold, and traded, restored formally free African-Americans to a status not unlike that of chattel slaves, i.e., to the status of commodities whose disposition was determined by white owners. That castration accompanied many spectacle lynchings, as was also done to many slaves accused of rape as late as the 1850s, should come as no surprise. Through this means, the white community literally emasculated (and so feminized) black men, thereby eliminating them as perceived threats to Southern white women, but also rendering them figuratively ineligible to enter into the company of formally equal male citizens.

B. Law/Underlaw

Conventional definitions of lynching, virtually without exception, either presuppose or expressly draw a sharp line of demarcation between violence inflicted in the name of the law and that which stands outside or in violation of the law (the extralegal and the illegal, respectively). The *Oxford English Dictionary*, for example, defines lynching as "the practice of inflicting summary punishment upon an offender, by a self-constituted court armed with no legal authority." In much the same vein, in their *A Festival of Violence*, Stewart Tolnay and E. M. Beck, maintain that "[a]ll lynchings . . . share one commonality: The mob acted illegally, choosing to circumvent the formal system of criminal justice in order to carry out the lethal punishment personally."[20] Similarly, Richard Maxwell Brown, in his oft-cited *Strain of Violence*, characterizes lynching as "the practice or custom by which persons are punished for real or alleged crimes without due process of law."[21] Finally, and as one would expect in a criminal code, much the same bifurcation was implicit in the antilynching statutes passed by various states during the late nineteenth and early twentieth centuries, beginning with Ohio in 1896: "That any collection of individuals, assembled for any unlawful purpose, intending to do damage or injury to any one or pretending to exercise correctional power over other persons by violence, and without authority of law, shall for the purpose of this act be regarded as a 'mob,' and any act of violence exercised by them upon the body of any person, shall constitute a 'lynching.' "[22] Lynching, according to each of these definitions, is construed as a paradigmatic instance of the extralegal or illegal, which, in turn, is typically taken to imply that the aim of reform is to secure state control over the exercise of such unauthorized violence and so bring this criminal practice to a halt.

Such definitions are of considerable utility to those who wish to tell a self-congratulatory tale about the ultimate victory of civilization over barbarism, of the duly constituted forces of law and order over lawless mobs acting absent all authority. However, they are a poor guide to a significant number of lynchings, and they are so precisely because they tacitly rely for their coherence on presuppositions drawn from the logic of the liberal social contract (which, in turn, renders them ill suited to an appreciation of the role of lynching in reproducing the racial contract). According to the terms of social contract theory, if it is to sustain its authority, the law of a liberal political order must distinguish unequivocally the harm it commands from that which it punishes. Thus, for example, the law must be able to differentiate the violence it inflicts when it carries out a death sentence from the violence for which that sentence is a punishment. The liberal state's capacity to create and sustain that distinction is, in turn, a function of its ability to demarcate the public from the private realms (just as the coherence of its abstract conception of citizenship presupposes that features of identity located in the private sphere, such as race, are formally irrelevant to determining one's participation in the social contract as well as membership in the political community it founds). One means of sustaining that demarcation is the state's adherence to norms of due process that are neither required nor expected of nonstate actors. It follows, accordingly, that the authority of the liberal state and, more particularly, the authority of its criminal law to punish are eroded when the distinction between lawful and unlawful violence, as well as that between public and private, are violated; and these distinctions are transgressed in an especially egregious way when the punishment of death, which is officially reserved to the state in a liberal political order on the ground that this penalty is the ultimate expression of its monopoly over the means of legitimate violence, is imposed by private agents who show no respect for the norms of due process. The integrity of liberal law therefore mandates, as the definitions cited above indicate, that official executions and unofficial lynchings be represented as categorically distinct events. Specifically, the former must be deemed a punishment performed by public officials, sworn to do their duty, after a dispassionate verdict has been reached following a fair trial before a jury of disinterested peers and supervised by an impartial judge, whereas the latter is prototypically construed as a lawless deed performed by an impassioned mob of private persons animated by a lust for vengeance and/or irrational race prejudice.

Yet, as the very phrase "lynch law" implies, and as Henry Smith's torture at the hands of the sheriff of Paris, Texas, suggests, the mutually exclusive opposition between the legal and the illegal fails to appreciate how unstable and often irrelevant was the liberal formulation of the distinction between the official and unofficial, public and private, in the conduct of lynching. Granted, the performance of spectacle lynchings did participate in elaborating a distinction between public and private, but the form assumed by that distinction was quite different from that mandated by the social contract. As a ritual that reaffirmed the racial contract, these lynchings were public not in the sense that they were authorized by a formal code of state law but, rather, in the sense that they ratified popular but unpromulgated norms regarding the superiority of the white race. Moreover, these lynchings were public not in the sense that they took place at sites officially designated by the state (e.g., a prison) but, rather, in the sense that they transpired at unbounded settings, typically outdoors, from which no one was excluded. Finally, spectacle lynchings were public not in the sense that they were accomplished by state agents acting in the name of a sovereign citizenry but, rather, in the sense that communal participation, often manifest in the traditional expectation that everyone present, without exception, fire shots at the victim's corpse, distinguished it from acts of private vengeance.

Spectacle lynchings, in short, are not well understood in terms of the oppositions conventionally drawn by social contract theory. A more promising route, one less prone to anachronism, is suggested not by the distinction between legal and illegal but between "law" and "underlaw." Jacquelyn Hall explains:

> [L]ynchings often took the form not of frenzied killings but of deliberate, purposeful extensions of the administration of justice. Blacks were eliminated from juries, and courts meted out disproportionately harsh sentences to black defendants. In a system of what one scholar has termed "underlaw," police officials exploited areas of discretion in the legal process to translate local white custom into effective social control, regardless of the letter of the statute books. The broad discretionary power in the hands of local and county officials routinely verged on vigilantism. Whites acting as special deputies or posse members eagerly assisted in manhunts. If the lawful authorities failed to measure up to community demands, the initiative for law enforcement could easily pass into the hands of private citizens. The lynchings that followed were modeled after the public hangings that, until the second decade of the twentieth century, were carried out by local and county government officials.[23]

As the above passage indicates, many lynchings, especially of the spectacle sort, should be located not in the domain of the illegal or the extralegal but, rather, near the heart of a more comprehensive structure of racial control, one that vested informal police powers in members of the white race and that encouraged vigilantism as a necessary complement to its weak agencies of formally authorized political discipline.[24]

The permeability of the border between the legal and the extralegal, a key element of the post-Reconstruction racial polity, can be illustrated from both sides of liberalism's conceptual divide: "The distinction between legal lynchings and mob lynchings," writes George Wright, "was blurred by instances when the court assumed the role of the mob by holding a 'trial' even though the defendant stood no chance of being found innocent, as well as instances when the mob assumed the role of the court and gave the victim a 'trial' and allowed members of the lynch mob to render a verdict and select the method of execution."[25] To appreciate Wright's point from the perspective of the underlaw, consider the following example:

> In 1917, in Memphis, Tennessee, Ell Persons was accused of raping and murdering a sixteen year old white girl by the name of Antoinette Rappel. While shuttling Persons back and forth between Memphis and Nashville, local authorities were intercepted and overpowered by members of a lynching committee calling themselves the Shelby Avengers and presided over by a designated "master of ceremonies." After the next morning's newspaper announced that the Avengers intended to lynch Persons, several hundred persons gathered at the designated location, where the mother of Antoinette was given an opportunity to identify her alleged assailant and then to offer something akin to a victim impact statement, which included an expression of her desire that "the Negro" should "suffer as my little girl suffered, only ten times worse." Respecting her wishes, the Avengers collectively agreed to burn Persons, and to refrain from shooting him first, since that would abbreviate his agonies. On the day following Person's death and dismemberment, which included his decapitation, the *Commercial Appeal* reported that "throughout the entire proceedings there was perfect order. The crowd was dominated completely by the committee which had planned and executed the capture of the black slayer from the state authorities, and none offered violence not countenanced by the summary court." The *Appeal* concluded by praising the Avengers for their election of a treasurer who was assigned responsibility for securing compensation for those who had lost wages from their regular jobs while participating in the search for and execution of Persons.[26]

As the example intimates, it was not uncommon for lynching parties to mimic certain of the formal procedures that, according to the conventional definitions cited above, are said to distinguish lawful trials from extralegal lynchings.[27] In addition, a very large number of spectacle lynchings were conducted either with the active participation of police officers (along with other community elites), or with their obvious connivance.[28]

Moreover, as Brundage notes, it is not at all clear that these officers entertained the political convictions, crucial elements of the social contract, that might have invited them to deem their participation problematic: "[M]any local officials held a conception of law and order that neither stressed the abstract principles of justice nor drew precise distinctions between legal and extralegal justice. Instead, many saw mob violence as a means of carrying out the spirit of formal law, if not the letter."[29] In sum, many lynchings should be classified not as irrational deeds perpetrated by mobs of private persons, acting without legal authority but, rather, as ritualized enactments that drew their authority from the unwritten racial contract of the white community and that patterned their proceedings, to a greater or lesser extent, on the very judicial procedures they are characteristically said to flout.

In moving from the perspective of the underlaw to that of the law, again recognizing that these terms point not to a categorical distinction but to coconstitutive elements of a larger structure of racial domination, the historical record makes clear that many of the executions ordered by Southern courts and performed by public officials during the post-Reconstruction decades were only barely distinguishable from the lynchings I have recounted thus far. Consider, for example, the following account of a 1929 execution in Brazos County, Texas, as related by the Southern Commission on the Study of Lynching in its 1931 publication, *Lynchings and What They Mean*:

The sheriff arrested a Negro accused of raping a schoolteacher at Millican, just southwest of Bryan, and escaped with him. The mob followed. To prevent a lynching, a leading lawyer promised mob leaders that if they would leave the Negro in the custody of the law he would see to it that there would be an immediate conviction and death sentence. The case was called late one afternoon. The mob, jamming the courthouse, demanded that it be completed that night. Court officials, fearing that a recess would result in a lynching, went on with the case. The evidence and argument were finished by ten o'clock. The jury retired and in a few minutes returned a verdict of guilty. The lawyers appointed by the court for the defendant considered whether to appeal the case, calling into their deliberations other lawyers and leading citizens. They decided not to appeal, fearing that to do so would only result in a lynching that night. So it was that the Negro's case was not appealed and within a month he was executed. The mob dictated every move in this trial, and doubtless the Negro would have been lynched had the court at any point failed to carry out promises made the mob by leading citizens.[30]

As Southern newspapers were often quick to point out, and as this example makes evident, the members of a community who engaged in a lynching were often the same persons who, should the accused be tried, would sit on the grand and petit juries that would convict and sentence him. Should the accused in fact be tried, as was the case here, the coercive presence of a band of potential lynchers, either within or just outside the courthouse, virtually guaranteed that adherence to the forms of due process generated the same verdict and punishment that its members would otherwise mete out in the streets. Should such proceedings take place before a jury from which all African-Americans had been excluded, either by law or by custom; should the interval between that trial's beginning and end prove exceedingly brief, as it was in the case of Allen Mathias, who, accused of rape in 1906, was tried, convicted, and executed in the space of one hour and two minutes;[31] should that trial deny to the accused the right to self-defense, as was George Dinning, also of Kentucky, when in 1897 he killed a member of an armed white mob seeking to seize his cattle and force him off his farm;[32] should that trial be presided over by a judge who acquiesced in these counterfeit proceedings, as was routinely the case, it is difficult to know what to call such incidents other than "legal lynchings," even though that phrase cannot help but appear oxymoronic from the standpoint of the social contract.

IV. Capital Punishment and the Contemporary Racial Contract

The last recorded spectacle lynching occurred in 1937 in the town of Duck Hill, Mississippi, where, after being arraigned for the murder of a white store owner, Roosevelt Townes and "Bootjack" McDaniels were seized by a party whose members removed them to a site near the scene of their alleged crime, tortured them with a chain as well as a blowtorch, and, finally, after each had "confessed," shot, mutilated and incinerated the two men.[33] Five years later, the Commission on Interracial Cooperation published a major report on the history of lynching in the post-Reconstruction era.[34] Analyzing the data presented in that document, Jessie Daniel Ames, executive director of the Association of Southern Women for the Prevention of Lynching, noted that, leaving aside occasional spikes, the number of lynchings had declined steadily from a peak in 1893, when, by the Commission's count, more than 150 blacks were killed. Indeed, in May of 1940, she concluded that, for the first time since the end of Reconstruction, a full year had elapsed without a single lynching.[35] To explain this accomplishment, among other factors, she pointed to an increase in the number of state radio police patrols, which, on her account, had the effect of introducing law enforcement officials into rural areas where, traditionally, most lynchings occurred. Ames's reading of lynching's history, in sum, is one that commends the victory of the social contract over its racial counterpart, however precarious, and which accounts for that victory, at least in part, by pointing to the state's more effective monopoly over the deployment of violence.

A less sanguine reading was offered by the National Association for the Advancement of Colored People, which was quick to respond to Ames's proclamation by arguing that what appeared to be a dramatic reduction in the number of lynchings was in fact simply an indication of their changing character.[36] As Ames and the NAACP both acknowledged, beginning in the mid-1930s, white bands seized fewer prisoners from officers and jails (or, when the accused remained unincarcerated, engaged in the customary manhunt). When they did so, almost never did their members resort to public torture, dismemberment, and/or burning of their victims; and only very rarely did they claim to be motivated by a code of chivalry, which demanded that they respond to injuries allegedly committed against white women. Curtailment of these features, maintained Walter White, executive secretary of the NAACP, indicated not that lynching had ceased but that the practice had simply "gone underground."[37] Setting aside its earlier definition, which required a mob acting in the name of community sentiment in order to qualify a killing as a lynching, the NAACP contended that lynchings were now more often conducted by small groups of white men who planned their deeds with considerable care, killed their victims in secret, attempted to hide the evidence of their crimes, and usually succeeded in escaping public identification and prosecution as a result of the clandestine participation or indifference of local law officers.

On this analysis, the end of spectacle lynchings did indeed signify a shift in the relationship between the social and racial contracts, as Ames's argument implied, but not one that could easily be folded into a narrative about the victory of the legal over the extralegal or illegal. As local and state elites sought to stabilize the sort of predictable legal order required by the imperatives of a slowly modernizing economy, as liberal reformers continued to afford lynchings national publicity and to press for passage of a federal bill that would impose heavy penalties on those who engaged in this practice, it grew more costly to reproduce the racial polity through an irregular and heavily ritualized brand of popular justice that relied on the undisciplined energies of untrained amateurs who, all too often, left the evidence of their handiwork swinging from tree limbs. That such rough justice proved eliminable may indicate not the growing authority of the social over the racial contract but, rather, as Jacquelyn Hall proposes, the latter's incorporation within the less overtly violent operations of rationalized institutions and routinized practices operating within the underlaw and law alike:

> White supremacy, of course, did not rest on force alone. Routine institutional arrangements denied to the freedmen and women the opportunity to own land, the right to vote, access to education, and participation in the administration of the law. Lynching reached its height during the battles of Reconstruction and the Populist revolt; once a new system of disfranchisement, debt peonage, and segregation were firmly in place, mob violence gradually declined.[38]

In other words, more graphic forms of racial violence, such as spectacle lynching, became less imperative once white dominance was assured by less transparent but more calculable means (although cruder forms, such as privatized lynchings, remained available, should their more mundane kin fail). Perpetuation of the racial contract still required the coercive production of a class of subpersons, but no longer was it necessary to secure that end by visibly marking and publicly displaying the bodies of its members.

Taking Hall's contention as my cue, the question I wish to address in the remainder of this essay is not whether capital punishment is one of the political practices that now serves to reproduce the racial polity (which, for the purposes of this essay, I will assume to be the case).[39] Rather, I mean to ask how transformations in the conduct of capital punishment contribute to what Mills calls "the epistemology of ignorance," i.e., the sort of ignorance that renders its participation in reinforcing the terms of the racial contract less transparent and so less susceptible to challenge on the grounds of its dissonance with the norms of the social contract. To address this question, in the remainder of this section, I will consider two overlapping ways in which the practice of capital punishment has been rendered formally more consistent with the legitimating imperatives of liberalism. Each corresponds to one of the two features of spectacle lynching I emphasized in parts A and B of section II. The first concerns the gradual elimination of race-specific penalties, as well as methods of inflicting them, which, at least formally, moves the law closer to the liberal ideal of equality under the law; and the second concerns the construction of a less permeable wall between official and unofficial realms, which enhances the appearance of state neutrality and hence its authority in upholding the law. Each, I will suggest, is a vital means of hiding the play of the underlaw within the law itself.

A. Masking Black Bodies

Although exceptional in its brutality, spectacle lynching was quite consistent with the long history of race-specific crimes and punishments in the antebellum South. Throughout the South, the list of crimes for which slaves could be sentenced to death was far longer than that for whites. In Texas, for example, slaves but not whites could be and were put to death for insurrection, arson, and, if the victim was white, attempted murder, rape, attempted rape, robbery, attempted robbery, and assault with a deadly weapon. Similarly, in Virginia, slaves were liable to the death penalty for any offense for which free persons could be sentenced to a prison term of three or more years. In addition, although hanging was the most common method of execution in North and South alike, slaves convicted of murdering their owners or of plotting to revolt were often burned at the stake.

Although Reconstruction brought an end to the express codification of race-specific punishments, the underlaw of the racial contract sometimes insinuated its way in barely less transparent form within statutory enactments governing the administration of capital punishment. For example, in most Southern states, legally authorized hangings remained public, and so retained much of their ritualistic and communal character, long after all states in the North had moved them behind penitentiary walls. Even so, by the turn of the twentieth century, public executions had been abolished in Virginia, Kentucky, Maryland, Louisiana, Missouri, South Carolina, and Tennessee. Arkansas, however, retained public hangings exclusively for the crime of rape, as did Kentucky, which had abolished this practice in 1880, only to restore it in 1920, at the discretion of local officials. Given the grossly disproportionate number of blacks executed for rape in the South relative to the number of whites, what might appear at first glance to express the law's race-neutral judgment concerning the exceptional heinousness of this crime is better understood as a means of ensuring that bodies continued to be marked in a way that publicly demonstrated the ineligibility of the race they personified for inclusion within the domain of equal citizenship.

Shortly after most Southern states abandoned public executions, many also shifted from hanging to electrocution as their statutorily mandated method of execution.[40] Simply in virtue of its technical imperatives, which required a generator, wiring, and a chair housed indoors, electrocution consolidated the "privatization" of capital punishment. Yet even electrocutions were sometimes conducted in ways that sought to preserve, so far as possible, the communal dimensions of spectacle lynching and so their role in visibly ratifying the terms of the racial contract. Consider, for example, the following: on November 3, 1945, Willametta Hawkins, of Laurel, Mississippi, alleged that she had been raped by a black man in her home. Shortly thereafter, on the basis of circumstantial evidence, Willie McGee was arrested, tried, convicted, and sentenced to death. In 1950, the U.S. Supreme Court stayed McGee's execution, and, shortly thereafter, his lawyers explained to the Mississippi Supreme Court that no white man had ever been executed for rape in that state, and that of the 108 people executed for any reason between 1930 and 1948, only 18 had been white. These pleas falling on deaf ears, McGee's execution by electrocution took place just after midnight on May 8, 1951:

> In Laurel, officials were completing preparations for the execution which, by Mississippi custom and law, was designed to resemble a lynching as closely as possible. In response to popular demand, official executions were carried out not at a prison, as in most other states, but in the same county courtroom where the condemned had been sentenced to death. To support this method of conducting legal executions while satisfying the community's interest in taking part, the state used a portable electric chair that, by 1951, had taken the lives of ninety people. Long before midnight, the hour when the switch would be thrown, upwards of five hundred men, women, and children gathered on the lawn of the Jones County courthouse. Some young men and boys climbed into the trees from which they could see the portable electric chair situated in the center of the courtroom. . . . Out on the lawn, when the portable generator stopped humming, indicating that the electrocution had taken place, the crowd burst into cheers, then crushed

forward in an effort to glimpse the corpse as it was removed from the building.[41]

For my purposes, what is noteworthy about the McGee execution is its ambiguous articulation of the forms of justice demanded by the social and racial contracts, respectively. On the one hand, the method of execution employed here meets the imperatives of liberalism's commitment to formal equality. Specifically, that method coheres with liberalism's abstract conception of citizenship in the sense that the law makes no provision for the infliction of death sentences upon any specified category of persons (or, more likely, subpersons) by means other than electrocution. In addition, and consistent with the requirement that the liberal state be rendered autonomous from the private sphere, the site of this execution, a county courthouse, is demarcated from the nonexclusive spaces where spectacle lynchings typically transpired, and from that site the bodies (but not the eyes) of all nonofficial agents have been excluded. On the other hand, this execution is located in a quasi-public context, which, quite deliberately, reproduces many of the defining features of a spectacle lynching and, in so doing, ensures that McGee's body, especially upon removal from the courthouse, will serve as a manifest sign that simultaneously regenerates and ratifies the racial boundary that is essential to the perpetuation of white supremacy.

Today, however, with the transformation of executions into rationalized procedures, conducted via the method of lethal injection (which is my principal concern in the remainder of this part) and hidden behind the walls of state penitentiaries (which is my chief concern in the next), the ambiguity that marked McGee's execution has been resolved in favor of formal consistency with the imperatives of the social contract. With the exception of Nebraska, which retains electrocution, all states (as well as the federal government and the U.S. military) now designate lethal injection as their default method of execution. Even more so than electrocution, which, I suspect, bears race-specific connotations in virtue of its association with burning flesh, lethal injection is evacuated of the racist associations that are bound up with the noose. To see the point, consider the claim advanced by Judge Stephen Reinhardt, of the Ninth Circuit, in a 1994 dissenting opinion in which he argued that execution by means of hanging violates the Eighth Amendment and, on that basis, urged its replacement by lethal injection: "Hanging is associated with lynching, with frontier justice, and with our ugly, nasty, and best-forgotten history of bodies swinging from the trees or exhibited in public places."[42] (To grasp Reinhardt's point, one need only imagine what race-specific meanings the execution of Gregory Resnover would have borne had he been killed by means of hanging in downtown Marion, Indiana.) More important, Reinhardt's reference to our "best-forgotten history" is expressive of the collective amnesia, "the epistemology of ignorance," that must be continuously produced if capital punishment's contemporary contribution to the racial polity is to be elided.

To better specify this amnesia's character, consider the opening sentence in a front-page article published in the New York Times of 1899: "Richard Coleman, colored, the confessed murderer of Mrs. James Lashbrook, wife of his employer, expiated his crime in daylight to-day by burning at the stake after suffering torture and fright beyond description, at the hands of a mob of thousands of citizens."[43] In this account, whose first sentence is followed by a lurid account of Coleman's alleged crime, his capture by agents of the underlaw, his "confession," his torture, and, finally, his death by incineration, the racial identity of all parties involved, even those left unspecified, is transparently clear, and there can be no doubt that this incident, in large part because of its specific method of killing, is bound up with reproduction of the racial polity. Now consider the complete account, taken from a back page of the New York Times, of the execution of Alton Coleman in April 2002: "Alton Coleman, who was sentenced to death in three states for four killings during a 1984 crime spree, was executed by lethal injection. Mr. Coleman, 46, was put to death at the Southern Ohio Correctional Facility in Lucasville for beating to death Marlene Walters, 44, in her home in a Cincinnati suburb. Mr. Coleman also faced execution for the murder of Tonnie Storey, 15, of Cincinnati; Vernita Wheat, 9, of Waukegan, Ill.; and Tamika Turks, 7, of Gary, Ind."[44] Here, the racial identity of the condemned (black) and his victims (white) is left entirely unspecified; and the particulars of the execution method offer no clues in this regard, as they so clearly do in the case of Richard Coleman. In effect, in this latter instance, the body of the condemned (as opposed to the disembodied legal subject who bears a proper name) is simply absent from the account, and so the question of the state's implication in the dynamics of racial subordination is far less likely to arise.

Although lethal injection is neutral in the sense that its statutorily mandated application is no longer bound up with race in the way that rope and faggot once were (and their colloquial connotations still are), paradoxically, it is this very absence of racial reference that is essential to this method's participation in reproduction of the racial contract. Precisely because execution by lethal injection, unlike spectacle lynching, does not color-code the body of the condemned, it engenders the sort of invisibility that normalizes and, indeed, legitimates the work accomplished by racism in less visible components of the state's machinery of death, including the unremarked decisions of prosecutors to seek (or not to seek) the death penalty; the use of barely disguised racist peremptory challenges to secure juries predisposed to vote for death; the mundane deployment of pernicious stereotypes about black defendants on the part of prosecuting attorneys; the race-specific construction of aggravating and mitigating circumstances after a death sentence has been imposed; and so forth and so on. Such invisibility, which is not to be equated with the mere absence of visibility, must be actively engendered, and it is in these terms that we might think about the nearly universal turn to lethal injection in an era when it is no longer possible to fashion the category of subpersons through slavery, lynchings, or the formally neutral but patently racist practices of the post-Reconstruction South.

Lethal injection, moreover, is one of the means by which those located in the category of persons accommodate the tension, what Mills labels "cognitive dissonance," between the formally race-less normative principles of the social contract and the production of a racially differentiated class of subpersons whose membership in the polity created by that contract remains partial. Or, rather, lethal injection is a technology of death that manufactures the "evasive 'color-blindness'" through which, according to Mills, the black body becomes "visibly invisible."[45] That body proclaims its differential status when, within a courtroom, for example, it comes to determining its availability for various forms and degrees of punishment, including the death sentence. Yet, within this context, the way this body announces its blackness is quite unlike the way bodies were made to proclaim their raced identity in the context of spectacle lynchings. There, the certification of a body's blackness occurred via an act of external branding on its visible surface, which in turn manufactured its distinction from, as well as its inferiority to, the unmarked bodies of the white race. Within the contemporary courtroom, by way of contrast, the disciplinary powers that are responsible for fashioning and sustaining racial categories, and hence the identity of any particular body as black, are veiled insofar as that body's racial identity appears "natural," i.e., an indisputable given rather than something etched into the flesh in the service of the racial polity. Moreover, when that body is in fact executed, the method employed no longer constructs that body as specifically black; and so its blackness evaporates—or, better, appears only to disappear—in the service of an abstract conception of formally equal universal citizenship, thereby occluding the living legacy of lynching. Just as lethal injection renders the violence inflicted by the state effectively invisible by leaving the body unmarked, just as the death it causes is abstract in the sense that it is not indicated by any visible alteration in the character of embodiment, so too does the needle help to efface the differential distribution of that violence throughout the racial polity.

B. Legal/Illegal

The rationalization of punishment that assumes the form of lethal injection, I suggested in the preceding part, helps to reproduce racial hierarchies through its active participation in the production of racial invisibility. The rationalization of the state that accompanies its more secure demarcation from the private domain in the imposition and infliction of punishment, I now want to suggest, serves a complementary end. That demarcation is itself a complex effect produced by the reiterated working of various practices that serve to effect a distinction between the state and that which, in coming to be deemed "external" to it, is constituted as the private realm. To stay with the example I introduced in the preceding part, the early twentieth century displacement of hanging by electrocution as the preferred method of inflicting death sentences confirmed the removal of executions behind prison walls. The adoption of electrocution excluded the public in a second way insofar as executions by this means could be performed only by those suitably trained. No longer were executions communal rituals that required no more expertise than that necessary to tie a noose and toss it over the branch of a maple tree, as was the case with Tom Schipp and Abe Smith. For both reasons, i.e., its transfer behind prison walls and its conduct by electrocution, execution was more securely defined as an act to be performed by duly authorized officials in the name of the state. That understanding was confirmed in yet another way because, unlike the readily available materials required for a hanging, the construction of electric chairs was quite expensive. Because individual counties, as a rule, could not afford to build and maintain their own devices, with the exception of Mississippi, all states that adopted electrocution soon moved executions to a single state facility, which effectively removed them from the communities in which convictions were secured and over which local sheriffs held sway. That, too, more clearly secured the distinction between violence inflicted in the name of the law and the illegal violence it was called upon to punish.[46]

To illustrate the relationship between visibility and invisibility that is produced through the more effective segregation of official from unofficial, and hence in the conduct of contemporary executions, it is useful to consider the sort of anonymity that was characteristic of spectacle lynchings. As a glance at the Beitler photograph makes chillingly clear, the participants in spectacle lynchings typically made no effort to hide their individual identities. Indeed, those identities were often made known well beyond the scene of any given lynching through commodification of such photographs in the form of postcards that were then circulated through the postal service. Curiously, though, as Bruce Baker points out, in lynching ballads, yet another means of circulating the racialized import of this spectacle beyond the community in which it occurred, the names of victims were almost always included, while the names of perpetrators never were. Baker is quite right to contend that recitation of the names of specific victims in lynching ballads "serves as a marker of the power relationships involved": "Since the mob is nameless, using the name of the victim while not mentioning the names of the mob reinforces the power conferred by anonymity. Lynch law, while applied at a specific point, draws its power to terrorize in large part from the uncertainty of the identity of mob members; anyone could be a potential lyncher, just as anyone could be a potential lynching victim."[47] This sort of anonymity secures its legal correlate in the statements issued by courts, coroners' juries, and other official bodies convened in order to investigate lynchings, which almost invariably concluded that black victims had met their deaths "at the hand of persons unknown." In one sense, this phrase represented a patent falsification, but in another and perhaps more profound sense, it spoke the truth: "The coroner's inevitable verdict," notes Philip Dray, "affirmed the public's tacit complicity: no *persons* had committed a crime, because the lynching had been an expression of the community's will."[48]

Yet an explanation of such anonymity through reference to community will leaves unexplained its character as a sort of visible invisibility, i.e., one that required namelessness but not facelessness. This apparent anomaly becomes intelligible, however, when we recall that the very purpose of a spectacle lynching was to produce and reproduce the conditions of racial domination within the context of a regime that openly affirmed white superiority. That in turn necessitated that specifically white faces be visible, and that those persons perceive a specifically black body, one defined by its corporeality as well as the racist discursive connotations that attend the identity ascribed to it. The success of this event, in other words, required that whiteness be visible, but also nameless so that the bearers of this property could sustain their collective self- representation as agents of a white race that was more than the sum of its named parts, but not for that reason abstract in the sense of color-free.

It was in 1908 that an amendment to the U.S. Postal Laws and Regulations was adopted, forbidding the mailing of "matter of a character tending to incite arson, murder or assassination."[49] The very abstraction of this language is worthy of note since it is clearly directed at lynching postcards but neither names them as such nor indicates that it is images of blacks killed by whites that have prompted the amendment. The nature of this prohibition thus gestures toward the quite different construction of the relationship between the visible and the invisible, as well as the official and the unofficial, that defines the contemporary execution of African-Americans. Most obviously, executions are now performed not in the name of white hegemony but in the name of a citizenry that, as liberalism requires, is abstract in the sense of without color. That citizenry is additionally abstract in the sense that, unlike its counterpart at a spectacle lynching, it has neither names nor faces, for executions are conducted in the name of the impersonal and disembodied imperatives of the law. Finally, that citizenry is abstract in the sense that its members become anonymous consumers of an event they never see, one in which the executed, as a rule, is now little more than a disembodied name available for appropriation not through the removal of a digit, nor through the visual imagery of a postcard, but, if at all, through the bloodless text of a newspaper account of the sort reproduced above.

And yet, of course, the abstraction of the liberal citizenry is itself a complex appearance, one that is generated by, among other things, the state's adherence to the norms of due process, which in turn helps to manufacture the state's appearance of autonomy from the private domain regulated by its criminal law. What that appearance masks, among other things, is the sense in which the normative vision of the liberal citizen in America, although acknowledged, remains raced. "Modern citizenship," writes Robin Wiegman, "functions as a disproportionate system in which the universalism ascribed to certain bodies (white, male, propertied) is protected and subtended by the infinite particularity assigned to others (black, female, unpropertied)."[50] As is the case with the lethal needle, the active production of this peculiarly liberal form of invisibility, which effectively denies the continuing validity of the distinction between persons and subpersons, serves to mask the equally active production of specifically black bodies at other sites of the criminal justice system (perhaps most notably in the prison system, which is extraordinarily effective not simply at containing and disciplining the economically superfluous population of African-American males but also at generating and confirming the stereotypical association of blackness with criminality). In any event, the achievement of a more complete categorical distinction between state executions, performed in the name of the law, and private acts of murder, performed outside the law, contributes to the larger logic whereby persons, in Mills's sense of the term, resolve the discrepancy between the imperatives necessary to reproduce the racial polity and a liberal creed that can no longer openly acknowledge those imperatives. Such denial, such willed ignorance, would be far more difficult to sustain were this distinction less secure, as was so often the case in instances of lynching.

V. Conclusion

In 1931, the authors of a report prepared by the Southern Commission on the Study of Lynching stated: "A lynching makes a lot of otherwise good people go blind or lose their memories."[51] Much the same is true, I have tried to show, of the contemporary administration of capital punishment, especially in relation to the reproduction of racial hierarchies. Ironically, though, this disability is, in large part, generated by what, from the perspective of the liberal social contract tradition, must be regarded as significant accomplishments. By eliminating the race-specific punishments that persisted in the South well after Reconstruction, the liberal state removes the dissonance generated by the persistence of such punishments, on the one hand, and the social contract's commitment to formal equality under law, on the other. By the same token, by drawing a sharper line of demarcation between public officials, who are authorized to take life in the name of the law, and private agents, who are not, the liberal state removes the dissonance generated when it fails to secure the sort of autonomy, which, according to the social contract tradition, is an indispensable condition of its authority. Both of these accomplishments, I have argued, render it more difficult to recognize how the liberal state remains implicated in perpetuating the racial polity.

If that is so, then efforts to reform the death penalty from within the confines of liberal political doctrine cannot help but prove double-edged at best. Consider, to illustrate, the title of a book recently published by the Reverend Jesse Jackson and his son, Jesse Jackson, Jr.: *Legal Lynching: Racism, Injustice, and the Death Penalty*. With this title, like those who displayed the Beitler photograph in 1994, the Jacksons mean to raise the possibility that the forms of criminal law may be merely formalistic, i.e., that their observance may do no more than paper over and so help to legitimate political practices that, in fact, are substantively unjust and, more specifically, profoundly racist. The Jacksons' aim, accordingly, is to dig beneath those forms in order to disclose "the terrible truth that bias and discrimination warp our nation's judicial system at the very time it matters most—in matters of life and death."[52] Construction of the dilemma of the death penalty in terms of "bias and discrimination," each of which, on their telling, represents an aberrational departure from America's true commitment to equal justice for all, dictates their understanding of an apt remedy: "This book is dedicated to the principle of equal protection under the law for all Americans contained in the Fourteenth Amendment to the Constitution."[53] Given this commitment, not surprisingly, their solution to the problem of "legal lynching" is to ensure that the liberal state be strictly segregated from the private realm via its strict adherence to the norms of due process, which, in turn, will compel it to live up to its self-proclaimed promise of color-blind justice.

What this analysis fails to grasp is what Mills demonstrates in his analysis of the racial polity: "[I]nstead of pretending that the social contract outlines the ideal that people tried to live up to but which they occasionally (as with all ideals) fell short of, we should say frankly that for whites the Racial Contract represented the *ideal*, and what is involved is not deviation from the (fictive) norm but *adherence* to the actual norm."[54] If Mills is correct on this point, then the problem of racism is not a problem illegitimately imported into the machinery of death by prejudiced nonstate actors, for it is the state that establishes and maintains the institutionalized practices through which black bodies are differentially fashioned long before the nonevent that is a lethal injection.[55] More specifically, the practices constitutive of due process, to return to the language of Gregory Resnover's attorney, are a "pretense" not in the sense that they render capital punishment and lynching identical but, rather, in the more subtle sense that they mask the continued articulation of the racial contract within a polity that no longer openly espouses the rhetoric of white supremacy.

A critique of capital punishment in terms of the workings of prejudice is, therefore, at best insufficient and at worst productive of "the epistemology of ignorance." A more promising route, I have suggested in this essay, must first acknowledge that the administration of capital punishment in the United States, like the practice of lynching, is one of the state practices by means of which the racial polity is reproduced; second, offer a detailed analysis of the specific ways the death penalty contributes to this end, for example, by creating spaces for the underlaw to do its work under the cover of law; and, finally, ask how that work, unlike the practice of spectacle lynching, is obscured by its institutionalization of the normative principles articulated by the liberal social contract. That sort of interrogation will almost certainly confirm the suspicion, entertained by Gregory Resnover and his attorney, that the practice of capital punishment in the United States is indeed a form of "diabolical" justice.

NOTES

1. For a careful account of the lynching of Abe Smith and Tom Shipp, see James H. Madison, *A Lynching in the Heartland* (New York: Palgrave, 2001).

2. This account of the protest organized by Amnesty International is taken from the *Indiana Daily Student,* December 5, 1994, 6. Thanks to Professor James Madison of Indiana University for making a copy of this article available to me.

3. Stephen Bright, "Discrimination, Death, and Denial: The Tolerance of Racial Discrimination in Infliction of the Death Penalty," *Santa Clara Law Review* 35 (1995), p. 439. See also Stephen Bright, "Legalized Lynching: Race, the Death Penalty, and the United States Courts," in William Schabas, ed., *The International Sourcebook on Capital Punishment* (Boston: Northeastern University Press, 1997), pp. 3–29.

4. For a recent example of this sort of Whiggish history, see Philip Dray, *At the Hands of Persons Unknown* (New York: Random House, 2002).

5. Charles Mills, *Blackness Visible* (Ithaca: Cornell University Press, 1998), p. 198.

6. Ibid., p. 192.

7. Ibid., p. 76.

8. Charles Mills, *The Racial Contract* (Ithaca: Cornell University Press, 1997), p. 72.

9. Ibid., p. 18.

10. Mills, *Blackness Visible*, p. 110.

11. For a useful account of the origins and history of the term "lynching," see James Cutler, *Lynch-Law* (Montclair, NJ: Patterson Smith, 1969).

12. The historical record explains and warrants these connotations. Specifically, in his *Lynching in the New South* (Urbana and Chicago: University of Illinois Press, 1993), W. Fitzhugh Brundage notes that, following the end of Reconstruction, the proportion of lynchings that occurred in the South rose each decade, increasing from 82 percent to 95 percent between 1880 and 1930. During these same decades, moreover, the proportion of lynching victims in the South who were black rose from 68 percent to 91 percent (pp. 8–9). The precise number of persons lynched following the withdrawal of Federal troops in 1877 will never be known with certainty, in part because many instances will remain forever unrecorded. That said, Brundage calculates that, between 1880 and 1930, 4,587 lynchings occurred in the United States, 3,943 in the South, and, of this number, 3,220 involved black victims.

13. For an overview of the principal accounts offered by scholars in order to explain lynchings in the post-Reconstruction South, see W. Fitzhugh Brundage's introduction to his *Under Sentence of Death* (Chapel Hill and London: University of North Carolina Press, 1997), pp. 1–20.

14. For an analysis of lynching in terms similar, but not identical, to those employed here, see Robyn Wiegman, "The Anatomy of Lynching," in *American Sexual Politics*, John Fout and Maura Tantillo, eds. (Chicago: University of Chicago Press, 1990).

15. Mills, *The Racial Contract*, p. 87.

16. See Brundage, *Lynching in the New South*, pp. 18–48, for a very helpful analysis of the principal types of post-Reconstruction lynchings. My particular concern is with those he labels "mass mobs," which, by his enumeration, accounted for 34 percent of all post-Reconstruction lynchings in Georgia and 40 percent of those in Virginia.

17. What I offer here is an abridged version of the more detailed accounts of the lynching of Henry Smith provided by Ida B. Wells, in her "A Red Record," in *Southern Horrors* (New York: Arno Press and the New York Times, 1969), pp. 25–32, as well as by Dray in his *At the Hands of Persons Unknown*, pp. 77–79.

18. Dray, *At the Hands of Persons Unknown*, p. 78.

19. Many of these photographs are reproduced in *Without Sanctuary: Lynching Photography in America* (Santa Fe, NM: Twin Palms Publishers, 2000).

20. Tolnay, Stewart, and E. M. Beck, *A Festival of Violence* (Urbana: University of Illinois Press, 1995), p. 56.

21. Richard Maxwell Brown, *Strain of Violence* (New York: Oxford University Press, 1977), p. 21. For another example of a definition that presupposes the coherence of the distinction between official and unofficial acts of violence, see Cutler,

Lynch-Law: "Lynch-law has always been considered as operating wholly without, or in opposition to, established laws of government" (p. 15).

22. Quoted in Cutler, *Lynch-Law,* p. 235.

23. Jacquelyn Hall, *Revolt Against Chivalry* (New York: Columbia University Press, 1993), pp. 140–41. Hall appropriates the term "underlaw" from Peter Teachout, "Louisiana Underlaw," in *Southern Justice,* Leon Friedman, ed. (New York: Meridian, 1967).

24. Throughout the nineteenth century and well into the twentieth, the South was distinguished from the North by its weak institutions of legal and, more generally, state authority. In the North, explains Brundage, in his *Lynching in the New South,* "the accelerating pace of economic development and the growth of cities required the permanent and dependable exercise of state authority on behalf of capital and property. Consequently, courts and law enforcement agencies, including recently created urban police forces, assumed a greater role in preserving social order. In the South, planters were wary of the establishment of any powerful legal institutions that might challenge their autonomy. . . . They preferred to rely on a code of honor and such traditional extralegal methods of punishment as whipping and ostracism to safeguard community morals and virtues" (p. 4).

25. George C. Wright, "By the Book: The Legal Executions of Kentucky Blacks," in Brundage, *Under Sentence of Death,* pp. 251–52.

26. I construct this account on the basis of the more extended version provided by Dray, *At the Hands of Persons Unknown,* pp. 231–34.

27. See George Wright, *Racial Violence in Kentucky* (Baton Rouge: Louisiana State University Press, 1990), pp. 93–95. For another example of a lynching party's respect for something akin to the norms of due process, see Leon Litwack, "Hellhounds," in *Without Sanctuary,* p. 18: In 1905, in Howard, Texas, after presenting a black man accused of rape to his alleged victim, so that she might confirm his identity before the community, the participants in his lynching elected to afford their victim two hours for prayers and family visitation prior to infliction of death. While waiting, they debated and then subjected to majority vote whether the sentence should be executed by means of hanging or by burning, with the latter eventually winning out on the grounds that the crime committed was unusually heinous. At the close of this "deliberately-planned and calmly-executed spectacle," reported the editor of a local newspaper, the crowd dispersed.

28. See Arthur Raper, *The Tragedy of Lynching* (New York: Negro Universities Press, 1969), for accounts of numerous lynchings in which police officers either actively participated or passively condoned the conduct of others. For a good example of official approval given to lynchings, consider the following example, taken from *Without Sanctuary,* pp. 20–21. In 1911, those who killed and dismembered Willis Jackson in Honea Path, South Carolina, were led by Joshua W. Ashleigh, who represented the district in the state legislature. When a group of South

Carolinians demanded a state investigation, Governor Cole Blease refused, stating that, had he deemed it necessary, he would have resigned his office, come to Honea Path, and led the mob himself. The local newspaper in Spartanburg, praising the governor's refusal to initiate an investigation, cautioned against indicting Jackson's killers because that "would make heroes of the lynchers and eminently qualify them for public office."

29. Brundage, *Lynching in the New South*, p. 180.

30. Southern Commission on the Study of Lynching, *Lynchings and What They Mean* (Atlanta: The Commission, 1931), p. 52.

31. See Wright, "By the Book," pp. 256–57.

32. See ibid., pp. 258–59. In response to the public outrage occasioned by his conviction, Dinning was given a full pardon by the governor of Kentucky ten days after his arrival at the state prison.

33. See Dray, *At the Hands of Persons Unknown*, pp. 359–60, for a complete account of the lynching of Townes and McDaniels.

34. Jessie Daniel Ames, *The Changing Character of Lynching* (Atlanta: Commission on Interracial Cooperation, Inc., 1942).

35. See Hall, *Revolt Against Chivalry*, p. 256.

36. To be properly understood, Ames's pamphlet, as well as the response issued by the NAACP, should be read against the backdrop of a protracted argument among various antilynching groups about whether the end of specifically spectacle lynchings signified the end of lynching more generally. For a helpful account of this controversy, see Christopher Waldrep, "War of Words: The Controversy over the Definition of Lynching, 1899–1940," *Journal of Southern History* 66 (2000): 75–100.

37. Quoted in Waldrep, "War of Words," p. 96.

38. Jacquelyn Dowd Hall, " 'The Mind That Burns in Each Body': Women, Rape, and Racial Violence," in *Powers of Desire*, Ann Snitow, Christine Stansell, and Sharon Tompson, eds. (New York: Monthly Review Press, 1983), p. 331.

39. Were I to offer evidence to sustain this contention, I would start with the following: Although blacks now make up approximately 13 percent of the U.S. population, 35 percent of those executed since 1976 have been African-American, as are 43 percent of the inmates currently on death row (see Death Penalty Information Center, at http://www.deathpenaltyinfo.org/race.html). Moreover, capital punishment remains a largely southern practice, although there is some dispute as to whether this is because the homicide rate is higher in the South than in other regions or because southern juries are more prone than those in other regions to impose death sentences. In any event, as Stuart Banner notes in his *The Death Penalty: An American History* (Cambridge, MA: Harvard University Press, 2002), of the 598 executions conducted between 1977 and 1999, the overwhelming majority took place in Texas (199), Virginia (73), Florida (44), Missouri (41), Louisiana (25), South Carolina (24), Georgia (23), Arkansas (21), Alabama (19), Arizona (19),

Oklahoma (19), and North Carolina (15) (p. 278). The geographical distribution of death sentences is not quite so unbalanced, but it is nonetheless true that of the 18 states that imposed more than 100 death sentences between 1973 and 1998, 13 are in the South. Furthermore, there are significant disparities in capital sentencing relative to race of the offender and the race of the victim. More specifically, as the U.S. General Accounting Office has indicated in the report "Death Penalty Sentencing: Research Indicates Pattern of Racial Disparities (1990)," reprinted in *The Death Penalty in America,* Hugo Bedau, ed. (New York: Oxford University Press, 1997), the percentage of death sentences imposed is highest in cases involving black defendants and white victims. This is so, explain William Bowers, Benjamin Steiner, and Marla Sandys in "Death Sentencing in Black and White: An Empirical Analysis of the Role of Jurors' Race and Jury Racial Composition," *University of Pennsylvania Journal of Constitutional Law* 3 (2001): 171–274, because, in black defendant/white victim cases, white male jurors are far less likely than are their black counterparts to experience doubts about the defendant's guilt, as well as far more likely to vote to impose a death sentence based on their perception of the defendant's future dangerousness. In terms of public opinion, the U.S. Department of Justice, in its Sourcebook of Criminal Justice Statistics 133, tbl. 2.60 (2000), available at http://www.albany.edu/sourcebook/1995/pdf/t260.pdf, shows that support for the death penalty is far more pronounced among whites, and especially white males, than it is among blacks. And, from the work of Steven Barkan and Steven Cohn, "Racial Prejudice and Support for the Death Penalty by Whites," *Journal of Research on Crime and Delinquency* 31 (1994), we learn that white support for capital punishment is predicated in large part on racial prejudice and stereotyping.

40. In 1889, New York was the first state to adopt electrocution as its method of execution. Ohio followed suit in 1896, followed by Massachusetts (1898), New Jersey (1906), Virginia (1908), North Carolina (1909), Kentucky (1910), South Carolina (1912), Arkansas, Indiana, Nebraska, Oklahoma, Pennsylvania, Tennessee, and Vermont (all in 1913), and Texas (1923). By 1950, the electric chair was also in operation in Alabama, Florida, Georgia, the District of Columbia, Illinois, New Mexico, Connecticut, South Dakota, Louisiana, Mississippi, and West Virginia.

41. Dray, *At the Hands of Persons Unknown,* p. 403.

42. *Campbell v. Wood,* 18 F.3d 662, 701 (9th Cir. 1994).

43. "Negro Burned at a Stake," *New York Times,* Dec. 7, 1899, 1.

44. "Killer of 4 is Executed," *New York Times,* April, 27, 2002, A15.

45. Mills, *Blackness Visible,* pp. 193, 16.

46. A detailed account of the practices that generated the state's appearance of autonomy in the decades following Reconstruction is beyond the scope of this essay. To tell that story adequately would require, among other matters, inquiry into the slow modernization of the criminal justice system in the South, which involved governmental assumption of responsibility for resolving disputes that in

the past would have been resolved informally and beyond the reach of the law; the uneven penetration of a salaried constabulary into the sparsely settled areas where lynchings, as I noted above, were most common; the state and local judiciary's more assiduous adherence to the formal due process protections that, at least in principle, distinguish the justice meted out by courts from that administered by their formally unauthorized counterparts; and, finally, the inconsistent and usually halfhearted efforts on the part of the federal government to guarantee the voting rights of African-Americans and, later, to extend the prohibitions of antidiscrimination law to private actors.

47. Bruce Baker, "North Carolina Lynching Ballads," in Brundage, *Under Sentence of Death,* p. 221.

48. Dray, *At the Hands of Persons Unknown,* p. ix.

49. Quoted in *Without Sanctuary,* p. 195.

50. Robyn Wiegman, *American Anatomies* (Durham: Duke University Press, 1995), p. 6.

51. Southern Commission on the Study of Lynching, *Lynchings and What They Mean,* p. 61.

52. Reverend Jesse Jackson, with Jesse Jackson, Jr., *Legal Lynching: Racism, Injustice, and the Death Penalty* (New York: Marlowe, 1996), p. 97.

53. Jackson, *Legal Lynching,* p. 5.

54. Mills, *The Racial Contract,* pp. 56–57.

55. For an analysis of lethal injection as a "nonevent," see chapter 6, "Needling the Sovereign," in Timothy V. Kaufman-Osborn, *From Noose to Needle: Capital Punishment and the Late Liberal State* (Ann Arbor: University of Michigan Press, 2002).

Chapter 2

Making Race Matter in Death Matters

Charles J. Ogletree, Jr.

In the modern era, many have characterized the use of capital punishment in America as "legal lynching,"[1] due to its historical inseparability from the issue of race. Since the mid-twentieth century, even those operating within the legal system have been aware of the influence that race discrimination has had in the administration of the death penalty and scores of scholars have written on the issue, many of them advocating for abolition as the only adequate remedy.[2] *Nevertheless, no American court has ever "upheld a legal claim alleging systemic race discrimination in the imposition of the death penalty," nor has Congress ever "adopted a law that would give murder defendants the right to advance claims of racial discrimination" in the same manner that racial minorities are empowered to raise claims in several less severe contexts, such as employment and housing.*[3] Sadly, although the racially disparate impact of capital punishment has been painfully obvious to scholars, practitioners, observers, and, above all, criminal defendants, for the past two decades, such disparity has not warranted any truly effective remedy from any branch of government—be it judiciary or legislature —to correct what has been perceived as a grave problem in the administration of criminal justice. This unfortunate lack of affirmative resolve had led commentators and advocates to question the fairness of the criminal justice system when evidence of racial disparity exists but not even modest reform has been embraced. The empirical evidence is clear and convincing, even though the rhetoric of courts and legislators proclaims that "death is different," the fact of the matter is that the combination of racial disparity and death has not led to meaningful and sustained efforts to eliminate these patterns. The racism pervasive in the application of the death penalty by both prosecutors and juries cannot be denied any longer;

if we are to continue as a civilized society, then we can no longer accept it either.

Upon analyzing capital sentencing data, it quickly becomes clear that sentencing disparities are based not only on the race of the victim but in some jurisdictions also on the race of the defendant.[4] However, claims based on such empirical data have widely been rejected by the courts, perhaps most prominently in the United States Supreme Court case of *McCleskey v. Kemp*.[5] Even in the face of such rejection, many scholars have continued to analyze such data in more recent years, creating further support for many of the same claims set forth in *McCleskey*. Although such arguments may accurately capture tangible effects of racial discrimination in the administration of the death penalty, they tend to serve only as a partial representation of the more deeply troubled relationship between race and the penalty of death rooted in our nation's history. The legal system has not yet acknowledged the extent to which, in many respects, much has remained consistent in the administration of injustice for black "defendants,"[6] and the extent to which hard data evidenced by sentencing studies are in many ways a manifestation of the same pervasive racism that has plagued our nation for centuries. From the age of slavery, when blacks had little to nothing in the way of legal recourse; to the early years of Reconstruction when many blacks were lynched by popular mobs before even reaching a court of law; to the present, when race continues to pervade our legal system, resulting in prisons—and particularly death rows—populated disproportionately by African-Americans, race has always had a profound effect on criminal sentencing, be it outside or inside the courtroom.

The effects of race on our system today, while widely acknowledged, have not been persuasive enough to convince those with the ability to change the system that it must be changed, even in the face of concrete data demonstrating the stark disparities that exist. Many of the effects of race felt within the criminal justice system, however, are elusive and intangible; they stem from years of history that cannot easily be calculated or analyzed. *They are the most difficult to quantify, but they have undeniably influenced how our criminal justice system views, processes, and penalizes black defendants.* They are why race matters not only in the results of our current capital sentencing scheme but in the way we conceptualize the death penalty and its relationship throughout our nation's history to those who are most familiar with its darkest aspects.

I. The "Peculiar Institution" and a "Mockery of Justice": The Historical Relationship between Race and the Death Penalty

The current statistics demonstrating racial disparities in the application of the death penalty are by no means an anomaly in America's larger criminal justice system. History, however, has revealed not only society's tendency to treat blacks more harshly than whites in meting out punishment but also its particular willingness to deliver a death sentence to blacks in legal and extralegal situations.

A. Injustice Beyond the Courtroom Walls

In 1857, Chief Justice Roger Taney summed up the nature of slaves' rights with his famous statement from *Dred Scott v. Sandford* that blacks were "so far inferior, that they had no rights which the white man was bound to respect."[7] Indeed, blacks had few rights, formal or informal, during the "peculiar institution" of chattel slavery.[8] Though evidence from early colonial times shows some instances of equality under the law,[9] laws dealing with law-breaking slaves grew more stringent as the slave population increased and threats of slave insurrections rose.[10] These "Slave Codes" were extreme laws reflecting white supremacy and fear, and allowing slaves to be put to death for transgressions ranging from helping a fellow slave escape to destroying property.[11] Such laws also revealed a penchant for valuing white life over black life.[12] Despite the statutes that existed during slavery, the controlling factor in a slave's life was not the legislation on the books but the master's whim. Though slaves were occasionally tried in courts and tribunals,[13] the chattel slavery system gave slaveholders almost total control over their "property," including the manner in which slaves were punished. Given the value of slaves as laborers, slaveowners often chose the lash over the noose as their means of control. Still, some slaves were put to death as punishment.[14]

During Reconstruction, once the era of slavery had formally ended, both black and white Southerners attempted to discern their roles in the new social system.[15] While the South was under federal control, black men won the right to vote and some had been elected to Congress.[16] Many whites resented the newfound rights of the freedmen and reacted violently, continuing in the trend devaluing black life that had begun during slavery. Federal workers stationed in the South observed these intentional killings that occurred over slight "offenses" by blacks.[17] One black man was killed in 1866 for failing to take off his hat in the presence of a white man.[18] Another report describes a black soldier killed at the hands of an identified (and unpunished) white man; fellow citizens justified the murder, describing the victim as "a damned nigger."[19] To solidify their continued domination, white Southerners enacted Black Codes to allow them to maintain some of the control of blacks they had during slavery.[20]

The treatment of African-Americans became more vicious as the twentieth century dawned. Though lynching had been used in the late 1800s as a form of punishment for whites, Mexicans, Chinese, and Native Americans, by the early 1900s, it had taken on a distinctively black/white racial character.[21] Some historians have attributed the rise of black deaths by lynching to the changed nature of relationships in the South.[22]

Whatever the exact cause of lynching's popularity, blacks could be lynched for a variety of reasons, including being too successful.[23] Suspicion of rape and murder (even in self-defense) were consistent reasons, but sometimes all that was needed was a suspicion or an allegation of a crime by a black person to result in a death sentence at the hands of a mob. Lynchings were characterized by their celebratory and public nature, their brutal method of killing, their disregard for any semblance of due process for the accused, and an absence of punishment for the killers. Some lynchings occurred when a black person did commit the act in question but had a justifiable reason for doing so, which was never heard. The lynching of Zachariah Walker in Pennsylvania in 1911 provides an apt example.[24] Walker was being arrested and got into an argument with the arresting officer, Edgar Rice. Rice threatened Walker and reached for his revolver. Walker reached his own gun first and fired two fatal shots at Rice.[25] A mob later grabbed Walker from the hospital where he was recovering from an attempted suicide and burned him alive.[26] Five thousand people were present for his killing, and some eager participants took Walker's fingers and bones as souvenirs after his body cooled.[27]

As troubling as a death like Walker's was, even more heartbreaking and shocking were the many killings where the victim was innocent of anything remotely resembling a capital crime. A pregnant Mary Turner (and her unborn baby) was killed for threatening to have the men who had lynched her husband arrested and brought to justice.[28] A man in Dawson, Texas, was killed in 1909 for allegedly sending an insulting letter to a white woman.[29]

Another example is provided by the background of the historic Supreme Court decision in *United States v. Shipp*.[30] In a case whose facts were painfully familiar for the time, Ed Johnson, a young, uneducated African-American man, was wrongly accused of raping a white woman. During his trial in the Tennessee courts, he was taunted by the press, the public, and even by a member of the jury. The court ignored these procedural injustices as well as proof of Johnson's actual innocence, allowing the all-white jury to convict Johnson of rape. In response, there was a public outcry for Johnson's lynching. In what was to be a historic first, two African-American lawyers—Noah Parden and Styles Hutchins—appeared before Supreme Court Justice John Marshall Harlan to plead for the Court to intervene in Johnson's case.[31] Parden and Hutchins were persuasive enough to convince the Court to "intervene to ensure an opportunity for appellate review of a fatally defective conviction" and Justice Harlan issued a stay of execution.[32] Unfortunately, such procedural protections were not enough to prevent a local mob from storming the jail where Johnson was being held. Assisted by local sheriff Joseph Shipp, the mob lynched, shot, and mutilated the body of Johnson on March 19, 1906.[33] Although the Department of Justice filed contempt of court charges against Shipp and several of his associates in the Supreme Court, all of them received sentences of less than three months.[34]

B. "Legal Lynching"

Several decades later, in the early 1930s, the landscape of the South still had not changed greatly, as evidenced by the trial of the Scottsboro boys. Nine young African-American boys were accused of raping two white women in what became known as the "nigger rape case."[35] While the boys sat in jail awaiting trial, another lynch mob attempted to storm the jail and failed only because local officials mobilized local law enforcement officers to prevent the lynching.[36] When the boys did eventually reach their day in court, it became clear that a "fair trial under the circumstances was impossible. The nine Negro boys had already been tried, found guilty, and sentenced to death by the news media."[37] The proceedings themselves appeared in retrospect to be a "mockery of justice," that was "conducted under the shadow of fixed bayonets and in a courtroom surcharged with racial hatred, while a crowd of ten thousand milled about the courthouse, and then thunderous applause as the guilty verdict was returned."[38]

Although the trial of one of the boys ended in a mistrial, the eight others were convicted and sentenced to death.[39]

Around the time of the Scottsboro boys' trial, another young African-American by the name of Willie Peterson experienced a similar subversion of justice. Although he did not in any way resemble the description of the man accused of raping and murdering two white women, Peterson was labeled as the accused, stopped on the street, and taken into custody.[40] Knowing Peterson was innocent, state officials nonetheless indicted and tried him. At trial, it took the jury only twenty minutes to return with a guilty verdict and Peterson was sentenced to death. As Dan Carter observes, "[r]ather than humiliate [the victim] by contradicting her story, the state of Alabama was willing to convict an innocent man. The 'honor' of one white woman was more important than the life's blood of a black man."[41] The governor was ultimately persuaded to commute Peterson's sentence to life imprisonment. Peterson died in prison of tuberculosis just several years later.[42]

Lynchings had declined by the end of World War II, but as evidenced by the tragic anecdotes above, similar results still occurred because of biased court systems.[43] With these "legal lynchings," whites deferred to the courts but remained ready to return to mob justice if the results were not favorable to them. The case of four black men accused of raping a white woman in Groveland, Florida, further illustrates this trend.[44] In that case, the alleged victim, her husband, and the sheriff had reason to fabricate the crime.[45] A grand jury that contained one lone black in order to give the appearance of fairness indicted the defendants.[46] They were convicted during a trial based on questionable evidence, including shaky information about whether there had been a rape at all.[47] The United States Supreme Court overturned the convictions on appeal.[48] Before a second trial ensued, the sheriff shot two of the defendants while he was transferring them, claiming they assaulted him.[49] One defendant survived, and he was sentenced to death at trial. In a bittersweet end to the case, the Supreme Court granted a stay two days before the execution, and a newly elected governor commuted the sentence to life in prison.[50]

In June of 2005, the Senate voted to issue a formal apology for its failure to pass antilynching legislation. Seven presidents had asked Congress to pass a bill that would make lynching a federal crime. In fact, the House passed an antilynching bill four times. Nevertheless, the Senate's powerful southern senators used the filibuster to ensure that the bill never got a vote.[51] In the absence of a federal law, the task of prohibiting lynching was left up to local officials. As the preceding pages indicate, local police officers and sheriffs were often either unwilling or unable to stop lynchings. Given that lynching was a well-known phenomenon, Congress's failure to make lynching a crime is a tragic example of blacks literally being denied equal protection of the laws. Moreover, the Senate's failure to pass an anti-lynching bill despite the plethora of needless, lawless killings demonstrates the way in which the government systematically undervalued the lives of black people. To be sure, the Senate's apology for its inaction is a step in the right direction, but nothing can change the fact that at least 4,742 Americans were lynched while Congress failed to act.[52]

II. *"Tinkering with the Machinery of Death": Race, the Death Penalty, and the Supreme Court*

The application of death as a punishment for black Americans in unique and cruel forms throughout American history is undeniable. The underlying currents involved in this sordid history—fear, white supremacy, devaluation of black life, hatred, and a desire to control—may not be exact reasons for the suspicious disparities in capital punishment today, but one cannot help but wonder whether some of the same impulses are at work. In its reluctance to address the impact of race on the death penalty, the Supreme Court has offered little assistance in confronting or discontinuing the trend.

When the Court first addressed the constitutionality of the death penalty in 1972, it did so without focusing on the varying effects of the punishment on defendants of different races. In *Furman v. Georgia*,[53] the Court found that the death penalty as applied in the cases before the Court "constitute[d] cruel and unusual punishment in violation of the Eighth and Fourteenth Amendments."[54] The Justices agreed that, in these cases, the death penalty was cruel and unusual. In several per curiam opinions, they put forth differing bases for their reasoning. Although race had undeniably been a factor in the imposition of the death penalty to date, only a few of the Justices acknowledged its potential impact in the current state of the punishment's practice.[55] In contrast, the Court's per curiam opinion neglected to address directly the claims of racial discrimination asserted by the petitioner.

In his concurring opinion in *Furman*, Justice Douglas touched briefly on the impermissibility of considering race in the imposition of the death penalty but did not delve much deeper into its influence: "It would seem to be incontestable that the death penalty inflicted on one defendant is 'unusual' if it discriminates against him by reason of his race, religion, wealth, social position, or class, or if it is imposed under a procedure that gives room for the play of such prejudices. A penalty . . . should be considered 'unusually' imposed if it is administered arbitrarily or discriminatorily."[56]

Justice Marshall gave the greatest attention to the question of racial discrimination in his own concurring opinion. He wrote, "[C]apital punishment is imposed discriminatorily against certain identifiable classes of people."[57] There had been explicit racial discrimination in the imposition of the death penalty, and such discrimination played a crucial role in his analysis of the penalty as an "unusual" punishment. "[I]t is usually the poor, the illiterate, the underprivileged, the member of the minority group —the man who, because he is without means, and is defended by a court-appointed attorney—who becomes society's sacrificial lamb."[58] He continued, listing statistics that, in his characterization, "betray[ed] much of the discrimination" by demonstrating that "Negroes were executed far more often than whites in proportion to their percentage of the population [and although] [s]tudies indicate[d] that the higher rate of execution among Negroes [was] partially due to a higher rate of crime, there [was] evidence of racial discrimination."[59]

Although Justice Marshall and, to a lesser extent, several other Justices were willing to acknowledge the influence of race on the capital punishment system, race was by no means the primary focus of the other concurring opinions in the case. This refusal to consider seriously the effect of race on the imposition of the death penalty started the Court down a path of analyzing the nature of punishment without regard to race. A poignant example of its reluctance in the *Furman* era to enter the controversial race realm can be found in the 1970 case *Maxwell v. Bishop*.[60] In *Maxwell*, a black male defendant received the death penalty after being convicted of the nonfatal rape of a white woman.[61] Maxwell's attorneys included in their defense a claim based on statistical evidence that his sentence was "part of a racially discriminatory pattern."[62] Despite such a showing, the Eighth Circuit held that such statistics were insufficient to invalidate Maxwell's sentence on equal protection grounds.[63] The Supreme Court ultimately overturned the Eighth Circuit's decision on another constitutional basis, declining to review Maxwell's statistically based equal protection claim.[64]

Several years later in *Coker v. Georgia*,[65] the Court held that the death penalty was "grossly disproportionate and excessive" for the crime of rape and therefore constituted cruel and unusual punishment in such a case.[66] In *Coker*, the same data brought to the surface in *Maxwell* were brought to the Court's attention.[67] What the Court failed to acknowledge in *Coker* was that many of the cases in which a sentence of death had been imposed for the crime of rape involved black male defendants and white female victims.[68] Instead, the Court's reasoning completely excluded this racial dynamic.[69] As in most of the opinions in *Furman*, race in the context of capital sentencing remained the "elephant in the room"—while Justice Marshall, in particular, acknowledged that it had played a significant part in the decisions about which defendants would be sentenced to death, the Court was extremely hesitant to use racial disparity as a basis on which to declare the use of the death penalty unconstitutional. Furthermore, the Court was generally reluctant to confront directly the issue of race in this context—so much so that "[i]n a number of capital cases between 1962 and 1986, the Court either declined requests to hear issues of racial discrimination by denying certiorari or resolved the case on other grounds."[70]

In 1987, McCleskey v. Kemp directly confronted the Court with the question of racial disparity in capital sentencing.[71] It declared that statistics of racial disparity in imposition of the death penalty, as evidenced by the Baldus study,[72] were "insufficient to demonstrate discriminatory intent or unconstitutional discrimination in the Fourteenth Amendment context, [and] insufficient to show irrationality, arbitrariness and capriciousness under any kind of Eighth Amendment analysis."[73] The Court did not dispute the validity of the data presented by the Baldus study;[74] but the Court did state that its "assumption that the Baldus study is statistically valid does not include the assumption that the study shows that racial considerations actually enter into any sentencing decisions in Georgia."[75] By holding that the Baldus study did not establish "with exceptionally clear proof that the decisionmakers in McCleskey's case acted with discriminatory purpose,"[76] the Court in effect subjected claims like McCleskey's to a "heavier burden of proof than is applied to evaluate claims in ordinary jury and employment discrimination cases and claims of discrimination by white voters challenging racially motivated legislative redistricting."[77] Aside from holding that McCleskey had failed to present adequate proof of discrimination, the Court's hesitation to rule in favor of McCleskey likely arose from several factors: a fear of basing its findings on empirical data (lest subsequent, yet converse, empirical data undermine the previous findings); a concern that a finding of unconstitutional discrimination would significantly disrupt the criminal justice system in Georgia and in other states; and a fear that "recognition of a racial claim in a death case by the high court would discredit the death penalty and enhance public perceptions that the Court was responsible for the 'failure' of the death penalty in the post-*Furman* period."[78]

McCleskey seemed to foreclose any possibility of successfully using statistically based claims of racial discrimination in capital sentencing. Shortly after *McCleskey* was handed down, there was one instance of a federal district court's granting a hearing on such a claim. The Eleventh Circuit affirmed that lower court's judgment[79] in *Dobbs v. Zant*,[80] holding that defendant Dobbs had to prove that his sentencing decision was motivated by racial prejudice and, more specifically, that the jurors in his case "were influenced by racial prejudices that would make them more likely to impose the death penalty when the defendant is black than when the defendant is white."[81] In *Dobbs,* some or all of the sitting jurors admitted to "reservations about interracial marriage, fear of blacks as more violent than whites, opposition to the methods of Martin Luther King, Jr.,"[82] and to the use of words such as "colored" and "nigger."[83] Furthermore, both the judge and the trial attorney contributed to this racially hostile environment because the judge also used the word "colored" (likely endorsing and fanning the flames of the jurors' existing racial prejudices) and Dobbs's attorney made his own opinions clear that blacks were less intelligent, less educated, had "inferior morals," and Dobbs's lawyer also used the word "nigger."[84] In spite of such evidence, the circuit court found Dobbs's argument insufficient to demonstrate a constitutionally unacceptable risk that racial prejudice affected his sentencing proceeding and affirmed the denial for habeas corpus relief.[85] Thus, any hope that there might remain some possibility for any similar such claims was soundly dismissed.

At the time of *McCleskey* and since, racial disparities in capital sentencing have continued in a similar trend to that of prior years. Of the 500 prisoners executed between 1977 and the end of 1988, 81.80% were convicted of the murder of a white victim, "even though blacks and whites are the victims of homicide in almost equal numbers nationwide."[86] Of those on death row on January 1, 1999, 42.24% were black and 46.75% were white.[87] A report released by the Death Penalty Information Center in 1998 concluded that in 96% of the reviews of the relationship between race and the death penalty in almost every death penalty state, there was a pattern of either race-of-victim or race-of-defendant discrimination, or both.[88] A

1999 Amnesty International report concluded: "Race is more likely to affect death sentencing than smoking affects the likelihood of dying from heart disease. The latter evidence has produced enormous changes in law and societal practice, while racism in the death penalty has been largely ignored."[89]

III. The Legislative Reaction to Race and the Death Penalty

While *McCleskey* and the cases leading up to *McCleskey* demonstrated the courts' hesitance to fully acknowledge (or at least to react based on) the historical relationship between race and the death penalty, they did not preclude further consideration of the issue by Congress. In fact, in *McCleskey*, the Supreme Court explicitly deferred decisions based on empirical racial disparities in imposition of the death penalty to the legislature. Toward the end of its opinion, the *McCleskey* Court stated that legislatures "are better qualified to weigh and 'evaluate the results of statistical studies in terms of their own local conditions and with a flexibility of approach that is not available to the courts' "[90] and confined its own responsibility to ensuring that the law had been "properly applied."[91] Ultimately, the Court concluded, "McCleskey's arguments are best presented to the legislative bodies."[92]

Under Section Five of the Fourteenth Amendment, Congress is vested with the power to provide additional protections against such forms of racial discrimination, and the Supreme Court has long acknowledged Congress's power to "enact statutes designed to redress racial discrimination, *even in the wake of Supreme Court decisions holding that such redress is not directly mandated by the Constitution.*"[93] Under that provision of power, Representative John Conyers of Michigan proposed the Fairness in Death Sentencing Act (also known as the Racial Justice Act) in April 1988.[94] Over the next several years, the act was reproposed in different forms, and although it was passed by the House of Representatives twice, it was not passed by the Senate and was eventually dropped from a more comprehensive version of the 1994 Crime Bill in a political effort to get both sides to agree.[95]

Absent a Racial Justice Act, death penalty act, defendants must prove discriminatory intent in order to make an effective equal protection claim, a burden that has proven very difficult to meet.[96] Under the proposed bill capital defendants could challenge their death sentences using statistical evidence of discriminatory impact, thereby presenting a prima facie case.[97] In making an "impact" claim defendants could demonstrate that within "the state in which they were convicted, a disproportionately higher number of one particular race is given the death penalty."[98] The bill places the burden of proof on the defendant that there exists a significant pattern of disproportionate sentencing in the jurisdiction where he or she was convicted.[99] Once a prima facie case is established, the burden shifts to the state, which may rebut the defendant's claim with "clear and convincing evidence that the disparity is due to nonracial factors."[100] If the state meets that burden, the claim is dismissed and the death sentence is upheld; if the state does not do so and the defendant's evidence prevails, the death sentence will be overturned. It is important to note that the primary responsibility remains on the defendant to make out a prima facie case. If there are race-neutral reasons for the discrepancy, the state should be able to provide effective rebuttal evidence. Everyone can then be assured that, at the very least, the relevant procedural safeguards are at work. Such a system will not allow for a death sentence to be overturned based on that evidence, if the state successfully rebuts it with evidence of non-racial reasons.[101]

Many who opposed the bill claimed that it was, in reality, an anti-death-penalty bill in disguise.[102] Its opponents in the Senate asserted that it resembled a quota system[103] and that it was problematic in that it attempted to counter racial discrimination by explicitly taking the race of the defendant into consideration during sentencing.[104] They also claimed that the burden on the states was unreasonable and that the existence of such statistical evidence proceedings would place a "tremendous cost and burden on the states."[105] Opponents argued that the bill, if passed, would undermine the Supreme Court's decision in *McCleskey*,[106] although in *McCleskey*, the Court declined only to assign constitutional legitimacy to statistical evidence of racial disparity in the context of capital sentencing —it by no means closed the door on legislative solutions. Quite to the contrary, it explicitly deferred to the legislature, given the Court's perceptions of its own limits.[107]

Many opposing the bill also agreed with the Court in *McCleskey* that capital sentencing could not be judged on statistical evidence alone, given the nature of individual sentencing and the fact that each case is an amalgam of facts and circumstances that is never exactly replicated in any other case.[108] The Supreme Court has required in capital sentencing that each defendant be sentenced based on the circumstances of the particular crime and of the individual defendant.[109] Many observers perceive logical inconsistency in a system that would allow the death sentence of one defendant sentenced under the combination of a given set of jurors, judge, prosecutor, and circumstances of the crime to be overturned based on statistical evidence that is premised on the sentencing of many other defendants, all with their own particularized sentencing proceedings. Furthermore, many might see such a system as producing its own unequal inconsistencies—consider the following example.

Assume, for example, that persons A and B have identical cases (as defined under the bill) and are equally deserving of the death penalty. Neither produces the slightest evidence that racial factors influenced his or her death sentence. A, who comes from a jurisdiction in which there is a "statistical disparity" under the bill, is not executed. B comes from a jurisdiction where there is no "statistical disparity" and is executed. All other factors being the same in each case (as the bill assumes), this circumstance fails to furnish a "meaningful basis for distinguishing the . . . cases in which [the death penalty] is imposed from the . . . cases in which it is not." Under the bill, A simply is fortunate to be able to point to the statistical disparity and B is not, although both are equally deserving of the death penalty. B, knowing of A, might feel that the imposition of the death penalty is "cruel and unusual in the same way that being struck by lightning is cruel and unusual. . . . The Eighth and Fourteenth Amendments cannot tolerate the infliction of a sentence of death under legal systems that permit this unique penalty to be so wantonly and so freakishly imposed."[110]

Although such an argument may intuitively sound correct, it fails to take account of the fact that the Supreme Court has always allowed lower courts to exercise discretion in showing mercy to individual defendants.[111] Even though two defendants may be equally eligible for the death penalty, it would not be unconstitutional for one court to decide to show one defendant mercy while it does not do the same for another.[112] The "meaningful basis" in the case of statistical evidence provided under an RJA scheme would be the conclusion that the statistical evidence presented is indicative of underlying racial prejudices within the jurisdiction that cannot be rooted out by the other procedures already in place (e.g., voir dire). Far from "wantonly and freakishly" imposing a death sentence, a remedy that recognizes the inability of the current system to account for and eliminate the influence of racial bias, and therefore implements a scheme to address that inability, should be seen as trying to *minimize* the arbitrariness of the death penalty.[113] It may be that in both cases, underlying racism was at play and only one defendant was able to demonstrate that effectively—does that mean that both defendants should nonetheless be sentenced to death?[114] Professor David Cole seems to agree that fears that the bill will overturn large numbers of death sentences assume that a high level of racial bias *is* at work in the system by noting that "[i]f the death penalty were already being imposed on race-neutral terms, the Racial Justice Act would have little or no effect, and there would be no cause for concern among death-penalty supporters. Their fears that the act might end the death penalty are, as then Justice William Brennan Jr. said in reference to the *McCleskey* majority, 'a fear of too much justice.' "[115] There may in fact be validity to the argument that systemic evidence (i.e., the Baldus study) is better suited to drawing conclusions about the system as a whole than about an individual sentencing hearing. However, we have already seen that argument soundly rejected—at least, for now—in *McCleskey*; in the resulting void, it seems preferable to have justice in the case of the individual than to have no justice at all.[116]

Another benefit of allowing a defendant to pursue equal protection claims based on disparate impact arguments is that it enables the defendant to root out subtle, more pervasive racism, while also preserving the "sanctity of both jury and prosecutorial discretion."[117] Restricting defendants to claims where they must prove intent requires them to go to such lengths as "prob[ing] into the mental processes of jurors," and "rummaging through the files of the district attorney";[118] even then, the defendant and his or her attorneys will likely come up empty-handed, or without a sufficiently "smoking" gun.[119]

The greatest achievement of the racial justice bill as proposed in Congress and the Racial Justice Act adopted by Kentucky is that the latter takes a major step toward acknowledging the presence and influence of subtle racism in capital sentencing.[120] Although other similar contexts in which disparate impact claims are available due to legislative action (e.g., employment, housing) can certainly be distinguished,[121] it does seem somewhat odd that we are willing to acknowledge the influence of underlying societal racism in those contexts but are more hesitant to do so when a life is at stake. It would be difficult—likely impossible—to define a common standard by which to evaluate all defendants who have or have not received the death penalty, yet such a fact should not be an obstacle in the provision of individual mercy. It may be impossible to prove that the difference between one defendant's sentence and those of another group is due solely to race, but it would seem equally impossible to prove that race was *not* a factor, especially when all of the other measured variables appear to be equivalent. At the very least, because under such a scheme the state will be forced to rebut such claims made by defendants, a racial justice act may encourage the state to adopt more uniform standards for imposition of the death penalty, which, when followed consistently, would leave little room for the influence of racial bias to have any effect.

Whatever the benefits of the act may have been, its passage did not take place. Although the *McCleskey* Court may have meant well in addressing such questions to the legislature, the history of the legislation makes clear that Congress is ultimately no more willing than the courts to give significant weight to objective evidence of the racially disproportionate impact of the death penalty. Congress cannot be expected to serve as any kind of protectionist backstop in ensuring that capital sentencing is free of discrimination.[122]

Once it had become clear that the bill would not be passed by the Senate, the Equal Justice bill was introduced as an alternative. It would have provided ex ante safeguards against racial bias and racial discrimination throughout the trial, and it would have applied to all penalties, not just to capital punishment.[123] One originally proposed provision was that the judge presiding over a capital sentencing proceeding must instruct the jury that it may not consider the "race or color of the defendant or victim in considering whether a sentence of death is justified" and that upon returning a death sentence, the jury would have to return as well a certificate signed by each juror testifying to the fact it had adhered to these instructions.[124] Although the equal justice bill was not a part of the omnibus crime bill legislation of 1994, Congress adopted a provision similar to it in the Federal Death Penalty Act of 1994.[125]

The equal justice provision is clearly aimed at minimizing the risk of racial bias or prejudice in sentencing proceedings. One initial advantage of the provision is that it addresses racial prejudice in capital sentencing by attempting to preempt such prejudice from ever coming into play. Although in the context of statistical evidence of racial disparity, the Court told us in *McCleskey* that statistical parity is not constitutionally required, it has never declared that a provision like that in the equal justice bill is not required if specifically requested by the defendant. In fact, the equal justice bill seems to stem from the same motivating impulse found in *Turner v. Murray*;[126] relying on the constitutional guarantees provided by the Sixth and Fourteenth Amendments, it seems eminently reasonable to put safeguards in place to ensure that any risk of racial bias in the jury could be minimized. The question as to whether such a measure is constitutionally required, however, is as posed in *Turner*: at which point does the risk that racial prejudice will "infect[ ] the capital sentencing proceeding" become "constitutionally unacceptable"?[127]

Currently, this provision of the Federal Death Penalty Act applies only to federal capital cases. Given the rationale in *Turner*—to minimize the risk of racial prejudice in capital sentencing—it might appear as if a request for a similar procedure in state court must be granted on the ground that a failure to instruct the jury not to consider race or color might present an unacceptable risk of racial bias. Still, based on a close analysis of *Turner's* reasoning and the Court's tendency to construe such precedents narrowly, it seems that the request for voir dire questioning of jurors regarding racial prejudice in *Turner* can be distinguished. In *Turner*, such questioning was required as a necessary step toward securing an impartial jury.[128] Without informing the jurors of the victim's race and by questioning them as to their own racial bias, it is likely that partial jurors could be selected to the jury; in that sense, the *Turner* requirement is an ex ante, preventive measure. In comparison, the requirement that a sitting jury be instructed that they may not consider the race or color of the defendant or victim and that they sign a certificate promising that they did not, in fact, consider such factors, is an ex post measure. Arguably, although such a measure may minimize the risk of racial prejudice, it does not affect the composition of the jury. *Turner's* rationale could still apply in the sense that this measure may still affect the impartiality of the jury by acting as one last fail-safe to avert the jurors' succumbing to racial prejudice. One may ask, however, if we have any faith in the all of the other safeguards in place, why would we need such a measure? The rationale itself then seems to admit that other procedures have failed in attempting to keep racially biased jurors from sitting on the jury (and, at that point, it is not at all certain that one last warning will do anything to counter that circumstance).

Aside from whether such a procedure could ever be required in state courts, a separate set of issues surrounds the desirability of such a procedure. On one hand, the ability to place race so squarely on the table may force some jurors to be more honest with themselves as to their own prejudices and, confronted with the requirement of having to sign a document acknowledging that they were not influenced by such prejudices, might actually impel them to reach their decision differently. In addition, the ability to utilize such a requirement as a tool in opening and closing arguments may be a powerful way to sway the jury—or at the very least, openly place race on the table as something of which jurors should be conscious (acknowledging the proverbial "elephant" in the room). On the other hand, such a strategy might also backfire in the sense that warnings about racial bias could potentially "actually inject bias into the minds of jurors, and jurors may subconsciously interpret the formal warnings as a cynical statement that jurors may act on racial biases as long as they do not admit to them."[129] Representative Conyers, a proponent of a racial justice bill who viewed the equal justice bill as an inadequate substitute, argued that "[t]o have any effect, the equal justice bill's provisions must assume, unrealistically, that biased jurors will recognize their own racial biases and either stymie them or confess them to the court."[130]

The implementation of such a strategy might also have damaging implications for defendants attempting to prove discriminatory intent, or —in a jurisdiction that has adopted some version of the racial justice bill[131]—to collect statistical evidence of racial disparity in capital sentencing. Faced with a multitude of signed documents certifying that jurors specifically did *not* take race into account, it would certainly be more difficult to prove that racial factors were impermissibly at play and perhaps more difficult to support statistical evidence showing the same (when there are documents pointing toward exactly the opposite conclusion).[132] Furthermore, if one were to respond in defense to such a critique that such procedures should not be imbued with meaning sufficient to defeat a showing of discriminatory intent, given their potentially superficial nature or impact, one may then question the very usefulness of such a requirement in the first place.

Bottom line: the question that must be asked is whether there is an unacceptable risk that racial prejudice might remain at play if not for the equal justice bill's provision. Given that there seem to be few strong arguments for its effectiveness, and even several arguments that it might actually produce an unintended "backfiring," it appears difficult to argue that the failure to include such a provision, would, in and of itself, create an unacceptable risk of bias. Although such a provision would certainly not be unconstitutional, it is doubtful that it would be constitutionally required. It is clear, nonetheless, that the bill's adopted provision acts modestly at best as an additional procedural safeguard. It does not go nearly as far as the racial justice bill in attempting to prevent racial bias so deep that it cannot be rooted out by questioning alone. In that sense, it appears to be a half-hearted response to the Court's legislative deferral in *McCleskey*—and many of us are left wanting more.

IV. Out of Step: A Comparative Perspective on Race and the Death Penalty

Although the American judiciary and Congress have failed to fully acknowledge or react to the discriminatory role race plays in the administration of the death penalty, there is growing domestic and international concern that the death penalty is a troubled doctrine—in part due to the significance of race in its imposition—demonstrating that the United States has fallen completely out of step with international norms with regard to capital punishment. On the domestic front, this concern is reflected in the writings and speeches of former and current Supreme Court Justices and actions by several states that have imposed moratoria or are reviewing their death penalty statutes. *Internationally, the majority of countries around the world have abolished the death penalty, including South Africa, a nation plagued with a troubled racial history and significant crime problem.*

A. Domestic Concern with the Death Penalty

Several current and former Supreme Court Justices who in the past supported the death penalty have expressed opposition to or anxiety about the death penalty. Justice Blackmun, for example, who voted to uphold the death penalty in the landmark cases *Furman v. Georgia* and *Gregg v. Georgia,*[133] reversed his legal position in a strongly worded dissent in *Callins v. Collins:*[134]

> From this day forward, I no longer shall tinker with the machinery of death. For more than 20 years I have endeavored—indeed, I have struggled —along with a majority of this Court, to develop procedural and substantive rules that would lend more than the mere appearance of fairness to the death penalty endeavor. Rather than continue to coddle the Court's delusion that the desired level of fairness has been achieved and the need for regulation eviscerated, I feel morally and intellectually obligated simply to concede that the death penalty experiment has failed. It is virtually self-evi-

dent to me now that no combination of procedural rules or substantive regulations ever can save the death penalty from its inherent constitutional deficiencies. The basic question—does the system accurately and consistently determine which defendants "deserve" to die?—cannot be answered in the affirmative.[135]

Although Justice Blackmun did not base his position solely on evidence of racial disparities in the application of the death penalty, he did recognize that racial discrimination continues to infect the application of the death penalty "[e]ven under the most sophisticated death penalty statutes"[136]

Justices O'Connor and Ginsburg, who both consistently upheld the imposition of the death penalty, have each expressed skepticism about the use of capital punishment. In a speech to the Minnesota Women Lawyers Association in July 2001, Justice O'Connor observed that there are "serious questions being raised about whether the death penalty is being fairly administered in this country."[137] She commented that Minnesotans "must breathe a sigh of relief every day" because their state does not impose the death penalty.[138] Justice O'Connor based her skepticism on the number of death row inmates who have been exonerated and the dearth of competent counsel available to death row inmates. Similarly, Justice Ginsburg has stated that she would support Maryland's proposed moratorium on the death penalty.[139] Like O'Connor, Ginsburg pointed to the problem of inadequate representation of counsel as a justification for her position and observed that well-represented defendants do not get the death penalty. She stated that during her tenure on the Court, she had not seen "eve-of-execution stay applications in which the defendant was well represented at trial."[140]

The declining domestic support for the death penalty is also evident in recent actions by states. Perhaps most notable is that of former Illinois governor George Ryan, once a death penalty proponent, who in January 2000 imposed a moratorium on capital punishment and commuted 167 death sentences in his state.[141] Governor Ryan stated that he had decided to impose the moratorium because of his state's "shameful" record of wrongful convictions in capital cases: "If the system were making so many errors in determining whether someone was guilty in the first place, how fairly and accurately was it determining which guilty defendants deserved to live and which deserved to die? What effect was race having? What effect was poverty having?"[142]

On the heels of the Illinois example, several other states have begun to call into question the effectiveness of their own criminal justice systems, given their own concerns about racial bias and the number of wrongful convictions in their own courts. In 1999, a blue ribbon committee was appointed in Pennsylvania to review that state's practice of capital punishment. Among the committee's recommendations were enactment of a Racial Justice Act similar to that implemented in other states; commission of further studies to investigate the impact of the race of the defendant, the race of the victim, and prosecutorial discretion in seeking the death penalty in capital sentencing; and passage of legislation that would "declare a moratorium on the death penalty until such time as policies and procedures are implemented to ensure that the death penalty is being administered fairly and impartially throughout the Commonwealth."[143] The committee also observed that capital counsel services were not being sufficiently provided to indigent defendants in Pennsylvania, a phenomenon that disproportionately affects minority communities.[144] In 2002, Maryland Governor Parris Glendening announced a moratorium on executions pending the outcome of a study by the University of Maryland into the fairness of the state's death penalty, especially with regard to racial bias. In May 2004, a group of 400-plus Massachusetts attorneys, "[a]larmed that Boston [was] second only to Chicago in its number of wrongful convictions," was in the midst of preparing to file a petition with state officials requesting the formation of a formal "Innocence Commission," which would review "nearly two dozen case in which the wrong man was imprisoned."[145]

In June 2004, in *People v. LaValle,* the New York State Court of Appeals held that the state's death penalty statute contained a provision that is unconstitutional under the state constitution and could only be cured by passage of a new law by the legislature.[146] The provision required judges to instruct death penalty jurors that if they deadlocked during the penalty phase, the judge would impose a sentence that would allow the defendant to be eligible for parole in 20 to 25 years. The court ruled that this so-called deadlock instruction coerced the jurors to vote for execution fearing that if they did not, the defendant may be paroled from prison and pose a threat to society. This ruling has created uncertainty regarding the future of New York's death penalty statute.[147]

B. Declining International Support for Death Penalty

Support for the death penalty has waned in the international community, with 117 nations having abolished the death penalty or declared a moratorium concerning its application.[148] Most notable is South Africa, a nation plagued by high levels of violence. In spite of its significant crime problems, South Africa abolished the death penalty in *State v. Makwanyane*.[149] Although the South African Constitution does not expressly prohibit the death penalty, the *Makwanyane* Court relied on several expressed rights granted by the Constitution, namely, the right to equality before the law; the right to equal protection under the law; the right to life; the right to respect for and protection of dignity; and the prohibition on cruel, inhuman, or degrading treatment or punishment. Further, the South African Constitution provides that any limitations on the aforementioned rights be "reasonable, justifiable in an open and democratic society based on freedom and equality, and shall not negate the essential content of the right in question." The *Makwanyane* Court recognized the inconsistency in the death penalty and the Constitution's limitations clause. As one of the *Makwanyane* judges summarized this inconsistency: "Look here, old chap, I propose to execute you but I want you to know I'm not negating the essential content of your right to life."

The Court also surveyed international norms and precedent to guide its decision.[150] Regarding the United States, the Court concluded that

> United States jurisprudence has not resolved the dilemma arising from the fact that the Constitution prohibits cruel and unusual punishments, but also permits, and contemplates that there will be capital punishment. The acceptance by a majority of the United States Supreme Court of the proposition that capital punishment is not per se unconstitutional, but that in certain circumstances it may be arbitrary, and thus unconstitutional, has led to endless litigation. Considerable expense and interminable delays result from the exceptionally-high standard of procedural fairness set by the United States courts in attempting to avoid arbitrary decisions. The difficulties that have been experienced in following this path, to which Justice Blackmun and Justice Scalia [in *Callins v. Collins*] have both referred, but from which they have drawn different conclusions, persuade me that we should not follow this route.[151]

C. The Emergence of International Law, the Revival of *Batson v. Kentucky,* and the Future of Death Penalty Jurisprudence

Three cases decided during the Supreme Court's 2004 term, *Miller-El v. Dretke*,[152] *Johnson v. California*,[153] and *Roper v. Simmons*[154] indicate that

that the Supreme Court has begun to reevaluate the way the death penalty is applied and at the same time reexamine the process that has operated to produce all-white juries and sentence a disproportionate number of blacks to death. *Miller-El* and *Johnson* marked a revival of *Batson v. Kentucky,*[155] the case holding that excluding blacks because of their race denied both the defendant and the excluded jurors of equal protection of the laws.[156] Together, these cases suggest that race is once again at the forefront of the Court's thinking about the death penalty.

In *Miller-El,* the Court vacated the murder conviction and death sentence of a black man because Dallas County prosecutors had used peremptory challenges to exclude two black jurors whose pro-death-penalty answers to a questionnaire should have made them more attractive prospective jurors than several of the white jurors who ended up serving and sentencing the defendant to death.[157] Further indicating prosecutor's discriminatory motives, when asked to justify his decisions to exclude the two black jurors, the prosecutor gave answers that the record demonstrated to be false.[158] The Court noted that out of the 20 blacks in the 108-person venire panel, only one served on the jury, and while nine were excused by the agreement of both parties, 10, including the two that the Court found would have made ideal jurors, were struck.[159] Further, the Court found that prosecutors had essentially elicited responses from black jurors that were likely to get them struck from the panel by giving those jurors a graphic description of what would happen to the defendant if they imposed the death penalty.[160] Finally, the Court pointed out that Dallas County prosecutors had a history of excluding blacks from juries, and, in fact, in 1968 they had written a manual on how to do it, and that manual was still available to the prosecutors when Miller-El's case was tried.[161]

In *Johnson,* the Court vacated the conviction of a black man for assaulting and killing his girlfriend's white baby.[162] In doing so, the Court struck down a California law requiring defendants raising *Batson* challenges to prove that a prosecutor's motives were "more likely than not" the product of discrimination in order to make the prima facie case.[163] Writing for the majority, Justice Stevens emphasized that the high burden of persuasion was particularly inappropriate since *Batson* claims are, by nature, difficult to demonstrate "on the basis of all the facts, some of which are impossible for the defendant to know with certainty."[164] Ultimately, *Johnson* will ensure that states are not able to resurrect burdensome standards of proof to prevent black defendants from challenging prosecutor's decisions to strike black persons from juries.

It remains to be seen what influence *Johnson* and *Miller-El* will have on the way juries in death penalty cases are selected in courtrooms across the country. At minimum, *Johnson* will ensure that states do not pass laws requiring onerous burdens of proof. The decisions may breathe new life into *Batson,* and consequently, make sure that prospective black jurors will be given an equal opportunity to serve on juries in death penalty cases. Of course, it is important to bear in mind that one of the primary reasons Miller-El prevailed was that two of the black jurors who were peremptorily struck from the venire panel had given responses that were more pro–death penalty that the responses of whites who were placed on the jury.[165] Hence, although a strengthened *Batson* doctrine does not by any means guarantee juries less likely to impose the death penalty, the holdings in *Johnson* and *Miller-El* will ensure that the juries doling out death sentences in the twenty-first century will have more blacks than the juries in the first half of the twentieth century. Allowing African-Americans a fair opportunity to serve on juries will at least guarantee that blacks will have a meaningful role in the process that has long operated to discriminate against black defendants.

International law played a significant role in narrowing the scope of the death penalty. In *Roper v. Simmons,* the Court ruled that executing minors who committed crimes when they were younger than eighteen was unconstitutional because doing so violated the Eighth and Fourteenth Amendments.[166] As it had done the past, the Court "referred to the laws of other countries and to international authorities as instructive for its interpretation of the Eighth Amendment's prohibition of 'cruel and unusual punishments.' "[167] Justice Kennedy, writing for the Court, noted "the overwhelming weight of international opinion against the juvenile death penalty."[168] Kennedy cited Article 37 of the United Nations Convention on the Rights of the Child, the laws of the United Kingdom, and the fact that only seven other countries in the world—Iran, Pakistan, Saudi Arabia, Yemen, Nigeria, the Democratic Republic of Congo, and China—had executed juveniles since 1990.[169]

Writing in dissent, Justice Scalia criticized the Court's reliance on international law and bemoaned that the Court had "rejected a purely originalist approach to our Eighth Amendment."[170] Nevertheless, the Court declared, "it does not lessen our fidelity to the Constitution or our pride in

its origins to acknowledge that the express affirmation of certain fundamental rights by other nations and peoples simply underscores the centrality of those same rights within our own heritage of freedom." Justice
O'Connor also dissented, but pointed out that "[o]ver the course of nearly
half a century, the Court has consistently referred to foreign and international law as relevant to its assessment of evolving standards of decency."[171]

Roper was by no means the first instance in which Supreme Court Justices debated what role international norms should play in U.S. death
penalty jurisprudence. In Atkins v. Virginia,[172] for example, the Court held
that the death penalty was unconstitutional as applied to the mentally
retarded.[173] Writing for the majority, Justice Stevens observed that "within
the world community, the imposition of the death penalty for crimes
committed by mentally retarded offenders is overwhelmingly disap-
proved."[174] Likewise, in Thompson v. Oklahoma,[175] the Court held that the
Eighth and Fourteenth Amendments prohibit the execution of a defendant convicted of first-degree murder for an offense committed when
defendant was fifteen years old.[176] Writing for the plurality, Justice Stevens
argued that other nations support the notion that executing a person who
was less than 16 years old at the time of his or her offense offends civilized
standards of decency.[177] Stevens also cited laws of other countries that
prohibit execution of juveniles and maintains that the Court has "previously recognized the relevance of the views of the international community in determining whether a punishment is cruel and unusual."[178]
Finally, in Knight v. Florida,[179] in which the Court denied certiorari to
petitioners who challenged the constitutionality of the lengthy delay
between their sentencing and planned executions, Justice Breyer in his dissent relied heavily on international law that views such lengthy delays as
inhuman. Justice Breyer argued that U.S. courts should take into account
"foreign courts considering roughly comparable questions under roughly
comparable legal standards."[180]

Justice Scalia dissented in Thompson and Atkins and objected to the
majority's use of international law. In Atkins, he responded that the practices of the " 'world community,' whose notions of justice are (thankfully)
not always those of our people" are irrelevant.[181] Dissenting again in
Thompson, Justice Scalia called Stevens's reliance on Amnesty International's assessment of international death penalty laws "totally inappropriate as a means of establishing the fundamental beliefs of this Nation."[182]
Justice Scalia further argued, "[t]hat 40% of our States do not rule out
capital punishment for 15-year-old felons is determinative of the question

before us here, even if that position contradicts the uniform view of the rest of the world. [W]here there is [no] settled consensus among our own people, the views of other nations cannot be imposed upon Americans through the Constitution. [T]he fact that a majority of foreign nations would not impose capital punishment upon persons under 16 at the time of the crime is of no more relevance than the fact that a majority of them would not impose capital punishment at all, or have standards of due process quite different from our own."[183]

Justice Thomas apparently shares Justice Scalia's disdain for using international law as a guidepost for interpreting the "evolving standards of decency" that inform the Eighth Amendment. In *Knight*, Justice Thomas echoed Justice Scalia in his critique of using international law as a guidepost for determining what constituted inhumane treatment.[184] In his concurring opinion, Justice Thomas disagreed with Justice Breyer's reliance on international law, arguing that the lack of support in U.S. law for petitioners' claim is why proponents of these arguments are forced to resort to the laws of other countries to support their claim.[185]

The Court's references to international law have not been confined to death penalty cases. In *Lawrence v. Texas*,[186] the Court held that a Texas statute making it a crime for two persons of the same sex to engage in certain intimate sexual conduct was unconstitutional.[187] Justice Kennedy, writing for the majority maintained "[t]he right the petitioners seek in this case has been accepted as an integral part of human freedom in many other countries."[188] Again, not surprisingly, Justice Scalia dissented. Justice Scalia averred that "[t]he Court's discussion of these foreign views is meaningless dicta. Dangerous dicta, however, since this Court . . . should not impose foreign moods, fads, or fashions on Americans."[189]

The Court's reliance on international norms in cases dealing with the death penalty and in *Lawrence, Roper*, and the other cases is significant because it sheds light on competing views about the rights protected by the Bill of Rights and government of limited and enumerated powers set forth in the Constitution. The Court's references to international law suggest that Kennedy and the Justices who joined his opinions conceive of the "rights retained by the people" as emanating not exclusively from those rights in existence in America at the time of the founding, but from a more inclusive source common to all human beings. By contrast, Justice Scalia's approach yields a narrower understanding of the rights protected by the Constitution. As Justice Scalia made clear in his *Roper* dissent, he favors "a purely originalist approach to our Eighth Amendment."[190] Put simply, Justice Scalia believes that the Constitution and Bill of Rights only protect those rights recognized at the time or our nation's founding. This view is a stark contrast with Justice O'Connor's reference to "evolving standards of decency" in *Roper*.[191] For Justice Scalia, our protected rights are not "evolving," but are frozen at the moment of our nation's founding. Needless to say, confining one's view of standards of decency to a time when the vast majority of African-Americans in our country were enslaved and subject to virtually unchecked violence at the hands of their masters is unlikely to lead to a reexamination of the disproportionate application of the death penalty. On the other hand, it is more likely that reliance on "evolving standards of decency" informed by international norms would lead the Court to reconsider the role race has played in sentencing African-Americans to death.

Combined with the Court's increasing willingness to refer to international norms, *Roper*, *Miller-El*, and *Johnson*, three cases from the Court's 2004 term, highlight what may be a progressive trend in the Court's death penalty jurisprudence. *Roper*, *Miller-El*, and *Johnson*, taken together, suggest that the Court has begun to rethink the groups to whom the death penalty is applied as well as the role of race in the process by which it is applied. Since Justice O'Connor and Chief Justice Rehnquist were not members of the *Roper* majority, even if Chief Justice Roberts and Justice O'Connor's replacement share Justice Scalia's views, both the holding and the Court's more expansive vision of rights informed by international norms should remain intact. While there is little evidence to indicate that the Court would reconsider the constitutionality of the death penalty, *Roper*, *Johnson*, and *Miller-El* and the concept of rights prompting the Court's references to international law may serve as basis for a serious reexamination of race and the death penalty.

V. Conclusion

Although far too many of our nation's courts and legislatures have heard —and then rejected—claims based on empirical data demonstrating racial disparities in the imposition of the death penalty, they have long underestimated the impact of this country's long history of providing black defendants, victims, and jurors with a criminal justice system that is far from fair. It may be that much of this injustice in the realm of criminal punishment now takes place within the courtroom, but it is clear that many black defendants, and especially those accused of murdering white victims, still do not experience the same system that many white defendants face—a burden that they have carried across centuries.

By the same token, the international intolerance of a form of punishment that involves the state in the taking of lives has been condemned with increasing urgency, and has at least drawn the attention of some members of our Supreme Court. The tolerance of discrimination in the application of the death penalty, and the continuing practice of ignoring the world's response in similar circumstances, must generate a call to action by those who believe that passive acceptance is tantamount to tacit approval. The time has come to finally embrace the moral courage to reject the tolerance of racial discrimination in the application of capital punishment, and also to follow the lead of progressive nations throughout the world, which cite various reasons to justify shutting down the state-operated machinery of death.

NOTES

1. E.g., Jesse Jackson, Legal Lynching: Racism, Injustice, and the Death Penalty (1996).

2. *See, e.g.,* Scott W. Howe, *The Futile Quest for Racial Neutrality in Capital Selection and the Eighth Amendment for Abolition Based on Unconscious Racial Discrimination,* 45 WM. & MARY L. REV. 2083 (2004) (demonstrating the ways in which race discrimination continues to play a significant role in capital sentencing and arguing that solutions other than abolition are inadequate to remedy that discriminatory phenomenon).

3. David C. Baldus & George Woodworth, *Race Discrimination and the Death Penalty: An Empirical and Legal Overview,* in America's Experiment with Capital Punishment: Reflections on the Past, Present, and Future of the Ultimate Penal Sanction 385, 385 (Acker et al., eds., 1998).

4. *See* Howe, *supra* note 2, at 2110–20.

5. 481 U.S. 279 (1987).

6. "Defendants" is placed in quotation marks to signify the fact that although some targeted African-Americans were actually defendants in a legal sense, others were those who had been accused or were believed to have committed some crime but had not actually been tried in a court of law. The injustice for the latter was often executed through extralegal means.

7. *Dred Scott v. Sandford,* 60 U.S. 393, 407 (1857).

8. John Hope Franklin & Alfred A. Moss, Jr., From Slavery to Freedom: A History of African Americans 141 (Alfred A. Knopf 2000) (1947).

9. *See* A. Leon Higginbotham, In the Matter of Color: Race and the American Legal Process, The Colonial Period 74 (1978) (discussing Massachusetts case from 1685, *Re Hannah Bonny,* in which a white woman was found guilty of fornication with two lovers, one black man and one white man; each received an equal punishment of whipping).

10. Franklin & Moss, *supra* note 8, at 141.

11. Higginbotham, *supra* note 9, at 252 (discussing a 1755 Georgia law, "An Act for the Better Ordering and Governing Negroes and Other Slaves in this Province").

12. Note the disparate treatment regarding murder of slaves: "A slave could not strike a white person, even in self-defense; but the killing of a slave, however malicious the act, was rarely regarded as murder." Franklin & Moss, *supra* note 8, at 141. Note that in much more recent years, murders involving white victims are still more likely to receive a death sentence. As I relate in my *Oregon Law Review* article, if asked by McCleskey whether he was likely to be sentenced to die, McCleskey's lawyer would have had to respond by saying that "[d]efendants charged with killing white victims in Georgia the odds would be 4.3 times as likely to be sentenced to death as defendants charged with killing blacks. In addition, frankness would compel the disclosure that it was more likely than not that the race of McCleskey's victim would determine whether he received a death sentence: 6 of every 11 defendants convicted of killing a white person would not have received the death penalty if their victims had been black. . . . Finally, the assessment would not be complete without the information that cases involving black defendants and white victims are more likely to result in a death sentence than cases featuring any other racial combination of defendant and victim." Charles J. Ogletree, Jr., *Wayne Morse Center for Law and Politics Symposium: The Law and Politics of the Death Penalty: Abolition, Moratorium, or Reform? Black Man's Burden: Race and the Death Penalty in America,* 81 ORE. L. REV. 15, 30 (2002).

13. Franklin & Moss, *supra* note 8, at 141–42.

14. *Id.* at 142.

15. *See generally* C. Vann Woodward, The Strange Career of Jim Crow (Commemorative Edition 2000). Woodward notes a shift in the popular white view of blacks during the twenty years between 1880 and 1900 from one of a harmless "Uncle Remus" type to one of a brute as depicted in the writings of Thomas Dixon. *Id.* at 93.

16. *Id.* at 123.

17. John A. Carpenter, *Atrocities in the Reconstruction Period,* 47 J. OF NEGRO HISTORY 234, 234 (October 1962).

18. *Id.* at 243.

19. *Id.* at 244.

20. Jerrold M. Packard, American Nightmare: The History of Jim Crow 42 (2002). Southern states "intended a return to virtually the same social relationship between whites and now-freed blacks as that which had existed before the Confederacy's defeat. To achieve it, the Black Codes were deliberately designed to be restrictive and harsh in their application." *Id.*

21. Barbara Holden-Smith, *Lynching, Federalism, and the Intersection of Race and Gender in the Progressive Era*, 8 YALE J.L. & FEMINISM 31, 36 (1996). The Archives at Tuskegee Institute indicate 4,742 total lynchings between 1882 and 1968, of which 3,445 were of blacks. *See* Robert L. Zangrando, The NAACP Crusade Against Lynching, 1900–1950, 68–69 (1980).

22. Brooks Miles Barnes, *The Onancock Race Riot of 1907*, 92 VIRGINIA MAGAZINE OF HISTORY & BIOGRAPHY 336 (July 1984). "[T]he new generation of whites experienced less personal contact and correspondingly less personal control over blacks than had their predecessors. Whites more frequently resorted to harsh tactics—segregation statute, lynch law, and race riot—to preserve their superiority." *Id.* at 350.

23. One example is the Memphis lynching of three businessmen whose "crime," according to antilynching advocate Ida B. Wells-Barnett, "had been to succeed in their grocery business at the expense of a competing white grocer." Packard, *supra* note 20, at 138.

24. William Ziglar, *'Community on Trial': The Coatesville Lynching of 1911*, 106 PENNSYLVANIA MAGAZINE OF HISTORY AND BIOGRAPHY 245 (April 1982).

25. *Id.* at 246.

26. *Id.* at 248–50.

27. *Id.* at 250.

28. Leon F. Litwack, *Hellhounds, in* Without Sanctuary: Lynching Photography in America 14 (2000). After burning the clothes from Mrs. Turner's body, the mob sliced open her abdomen, releasing the baby. A member of the crowd stepped on the baby's head, crushing its skull.

29. Herbert Shapiro, White Violence and Black Response: From Reconstruction to Montgomery 114 (1988).

30. 214 U.S. 386 (1909).

31. *See* Mark Curriden & Leroy Phillips, Jr., Contempt of Court: The Turn-of-the-Century Lynching That Launched 100 Years of Federalism 3–4 (1999).

32. Ogletree, *supra* note 13, at 15, 20.

33. Curriden & Phillips, *supra* note 31.

34. Ogletree, *supra* note 12, at 21. Another example of such an incident occurred in 1906, when a man was hanged immediately after an hourlong trial in Mayfield, Kentucky: "The editorial [in the Louisville *Courier-Journal*] noted that, although the trial was hasty, 'at least it was not a lynching.' Adding that since a Negro had raped a white woman, 'no other result could have been reached, how-

ever long the trial.' " *Killing with Prejudice: Race & the Death Penalty in the USA* (Amnesty International, May 1999), at 3–4 (citing Stephen Bright, *Discrimination, Death and Denial: The Tolerance of Racial Discrimination in Infliction of the Death Penalty*, 35 SANTA CLARA L. REV. 433–483 (1995)).

35. Dan T. Carter, Scottsboro: A Tragedy of the American South 12 (rev. ed. 1979).

36. *Id.* at 8–9.

37. *Id.* at 20.

38. *Id.* at 113 (quoting *Selma Times-Journal,* quoted in the *New York Times,* July 27, 1931, at 14) (internal quotation marks omitted).

39. *Id.* at 48.

40. *Id.* at 133.

41. *Id.* at 134.

42. *Id.* at 135.

43. Steven F. Lawson, David R. Colburn, & Darryl Paulson, *Groveland: Florida's Little Scottsboro,* 65 FLORIDA HISTORICAL QUARTERLY 1 (July 1986).

44. *Id.*

45. *Id.* at 8–9.

46. *Id* at 10.

47. *Id.* at 13.

48. *Id.* at 16. Justice Jackson felt that the pretrial publicity involved in the case, *inter alia,* prevented a fair hearing.

49. *Id.* at 18.

50. *Id.* at 23.

51. Sheryl Gay Stolberg, *Senate Issues Apology Over Failure on Antilynching Law,* N.Y. TIMES, June 14, 2005.

52. *Id.* According to Senator Landrieu of Louisiana, 4,742 is the number of recorded lynchings.

53. 408 U.S. 238 (1972).

54. *Id.* at 240.

55. Three concurring opinions and one dissenting Justice expressed a concern that the jury sentencing practices being examined in *Furman* created a danger of racial discrimination.

Before the landmark Supreme Court case of *Furman v. Georgia* was decided, it was clear that the death penalty, even as imposed in more modern cases, had a dramatically disproportionate effect on blacks. For example, 49 percent of 3,334 defendants executed for murder in the pre-*Furman* era were black; from the 1910s to the 1950s, between 60 and 70 percent of people executed in the South for murder were black. Baldus & Woodworth, *supra* note 3, at 397.

56. *Furman,* 408 U.S. at 242 (Douglas, J., concurring).

57. *Furman,* 408 U.S. at 364 (Marshall, J., concurring).

58. *Id.* at 364 (Marshall, J., concurring) (quoting Hearings on S. 1760 before the

Subcommittee on Criminal Laws and Procedures of the Senate Committee on the Judiciary, 90th Cong., 2d Sess. n. 80, at 11 (1968) (statement of M. DiSalle)).

59. *Id.*

60. 398 U.S. 262 (1970).

61. *Maxwell v. State,* 263 Ark. 694, 697–98 (1963). The Arkansas Supreme Court reveals the race of both the victim and the perpetrator when it states that the police were able to ascertain the identity of the rapist from a strand of "Negroid hair" found in the victim's home. *Id.* at 698.

62. Baldus & Woodworth, *supra* note 3, at 405. Maxwell's attorneys cited an Arkansas study showing that "between 1945 and 1965, the probability that a black male raping a white woman would receive the death sentence in Arkansas was about 50 percent, while the death-sentencing rate for cases involving an interracial rape was only 14 percent." *Id.*

63. *Id.*

64. *Id.*

65. 433 U.S. 584 (1977).

66. *Id.* at 587.

67. Baldus & Woodworth, *supra* note 3, at 405 n.1.

68. Before 1977, when the death penalty could still be imposed for the crime of rape, "the death penalty was used overwhelmingly against African-American men convicted of raping white women." Phyllis L. Crocker, *Feminism and the Criminal Law: Is the Death Penalty Good for Women?,* 4 BUFF. CRIM. L. REV. 917, 944 (2001). As Crocker observes, this "was true as a legal matter in the criminal justice system as well as outside of the legal system where African-American men were often lynched under the pretext of having raped a white woman." *Id.; see also* Jacquelyn Dowd Hall, Revolt Against Chivalry: Jessie Daniel Ames and the Women's Campaign Against Lynching 154 (1979) (noting that "popular opinion [and] very often in law [presumed] that any white woman having intercourse with a black man had been 'raped'" and that this was used to justify lynchings and legal executions).

Marvin Wolfgang and Marc Riedel conducted an extensive study of rape-murder cases in Florida, Ohio, Colorado, and Oregon and discovered dramatic racial disparities. Marvin E. Wolfgang & Marc Riedel, *Race, Judicial Discretion and the Death Penalty,* 407 ANNALS AM. ACAD. POL. & SOC. SCI. 119 (1973). The study found that 36 percent of African-American defendants convicted of raping white women were sentenced to death and that only 2 percent of defendants in all other racial combinations were sentenced to death; thus, African-American defendants convicted of raping white women were sentenced to death approximately eighteen times more often than defendants in any other racial combination. *Id.* at 129 tbl. 2, 130. By also examining a series of nonracial variables, Wolfgang and Riedel concluded that "in none of the seven states carefully analyzed can it be said that any of the nonracial factors account for the statistically significant and disproportionate number of blacks sentenced to death for rape." *Id.* at 132.

The apparent overt racism against African-American defendants in rape cases has diminished, but it has not vanished. Phyllis Crocker recalls a more recent example in the case of *Robinson v. State*:

> [In this] Florida case, an all white jury convicted Johnny L. Robinson, an African-American, of the sexual battery, kidnapping, robbery, and murder of a white woman. At the punishment phase the prosecutor elicited testimony from the defendant's medical expert that Robinson told him he had sexual encounters with several other white individuals, who were presumably female. The trial court denied the defense attorney's objection to this line of questioning, but the Florida Supreme Court vacated the death sentence, finding that this was a deliberate attempt to inject racial bias and prejudice into the case.

Crocker, *supra*, at 947 (citing *Robinson v. State*, 520 So. 2d 1, 6–7 (Fla. 1988)).

69. As David Baldus and George Woodworth write, "The Court barred the use of capital punishment for rape on Eighth Amendment 'excessiveness' grounds, and it pointedly made no reference to the racial issue presented by the case." Baldus & Woodworth, *supra* note 3, at 405 n.1.

70. Baldus & Woodworth, *supra* note 3, at 405.

71. 481 U.S. 279 (1987).

72. For example, the Baldus study demonstrated that prosecutors sought the death penalty more often in cases involving black defendants and white victims and that the death penalty was imposed more often in cases involving black defendants and white victims. *See McCleskey*, 481 U.S. at 286–87.

73. *Id.* at 289 (quoting *McCleskey v. Kemp*, 753 F.2d 877, 891 (11th Cir. 1985)) (alteration in original). As an example of the drastic claims of disproportionality that were nonetheless found unacceptable under *McCleskey*, see *Stephens v. State*, 456 S.E.2d 560, 561 (Ga. 1995) (finding insufficient for federal and state due process and equal protection challenges Stephens's evidence that "[i]n Hall County, where Stephens was convicted, the trial court found that one hundred percent of the persons serving a life sentence [were] African-American, although African-Americans make up less than ten percent of the county population and approximately fifty to sixty percent of the persons arrested in drug investigations. Relying on evidence provided by the State Board of Pardons and Paroles, the trial court also found that 98.4 percent of the persons serving life sentences for drug offenses were African-American, although African-Americans comprise only 27 percent of the state's population.").

74. Other data presented by the Baldus study included that

> [d]efendants charged with killing white victims the odds were 4.3 times as likely to receive a death sentence as defendants charged with killing blacks. According to this model, black defendants were 1.1 times as likely to receive a death sentence as other defendants. Thus, the Baldus study indicates that black defendants . . . who kill white victims have the greatest likelihood of receiving the death penalty.

McCleskey, 481 U.S. at 287.

Furthermore, the study concluded that "prosecutors sought the death penalty in 70% of the cases involving black defendants and white victims; 32% of the cases involving white defendants and white victims; 15% of the cases involving black defendants and black victims; and 19% of the cases involving white defendants and black victims." *Id.*

75. *Id.* at 291 n.7.

76. *Id.* at 297.

77. Baldus & Woodworth, *supra* note 3, at 407.

78. *Id.* at 409.

79. 963 F.2d 1403 (11th Cir. 1991).

80. 720 F. Supp. 1566 (N.D.Ga. 1989).

81. *Id.* at 1574.

82. Paul Schoeman, Note, *Easing the Fear of Too Much Justice: A Compromise Proposal to Revise the Racial Justice Act,* 20 HARV. C.R.-C.L. L. REV. 543, 556 (1995).

83. *Dobbs,* 720 F. Supp. at 1576.

84. *Id.* at 1577.

85. *Dobbs v. Zant,* 963 F.2d 1403, 1405 (11th Cir. 1991).

86. *See Killing with Prejudice: Race and the Death Penalty in the USA* (Amnesty International, May 1999), at 5.

87. *Id.* at 6.

88. *Id.* at 7 (citing *The Death Penalty in Black and White. Who Lives. Who Dies. Who Decides.* Available from: Death Penalty Information Center, 1320 18th St. NW, Washington, DC 20036, USA (www.essential.org/dpic)).

89. *Id.* at 8 (citing same source).

90. *Id.* at 319.

91. *Id.* (holding that "[d]espite McCleskey's wide-ranging arguments that basically challenge the validity of capital punishment in our multiracial society, the only question before us is whether in his case, the law of Georgia was properly applied" (citation omitted)).

92. *Id.; see also* David Cole, No Equal Justice 138–39 (1999) ("The *McCleskey* Court seemed to be saying that the significance of racial disparity in criminal justice poses a political, not a legal question, better decided by a politically elected branch.").

93. S. Rep. No. 170, 101st Cong., 1st Sess. 75 (1989) (citing *Katzenbach v. Morgan,* 384 U.S. 641 (1966)) (emphasis added). Historically, Congress has used its Section Five power to prohibit otherwise unexplainable racial disparities. For example, after the Court ruled that the plaintiffs in *Mobile v. Bolden,* 466 U.S. 55 (1980), had to prove discriminatory intent in order to declare the Voting Rights Act unconstitutional, Congress decided to amend the act to "allow proof of discriminatory result, rather than intent, to establish a prima facie case of discrimination" after recognizing that to require proof of intent would place too high of a burden on

plaintiffs. Rebecca A. Rafferty, Note, *In the Shadow of* McCleskey v. Kemp: *The Discriminatory Impact of the Death Sentencing Process,* 21 NEW ENG. J. ON CRIM. & CIV. CONFINEMENT 271, 298 & n.193 (1995) (citing S. Rep. No. 417, 97th Cong., 2d Sess. 16 (1982)).

94. 134 Cong. Rec. E1175 (daily ed. Apr. 21, 1988). The act was reintroduced to the 100th Congress as H.R. 4442. Comprehensive Crime Control Act of 1990, H.R. Rep. No. 631, 101st Cong., 2d Sess. 160 (1990). As included in the House Crime Bill adopted in April of 1994, the act stated:

> (c) Relevant Evidence—Evidence relevant to establish an inference that race was the basis of a death sentence may include evidence that death sentences were, at the time pertinent under subsection (b), being imposed significantly more frequently in the jurisdiction in question—
>
> (1) upon persons of one race than upon persons of another race; or
>
> (2) as punishment for capital offenses against persons of one race than as punishment for capital offenses against persons of another race.

H.R. 4092, §2921(c), 140 Cong. Rec. H2655–56 (daily ed. Apr. 15, 1994).

95. *See* Rafferty, *supra* note 93, at 271, 299.

96. The defendant "must produce 'smoking gun' evidence of racially discriminatory intent by the decisionmakers in the case [and of] course, that is an impossible burden—no prosecutor, judge, or juror is going to admit to the type of conscious and subconscious racial bias which the statistics demonstrate exists." Death Penalty: Hearing Before the Subcomm. on Criminal Justice, 100th Cong., 1st Sess. 74 (1987) (statement of Robert McDuff, Staff Attorney, Lawyers Committee for Civil Rights Under Law).

97. *See id.*

98. Rafferty, *supra* note 93, at 304 (citing 135 Cong. Rec. S1880 (daily ed. May 24, 1989) (statement of Rep. Conyers)); *see also id.* at n. 244 ("Defendants may use the evidence to show that either the race of the victim or the defendant influenced the sentencing process.") (citing 135 Cong. Rec. S1881 (daily ed. May 24, 1989)).

99. S. Rep. No. 170, 101st Cong., 1st Sess. 25 (1989). The evidence presented by the defendant must include evidence of the aggravating factors involved in the crimes on which the statistical evidence is based, to ensure that the statistical evidence is both valid and relevant. The Comprehensive Crime Control Act of 1990: Hearing Before the Committee on the Judiciary, 101st Cong., 2d Sess. 161 (1990).

100. Rafferty, *supra* note 93, at 305. Note that the state can challenge the defendant's proffered statistical evidence either by challenging the "validity of its analysis and its relevance to the present case" or by offering "nonracial factors that account for the racial disparities." *Id.* at 306.

101. The "defendant never escapes punishment [but] has the added opportunity to defend his or her life against discrimination in the imposition of the death penalty." *Id.* at 306.

102. In Senate hearings, the proposed bill was referred to by an opponent of

the Act as the so-called Racial Justice Act: "[T]he racial quota death penalty provision—the so-called Racial Justice Act is really a death penalty abolition act." 140 Cong. Rec. S12269, 103d Cong., 2d Sess. (1994).

103. Some commentators claim "the RJA changes the focus of our criminal justice system from case-specific fairness to quota-based 'equivalence.' " Daniel E. Lundgren & Mark L. Krotoski, *The Racial Justice Act of 1994—Undermining Enforcement of the Death Penalty Without Promoting Racial Justice*, 20 U. Dayton L. Rev. 655, 661 (1995).

104. *Id.* These same opponents cited this as a reason for their preference of the Equal Justice Act, which deals with race in a more neutral manner—only attempting to ensure that it was *not* taken into consideration at all.

105. Lundgren & Krotoski, *supra* note 103, at 671. There might also be a fear that because statistical evidence is of a more technical nature, a "war of the experts," similar to that possible in the context of psychological or mental health testimony, might arise. *Cf. Ake v. Oklahoma,* 470 U.S. 68 (1995); *see also* Lundgren & Krotoski, *supra* note 103, at 679 (discussing the possibility for "statistics shopping").

106. In Senate floor debates regarding the act, Senator Kennedy argued that "the *McCleskey v. Kemp* decision was wrongly decided." Lundgren & Krotoski, *supra* note 103, at 657.

107. *See* Cole, *supra* note 92, at 139.

108. David Cole also suggests several arguments as to why statistics can rarely prove intentional discrimination, but he does state that, at the very least, they do "raise serious questions about the racial fairness of our criminal justice policy." Cole, *supra* note 92, at 151. It is also important to note that in the context of the RJA, statistics are not being used to prove intent but, instead, only impact.

109. *See Woodson v. North Carolina,* 428 U.S. 280 (1976); *see also Proffitt v. Florida,* 428 U.S. 241 (1976).

110. Lundgren & Krotoski, *supra* note 103, at 666–67 (quoting *Gregg v. Georgia,* 428 U.S. 13 (1976) (footnotes omitted).

111. *McCleskey v. Kemp,* 481 U.S. 279, 306–07 (1987) ("Nothing in any of our cases suggests that the decision to afford an individual defendant mercy violates the Constitution." (quoting *Gregg,* 428 U.S. at 199)).

112. In fact, the Court struck down a mandatory death penalty scheme that would have ensured such an outcome in *Woodson v. North Carolina. See Woodson,* 428 U.S. at 305.

113. There is also an argument to be made that a showing of racial disparity is not even equivalent to a showing of arbitrariness, given that the racism at play provides exactly the opposite result. The imposition of the death penalty is not arbitrary insofar as there is a certain measure of higher predictability that cases involving a black defendant and a white victim will be most likely to face and be sentenced to the death penalty. The Eighth Amendment is therefore more relevant

in the sense that no punishment should be imposed based on race. *See Furman v. Georgia*, 408 U.S. 238, 242, 249 (1972) (Brennan, J., concurring) ("It would seem to be incontestable that the death penalty inflicted on one defendant is 'unusual' if it discriminates against him by reason of his race, religion, wealth, social position, or class, or if it is imposed under a procedure that gives room for the play of such prejudices. A penalty . . . should be considered 'unusually' imposed if it is administered arbitrarily or discriminatorily." (quoting Goldberg & Dershowitz, *Declaring the Death Penalty Unconstitutional*, 83 HARV. L. REV. 1773, 1792 (1970)).

114. *Cf. Woodson*, 428 U.S. at 303–04.

115. David Cole, *A Fear of Too Much Justice*, Legal Times, May 9, 1994, at 41.

116. To me, these difficult questions only add more fuel to the argument that the death penalty cannot be administered fairly in our society, an argument that should point toward abolition even more strongly than to reform.

117. Schoeman, *supra* note 82, at 558.

118. *Id.* at 558–59.

119. Schoeman also notes that "a comprehensive effort to discover and expose purposeful discrimination in the jury room would likely run afoul of *Federal Rule of Evidence 606(b)* and its state equivalents, which embody a policy of insulating jury deliberations from scrutiny." *Id.* at 559. The *Dobbs* court picked up on this tension as well, noting that "a conflict emerges between [Rule 606(b) and the *McCleskey* decision]: whereas the *McCleskey* standard requires a petitioner to show actual bias in the sentencing decision, Rule 606(b) precludes inquiry into the decision making process." *Dobbs*, 720 F. Supp. at 1573. The RJA avoids this problem altogether.

120. Many commentators have written on the nature and effects of subtle, or unconscious, racism. *See, e.g.,* Darren Lenard Hutchinson, *"Unexplainable on Grounds Other Than Race": The Inversion of Privilege and Subordination in Equal Protection Jurisprudence*, 2003 U. ILL. L. REV. 615, 670 (2003) (observing that "[p]rocess distortion exists where the unconscious motive of racial prejudice has influenced the decision. It matters not that the decisionmaker's motive may lie outside her awareness. If we accept the existence of unconscious or subtle bias or prejudice, then impact data should have relevance in equal protection litigation."); Charles R. Lawrence III, *The Id, the Ego, and Equal Protection: Reckoning with Unconscious Racism*, 39 STAN. L. REV. 317, 318 (1987) (retelling the story about how one of the author's college companions attempted to compliment him by saying that he didn't "think of [him] as a Negro."). Lawrence also writes: "[R]equiring proof of conscious or intentional motivation as a prerequisite to constitutional recognition that a decision is race-dependent ignores much of what we understand about how the human mind works. It also disregards both the irrationality of racism and the profound effect that the history of American race relations has had on both the individual and collective unconscious." *Id.* at 323.

121. The argument that this is not a fair analogy contends that in employment

decisions, for example, the decision to hire any given employee is made by a single decision maker and based on variables that remain uniform for each employee, whereas "capital decisions involve the assessment of numerous variables, which will differ in every case, and the actions of several decision makers, including juries, which may not readily be captured by statistics." Lundgren & Krotoski, *supra* note 103, at 664.

122. *See* Ronald Tabak, *Is Racism Irrelevant? Or Should the Fairness in Death Sentencing Act Be Enacted to Substantially Diminish Racial Discrimination in Capital Sentencing?* 18 N.Y.U. Rev. L. of Soc. Change 777 (1990–91).

123. See *id.* at 659.

124. As introduced during the House Crime Bill Debate in April of 1994, the act stated:

> (a) Jury Instructions and Certification—In a prosecution for an offense against the United States in which a sentence of death is sought, and in which the capital sentencing determination is to be made by a jury, the judge shall instruct the jury that it is not to be influenced by prejudice or bias relating to the race or color of the defendant or victim in considering whether a sentence of death is justified, and that the jury is not to recommend the imposition of a sentence of death unless it has concluded that it would recommend the same sentence for such a crime regardless of the race or color of the defendant or victim. Upon the return of a recommendation of a sentence of death, the jury shall also return a certificate, signed by each juror, that the juror's individual decision was not affected by prejudice or bias relating to the race or color of the defendant or victim, and that the individual juror would have made the same recommendation regardless of the race or color of the defendant or victim. 140 Cong. Rec. H2518-01 (1994)

Note that this provision, in addition to the provision of the Federal Death Penalty Act below, applies only to federal capital cases. The EJA as initially proposed also provided that on motion of the defense attorney or prosecutor, given a substantial likelihood of the influence of racial prejudice or bias, the risk of racial prejudice or bias shall be examined on voir dire. *Id.* If it is found that an impartial jury could not be obtained because of racial prejudice or bias, the act stated that a motion made for change of venue would be granted. *Id.* Last, the act provided that "neither the prosecutor nor the defense attorney shall make any appeal to racial prejudice or bias in statements before the jury." *Id.*

125. The Federal Death Penalty Act of 1994 (FDPA) provides:

> (f) Special precaution to ensure against discrimination. In a hearing held before a jury, the court, prior to the return of a finding under subsection (e), shall instruct the jury that, in considering whether a sentence of death is justified, it shall not consider the race, color, religious beliefs, national origin, or sex of the defendant or of any victim and that the jury is not to recommend a sentence of death unless it has concluded that it would recommend a sentence of

death for the crime in question no matter what the race, color, religious beliefs, national origin, or sex of the defendant or of any victim may be. The jury, upon return of a finding under subsection (e), shall also return to the court a certificate, signed by each juror, that consideration of the race, color, religious beliefs, national origin, or sex of the defendant or any victim was not involved in reaching his or her individual decision and that the individual juror would have made the same recommendation regarding a sentence for the crime in question no matter what the race, color, religious beliefs, national origin, or sex of the defendant or any victim may be. 18 U.S.C. §3593(f) (2000)

126. 476 U.S. 28 (1986). In *Turner,* the Supreme Court seemed briefly to acknowledge the importance of rooting out racial bias. A fundamental case in this regard, *Turner* stated that, in a trial for an interracial crime and if the defendant requested such a proceeding, prospective jurors had to be informed of the victim's race and then questioned as to racial bias before they could be selected on to the jury. *Id.* at 36–37. In requiring such measures, the Court reasoned that "the risk that racial prejudice may have infected petitioner's capital sentencing [was] unacceptable in light of the ease with which that risk could have been minimized." *Id.* at 35. Here, the Court seemed to acknowledge that "[b]ecause of the range of discretion entrusted to a jury in a capital sentencing hearing, there is a unique opportunity for racial prejudice to operate but remain undetected. More subtle, less consciously held racial attitudes could influence a juror's decision in [a given] case." *Id.* at 35. The Court concluded that because Turner's request to question potential jurors about racial bias during voir dire had a "constitutionally significant likelihood" of minimizing the risk of racial prejudice in his capital sentencing hearing, such a request could not be denied. *Id.* at 33.

127. *Turner v. Murray,* 476 U.S. 28, 36 n.8 (1986).

128. *Id.* at 36.

129. Schoeman, *supra* note 82, at 555.

130. *Id.* at 554–55.

131. *Id.* at 555.

132. Paul Schoeman writes that "by ensuring that there is written evidence of each juror's promise not to have discriminated, the EJA seems designed to prevent defendants from ever being able to prove purposeful discrimination. The written certification could create a presumption that jurors did not discriminate—a presumption that, in practice, defendants would be unable to rebut." *Id.* at 555.

133. 428 U.S. 153 (1976)

134. 510 U.S. 1141 (1994).

135. *Id.* at 1145 (Blackmun, J., dissenting).

136. *Id.* at 1153.

137. *See* O'Connor Questions the Death Penalty, San Diego Union-Tribune, July 4, 2001 at A6.

138. *Id.*

139. Ginsburg Backs Ending Death Penalty, Associated Press, Apr. 9, 2001.

140. *Id.*

141. *See* Jeffrey L. Kirchmeier, *Another Place Beyond Here: The Death Penalty Moratorium Movement in the United States,* 73 U. Colo. L. Rev. 1 (2002) (maintaining that Governor Ryan's decision was not based on a moral opposition to the death penalty but rather on concerns about systemic problems and that 66 percent of Illinois residents approved of the governor's moratorium).

142. *See* Amnesty International, *United States of America: Death by Discrimination—The Continuing Role of Race in Capital Cases,* April 2003.

143. Penn. Sup. Ct. Comm. on Racial and Gender Bias in the Justice System: Final Report at 220–21 (1999).

144. *Id.* at 218.

145. Maggie Mulvihill & Franci Richardson, *It's Time for Age of Innocence: A Call for Commission on Wrongful Convictions,* Boston Herald, May 7, 2004.

146. In *People v. La Valle,* 2005 WL 1402516 (2004) the provision CPL 400.27(10) declares, in pertinent part, that "the court must instruct the jury that with respect to each count of murder in the first degree the jury should consider whether or not a sentence of death should be imposed and whether or not a sentence of life imprisonment without parole should be imposed, and that the jury must be unanimous with respect to either sentence The court must also instruct the jury that in the event the jury fails to reach unanimous agreement with respect to the sentence, the court will sentence the defendant to a term of imprisonment with a minimum term of between twenty and twenty-five years and a maximum term of life."

147. *See* William Glaberson, *Across New York, a Death Penalty Stuck in Limbo,* N. Y. Times, Aug. 21, 2004.

148. The Death Penalty: An International Perspective, *available at* http://www.deathpenaltyinfo.org/article.php?did=127&scid=30.

149. 1995 (3) SALR 391 (CC).

150. Peter Norbert Bouckaert, *Shutting Down the Death Factory: The Abolition of Capital Punishment in South Africa,* 32 Stan. J. Int'l L. 287 (1996).

151. 1995 (3) SALR 391 (CC).

152. 125 S. Ct. 2317 (2005).

153. 125 S. Ct. 2410 (2005).

154. 125 S. Ct. 1183 (2005).

155. 106 S. Ct. 1712 (1986).

156. *Id.* at 1716.

157. *Miller-El,* 125 S. Ct. at 2328.

158. *Id.* at 2327.

159. *Id.* at 2326.

160. *Id.* at 2334. The Court described the difference between the description given to white and black jury members:

As we pointed out last time, for 94% of white venire panel members, prosecutors gave a bland description of the death penalty before asking about the individual's feelings on the subject. *Miller-El v. Cockrell*, 537 U.S., at 332, 123 S. Ct. 1029. The abstract account went something like this: "I feel like it [is] only fair that we tell you our position in this case. The State of Texas . . . is actively seeking the death penalty in this case for Thomas Joe Miller-El. We anticipate that we will be able to present to a jury the quantity and type of evidence necessary to convict him of capital murder and the quantity and type of evidence sufficient to allow a jury to answer these three questions over here in the affirmative. A yes answer to each of those questions results in an automatic death penalty from Judge McDowell." App. 564–565.

Only 6% of white venire panelists, but 53% of those who were black, heard a different description of the death penalty before being asked their feelings about it. This is an example of the graphic script: "I feel like you have a right to know right up front what our position is. Mr. Kinne, Mr. Macaluso and myself, representing the people of Dallas County and the state of Texas, are actively seeking the death penalty for Thomas Joe Miller-El. . . ."

"We do that with the anticipation that, when the death penalty is assessed, at some point Mr. Thomas Joe Miller-El—the man sitting right down there—will be taken to Huntsville and will be put on death row and at some point taken to the death house and placed on a gurney and injected with a lethal substance until he is dead as a result of the proceedings that we have in this court on this case. So that's basically our position going into this thing."

161. *Id.* at 2339.
162. *Johnson,* 125 S. Ct. at 2416.
163. *Id.*
164. *Id.* at 2417.
165. *Miller-El,* 125 S. Ct. at 2328.
166. *Roper,* 125 S. Ct. 1200.
167. *Id.* at 1198.
168. *Id.*
169. *Id.* at 1199.
170. *Id.* at 1228.
171. *Id.* at 1200.
172. 536 U.S. 304 (2002).
173. *Id.* at 321.
174. *Id.* at 316 n. 21.
175. 487 U.S. 815 (1988).
176. *Id.* at 838.
177. *Id.* at 830.
178. *Id.* at 830, n.31.
179. 120 S. Ct. 459 (1999).

180. *Id.* at 463.
181. *Atkins,* 536 U.S. 347–48.
182. *Thompson,* at 869, n.4.
183. *Id.*
184. *Knight,* 120 S. Ct. 459–60.
185. *Id.* at 459. The role of international death penalty jurisprudence has been discussed in other cases as well. *See, e.g., Campbell v. Wood,* 511 U.S. 1119 (1994) (Blackmun, J. dissenting in a denial of review of state-sponsored hangings, arguing that only three jurisdictions in the English-speaking world impose state-sponsored hangings — Washington, Montana, and South Africa); *Coker v. Georgia,* 510 U.S. 1009 (1993) (maintaining that international practice regarding death penalty for rape was relevant to the evolving standards analysis). Outside the Court, Justice Blackmun has argued that "if the substance of the 8th amendment is to turn on 'evolving standards of decency' of the civilized world, there can be no justification for limiting judicial inquiry to the opinions of the US." *See* Harry A. Blackmun, *The Supreme Court and the Law of Nations,* 104 YALE L.J. 39 (1994). Similarly, Justice O'Connor has also advocated for U.S. courts to look to international law in making decisions. *See* Broadening Our Horizons: Why American Judges and Lawyers Must Learn About Foreign Law, Int'l Jud. Observer, June 1997, at 2 (adapting Justice O'Connor's speech at 1997 spring meeting of American College of Trial Lawyers). *See also* O'Connor Speech Puts Foreign Law Center Stage, Jonathan Ringel, *Fulton County Daily Report* 10-31-2003, available at http://www.law.com/jsp/newswire_article.jsp?id=1067350962318 (arguing that international decisions should be have persuasive authority in American courts).
186. 123 S. Ct. 2472.
187. *Id.* at 2484.
188. *Id.* at 2482.
189. *Id.* at 2495 (quoting *Foster v. Florida,* 537 U.S. 990, n., 123 S. Ct. 470 (2002) (Thomas, J., concurring in denial of certiorari)).
190. *Roper,* 125 S. Ct. at 1228.
191. *Id.* at 1200.

Chapter 3

Traces of Slavery
Race and the Death Penalty in Historical Perspective

Stuart Banner

One of the standard arguments against the death penalty is that it is imposed unequally by race. Until the 1970s, it was widely known that black defendants were sentenced to death more frequently than similarly situated white defendants. More recently, as the race-of-defendant disparity has been ameliorated in some jurisdictions, opponents of capital punishment have turned their attention to the race-of-victim disparity: holding all else equal, killers of white victims are more likely to be sentenced to death than killers of black victims.[1]

The argument from racial disparity may even be the one that resonates most strongly with general audiences, if the tactical decisions of death penalty opponents are any guide. The Web site of the Death Penalty Information Center, the most sophisticated and thorough of the abolitionist organizations, includes "Race" as the very first of the "Issues" surfers might wish to explore, ahead of competitors like "Innocence," "Costs," and "Deterrence."[2] Recent books urging the abolition of capital punishment include one called *Legal Lynching* and another in which capital defense lawyers are analogized to the Underground Railroad.[3] And supporters of the death penalty respond in kind. When the U.S. Department of Justice recently evaluated the first twelve years of the federal death penalty, it wasn't to see if the death penalty were a superior deterrent to prison, or if it were cost effective, or if there were lingering doubts about the guilt of any of the condemned. It was to see if white and nonwhite defendants were treated unequally.[4]

If we had no history—if we could make our policy decisions by considering the future but not the past—racial disparity would move far down the list of standard arguments, and might even drop off the list entirely. In every other area of public policy debate, the existence of racial disparities in a given practice is considered a reason to reform the disparities, not to abolish the practice. There are racial disparities in public education, for example, but that does not elicit calls to abolish public education. Or to pick an issue more similar to the death penalty, there are racial disparities in noncapital sentencing analogous to the disparities in capital sentencing.[5] Black robbers may get longer prison sentences, all else equal, than white robbers, but that would not be considered a reason to abolish incarceration for robbery. If history had no influence on us, we would draw the same conclusion about the death penalty. As with public education or incarceration, our response would be to try to make it fairer, not to get rid of it entirely.

But our history hangs over us. When we think about the death penalty, we think, in part, in race-tinged pictures—of black victims lynched by white mobs, of black defendants condemned by white juries, of slave codes and public hangings. For centuries capital punishment was, among other things, a method of racial control, particularly in the South but often in the North as well. These practices have almost entirely disappeared today, but they linger on in our memories, exerting their influence on the instinctive, prerational decision making that drives most of the death penalty debate. That makes them worth some attention, if only to understand how they can be so powerful today.

Race has interacted with capital punishment in two primary ways, both of which were products of slavery. First, for most of American history, capital crimes were defined unequally by race—as a matter of formal law before the Civil War, and then as a matter of unwritten practice after the Civil War, when formal racial discrimination became unconstitutional. Second, for a long time executions were staged so as to reinforce the racial hierarchy. From the content of gallows sermons to the choice of execution technique, the ceremony of execution included a variety of rituals intended to broadcast a message of white dominance. Until relatively recently, both the law and the drama of capital punishment were soaked in racism.

Unequal Penalties

Colonial and early state governments often had penal codes with certain crimes that were capital only for black defendants. The first of these—a statute setting death as the penalty for slaves convicted of attempted murder or attempted rape—was enacted in New York in 1712, after a slave revolt.[6] Most of these race-dependent capital crimes were created in the southern colonies, where the black population was the highest. To keep control over their growing number of slaves, the southern colonies resorted to ever-lengthening lists of capital statutes. In 1740, for example, South Carolina imposed the death penalty on slaves and free blacks for burning or destroying any grain, commodities, or manufactured goods; on slaves for enticing other slaves to run away; and on slaves maiming or bruising whites. Virginia, fearing attempts at poisoning, made it a capital offense for slaves to prepare or administer medicine.[7]

Some of these early statutes included preambles manifesting legislators' belief that noncapital penalties were not stiff enough to deter slaves from committing crimes. Slaves' lives were already very harsh, so slaves were widely understood to have less fear than whites of conventional punishments. Slaves were also widely believed to have less faith than whites in the system of eternal rewards and penalties provided by the Christian concepts of heaven and hell, so they were understood to need more conspicuous penalties in this life. Thus the Georgia legislature determined that crimes committed by slaves posed dangers "peculiar to the condition and circumstances of this province," dangers that meant that such crimes "could not fall under the provision of the laws of England." Georgia accordingly made it a capital offense for slaves or free blacks to strike whites twice, or once if a bruise resulted.[8] "The Laws in Force, for the Punishment of Slaves" in Maryland, its legislature found, were "insufficient, to prevent their committing, very great Crimes and Disorders." Slaves were accordingly subjected to the death penalty for conspiring to rebel, to rape a white woman, or to burn a house.[9]

Colonies with large numbers of slaves also expedited the procedures for trying them. As early as 1692, Virginia began using local justices of the peace rather than juries and legally trained judges to try slaves for capital crimes.[10] South Carolina adopted a similarly streamlined procedure in 1740.[11] These systems remained in place as long as slavery existed.[12] Execution rates for slaves far exceeded those for southern whites. In North Carolina, for instance, at least one hundred slaves were executed between 1748 and 1772, well more than the number of whites executed during the colony's entire history, a period longer than a century.[13]

The southern states retained a formally unequal capital sentencing system until the Civil War. In the mid-nineteenth century, slaves in Texas (but not whites) were subject to capital punishment for insurrection, arson, and—if the victim were white—attempted murder, rape, attempted rape, robbery, attempted robbery, and assault with a deadly weapon. Free blacks were subject to capital punishment for all these offenses plus that of kidnapping a white woman. In Virginia, slaves were liable to be executed for any offense for which free people would get a prison term of three years or more. Free blacks, but not whites, could get the death penalty for rape, attempted rape, kidnapping a woman, and aggravated assault if the victim were white. Attempted rape of a white woman was a capital crime for blacks in Texas and Virginia, as well as Florida, Louisiana, Mississippi, South Carolina, and Tennessee.[14] In his 1856 treatise summarizing the slave laws of the southern states, George Stroud counted sixty-six capital crimes for slaves in Virginia against only one (murder) for whites. In Mississippi he found thirty-eight crimes capital for slaves but not whites. The ratios in the other southern states were less skewed, but all had a similar imbalance.[15]

The black-white divergence in southern criminal codes was reflected in actual practice. In many states, blacks were hanged in numbers far out of proportion to their percentage of the population. When the Reverend Preston Turley was executed in Charleston, Virginia, in 1858, observers remarked that although it was unusual to hang a minister, the real interest in the event arose "from the strange spectacle of the execution of a white man in this region. It was the first occurrence of the kind ever known to have taken place within the county."[16] Blacks were executed for many more crimes than whites were. All of the whites known to have been hanged in Virginia between 1800 and 1860 were hanged for murder. But of the hundreds of blacks hanged in Virginia in the same period, only about half were murderers. The other crimes for which blacks were commonly hanged included, in order of frequency, rape, slave revolt, attempted murder, burglary, and arson. In Louisiana, nearly all the whites executed were murderers, but the blacks hanged for murder were outnumbered by those executed for planning slave revolts, and several others were hanged for arson and attempted murder. Kentucky hanged whites only for murder, but hanged blacks for attempted murder, rape, attempted rape, arson, and slave revolt. The Carolinas were the states most likely to hang whites for crimes other than murder, but even they executed many more black non-murderers than white. Throughout the South, capital punishment for whites was in practice primarily for murder, but for blacks it was for a much wider range of crimes.[17]

A count of official executions underestimates the intensity with which capital punishment was used for black criminals in the South, for two reasons. First, it does not include the growing number of lynchings—that is, unofficial executions.[18] Blacks were of course the primary victims. They were often lynched because they were believed to have committed capital crimes, so we can assume that many would have been executed officially had they lived a bit longer. Second, many slaves who would have been executed were sold abroad instead. In Virginia (and perhaps in other southern states as well), condemned slaves were often sold to contractors who agreed to convey them outside the boundaries of the United States. Between 1801, when Virginia established the program, and 1858, when it was abandoned, nearly 900 condemned slaves were transported out of the country.[19] Because the state had to compensate the slaves' owners—a rule that prevailed in almost all the southern states, to assure that owners would not attempt to protect their property from the criminal justice system[20]—selling slaves rather than hanging them represented a substantial savings for the public treasury. If these slaves had been executed, the proportion of blacks hanged in the antebellum South would have been significantly higher.

After the Civil War, explicitly race-based sentencing became unconstitutional, so the southern states responded by vesting capital sentencing discretion in all-white juries, who could be trusted to sentence black defendants to death more frequently than white defendants, even when the law was formally equal. The practice actually began on a small scale before the Civil War, in the 1830s and 1840s, when three southern states—Tennessee, Alabama, and Louisiana—became the first in the nation to grant juries discretion to sentence all murderers to something short of death. The purpose of these early discretion statutes was almost certainly to allow jurors to take race into account in setting the penalty. In the years immediately following the Civil War, most of the southern states adopted the same strategy with respect to some crimes.[21]

This system—a formally equal criminal law that vested great discretion in white jurors—continued in the South through much of the twentieth century. With the end of slavery, whites turned toward alternative forms of racial subjugation, and one of them was the death penalty. The belief that capital punishment was necessary to restrain a primitive black population became an article of faith among white southerners lasting well into the twentieth century. As George W. Hays, a former governor of Arkansas, explained in 1927,

> One of the South's most serious problems is the negro question. The legal system is exactly the same for both white and black, although the latter race is still quite primitive, and in general culture and advancement in a childish state of progress.
>
> If the death penalty were to be removed from our statute-books, the tendency to commit deeds of violence would be heightened owing to this negro problem. The greater number of the race do not maintain the same ideals as the whites.[22]

As a result, most of the southern states' capital crimes on the eve of the Civil War were still capital nearly a century later, long after the northern states had limited the death penalty to murder. As of 1954, rape was punished with death in eighteen states, all but one (Nevada) in the South: Alabama, Arkansas, Delaware, Florida, Georgia, Kentucky, Louisiana, Maryland, Mississippi, Missouri, Nevada, North Carolina, Oklahoma, South Carolina, Tennessee, Texas, Virginia, and West Virginia. Robbery was capital in nine, again all but Nevada in the South: Alabama, Georgia, Kentucky, Mississippi, Missouri, Nevada, Oklahoma, Texas, and Virginia. Five states, all southern, still retained the death penalty for arson: Alabama, Arkansas, Georgia, North Carolina, and Virginia. Burglary was still capital in four: Alabama, Kentucky, North Carolina, and Virginia.[23] Death sentences were imposed disproportionately on black defendants.

Execution Ceremonies

Another way race affected the death penalty was in the staging of executions, which were held in public until the early nineteenth century in the North, and until the early twentieth in parts of the South. These ceremonies served to reinforce hierarchies of all sorts, including the racial hierarchy. The most obvious way they did so was by incorporating explicit messages encouraging blacks to defer to whites. For example, at the 1819 hanging of Rose Butler, a New York City slave convicted of setting fire to her owner's house, the Baptist minister John Sandford directed his remarks to the black spectators. "The wings of the Constitution of America are extended to defend and foster the property, the liberties, and the lives of all its citizens, without exception," he began.

> In this inestimable privilege, our fellow citizens of *color* enjoy a mutual share with us; and this unquestionably should dictate to them a correspondent spirit of gratitude and the practice of every social virtue. It is therefore deeply to be regretted that persons of color should either envy or attempt to destroy the safety and comfort to which we are justly entitled.[24]

Remarks like Sandford's sometimes came from black defendants themselves (often in language fluffed up by the publishers of their dying words). "I would solemnly warn those of my own Colour, as they regard their own Souls, to avoid Desertion from their Masters," a slave named Arthur declared.[25] Despite the fact that some of the condemned had flouted social convention most of their lives—Arthur, for instance, had by his own account run away and traveled widely among all different sorts of people[26]—the message of the gallows speech was normally one of black subservience to whites.

This was not always true. Cato, a New York slave, blamed his criminal career on the mistreatment he received as a child from his master, "a man of very corrupt and immoral habits," and urged slaveowners to "learn the necessity of paying due attention to the instruction of their servants."[27] The free black Abraham Johnstone, hanged in New Jersey, spent his last days in jail placing his execution in the context of American race relations at the close of the eighteenth century. Johnstone was concerned that his case would "be made a handle of in order to throw a shade over or cast a general reflection on all those of our colour, and the keen shafts of prejudice be launched against us by the most active and virulent malevolence." He hastened to point out that if one compared the numbers of blacks and whites executed with the racial composition of the population as a whole, "it will be found that as they claim a pre-eminence over us in every thing else, so we find they also have it in this particular, and that a vast majority of whites have died on the gallows." He concluded "that there are some whites (with all due deference to them) capable of being equally as depraved and more generally so than blacks or people of colour."[28] Johnstone followed with an argument for abolishing slavery. But this point of view was rare on the scaffold. If a condemned person hoped to live another day, it was prudent to project an attitude of submission rather than defiance. With few exceptions, the execution ceremony served more to underscore than to undermine the racial hierarchy.

Hanging was the normal execution method before the end of the nineteenth century. For certain kinds of criminals, however, colonial Americans resorted to especially painful or degrading methods of execution. These forms of super-capital punishment were often imposed on black defendants, again as a means of reinforcing the racial hierarchy. One such method was burning alive.

Burning was reserved for two classes of offenders whose crimes were perceived to be unusually disruptive of the social order. The first was slaves convicted either of murdering their owners or plotting a revolt. In Virginia, a "Negro Woman who lately kill'd her Mistress" confessed to the crime, "and is since burnt."[29] Ten years later, in 1746, another Virginia slave, named Eve, murdered her master; she was incinerated soon after.[30] Two North Carolina slaves suffered the same fate in the 1770s.[31] A "Negroe fellow" who killed his owner in New Jersey in 1753 endured the pain of his burning skin long enough to threaten the spectators. "He stood the Fire with the greatest Intrepidity," it was reported in the newspaper, "and said they had taken the Root but left the Branches."[32] In New York, "a Negroe Man, belonging to Mr. George Trail of New Rochelle, killed his House keeper, by a Blow with a small Ax on the Head." He too was "ordered to be burnt: Which Sentence was put in Execution at New Rochelle last Week."[33] Thirteen of the black participants in the New York "Negro Plot" were burned at the stake; none of the whites was.[34]

The second and smaller class of offenders subject to being burned alive was women convicted of killing their husbands. The idea of burning as a punishment particularly associated with women was sometimes transferred to crimes committed by slaves, which resulted in several cases where groups of slaves convicted as accomplices were executed according to gender, even where the male offenders were in principle liable to be burned as well. "[A] most barbarous murder has been committed upon the Family of one Hallet by an Indian Man Slave, and a Negro Woman, who have murder'd their Master, Mistress and five Children," Lord Cornbury reported to the Board of Trade in 1708. Cornbury, the governor of New York, explained that he "immediately issued a special commission for the Tryal of them, which was done, and the man sentenced to be hanged, and the Woman burnt."[35] Three slaves convicted of murder in Annapolis, Maryland, in 1746 were sentenced to death, the two men to be hanged, and Esther Anderson to be burned.[36]

What these cases have in common is the reversal of the traditional hierarchy of the household, the revolt by slave against master or wife against husband. The legal name for such crimes, petit treason, suggests the strength of the analogy contemporaries drew between the household and the state.[37] Treason denoted "not only offences against the king and government," explained Blackstone, but also crimes "proceeding from the same principle of treachery in private life."[38] If treason, the subversion of the authority of the state, was the gravest of crimes, then petit treason, the subversion of the authority of the family, had to be punished especially harshly. The institution of slavery caused the law to be harsher in America than in England, where traditionally only women had been burned for petit treason.[39]

Another way to make a sentence worse than death was to display the corpse of the condemned in a public place. The body, covered with tallow or pitch to delay decomposition, was encased in a gibbet, an iron cage sturdy enough to hold the body high above the ground and with large enough spaces between the bars to permit easy viewing.[40] The practice was intended to magnify the deterrent effect of capital punishment, in two senses. First, by keeping the execution in public view for much longer than the ceremony itself, gibbeting allowed the state to play to a larger audience and to repeat its message of terror, day in and day out, for potential offenders whose routines took them by the site over and over again. Second, by denying the customary burial, and by permitting the condemned's body to decompose in full view; subject to weather, insects, and birds of prey; and giving off an unmistakable smell to anyone wandering close enough; the state could exploit the popular concern with the integrity of the body after death.

Unlike burning at the stake, for which by established practice only certain categories of offenders were eligible, the gibbet was a penalty applied in an ad hoc fashion. The gibbet would be in order whenever officials perceived the need for an extra dose of terror. Many of the people gibbeted were slaves, exhibited in a show of force to other slaves in communities where crime had occurred.[41] In colonial New York, for example, an unnamed slave believed to have murdered three people, including two of his owner's children, was found dead in a river. His body was retrieved and gibbeted.[42]

A third form of super-capital punishment involved the public display of the dismembered body. As with the gibbet, dismemberment was an extra punishment applied ad hoc, whenever disorder was believed to pose an exceptional threat. Slaves were often dismembered. The point was to put on the most vivid reminder possible of what the state could do to its criminals, a massive public display of the government's force at a time when that force might be in question. Thus in 1763, a local court ordered that a slave named Tom from Augusta County, Virginia, convicted of killing his owner, "be hanged by the neck until he be dead and . . . that then his head be Severed from his body and affixed on a pole on the Top of the Hill near the Road that lead from this Court House." Tom's head, high enough to be visible from a distance, and close to a heavily traveled road, was no doubt seen by many, but probably not by as many as the body parts of another slave named Tom, also convicted of killing his owner, in Amelia County, Virginia, in 1755. This Tom was sentenced to have his head

> severed from his body which is to be cut up in four quarters and disposed of in the following manner. His head is to be stuck up at the cross road near Major Peter Jones', one quarter near William Wiley's, one quarter at Farley's, and the other at any other public place within this County the Sheriff shall think proper.[43]

In 1729, the Maryland legislature found that "several Petit-Treasons, and cruel and horrid Murders, have been lately committed by Negroes, which Cruelties they were instigated to commit with the like Inhumanity, because they have no Sense of Shame, or Apprehension of future Rewards or Punishments." The ordinary manner of executing criminals, the legislature concluded, "is not sufficient to deter a People from committing the greatest Cruelties, who only consider the Rigour and Severity of Punishment." Maryland accordingly authorized its judges to sentence slaves in cases of murder or arson "to have the right Hand cut off, to be hang'd in the usual Manner, the Head severed from the Body, the Body divided into Four Quarters, and Head and Quarters set up in the most publick Places of the County where such Fact was committed."[44] Georgia gave its judges authority to sentence slaves to death by whatever techniques the judges believed "will be most effectual to deter others from offending in the like manner."[45]

These forms of aggravated capital punishment ceased to be used by the early nineteenth century, and then by the middle of the century the northern states had moved their hangings into the jail yard, out of the public eye. Public execution held on longer in parts of the South, largely on account of race. While northern whites were becoming increasingly squeamish about public hangings, the mounting frequency of lynchings prevented southern whites from growing too sensitive to the public display of violence. Many, and perhaps a large majority, of the public hangings in the late nineteenth-century South were of blacks, often before largely black crowds.[46] Genteel contempt for the crowd was most likely tempered by the feeling among whites that nothing short of a vivid display of force could deter such an audience.

Sensibilities eventually changed in the South as well, but even then the abolition of public executions sometimes occurred more slowly for black defendants. In 1901, giving a clear signal that government officials had differing expectations for the two races, Arkansas abolished public hanging except for rape, a crime for which the death penalty was almost exclusively imposed on black men who raped white women. Arkansas moved even rapists' hangings indoors five years later. Kentucky, which had abolished public hanging in 1880, brought it back for rape and attempted rape in 1920, at the option of local officials. Legislators explained that electrocution inside the state penitentiary, the execution method for other capital crimes, would not be adequate to deter rapists.[47] Kentucky did not move rapists' executions out of the public until 1938, when it became the last state to abolish public execution, more than a century after most of the northeastern states.

But even when official hangings moved indoors, unofficial hangings—lynchings—remained common public events. Lynching was a form of unofficial capital punishment, the adjudication of guilt and execution by groups lacking the formal authority to do either. The victims were usually black, the executioners usually white.[48] The line between a lynching and an official execution could be thin. The participants in lynchings often included the very same people who, in their official capacities, administered the criminal justice system. Official trials and executions in the South could be astonishingly fast, so fast as to closely resemble lynchings, when a case carried racial implications. In 1906, a black man in Kentucky convicted of raping a white woman was hanged only fifty minutes from the time the jury was sworn. In Galveston, a black defendant was indicted, tried, and hanged in less than four hours.[49] But if the line was thin, everyone knew it was there. Participants and victims alike could tell the difference between an official and an unofficial execution. At its peak, lynching was much more common than official capital punishment. In Kentucky, for instance, between 1865 and 1940 there were 229 executions, but 353 lynchings. In the 1870s, lynchings outnumbered executions 82 to 6; in the 1890s, lynchings outnumbered executions 92 to 40.[50] A culture that carried out so much public unofficial capital punishment could hardly grow squeamish about the official variety.

The relationship between lynching and capital punishment was a subject of considerable controversy in the late nineteenth and early twentieth centuries. Some took the position that the frequency of lynching demonstrated the need for capital punishment in the South. Without an officially sanctioned outlet, they argued, southerners' strong desire to exact retribution for crime would result in even more lynching than was already taking place.[51] Others replied that if lynching were a substitute for capital punishment, one ought to see considerable amounts of lynching in places like Michigan or Wisconsin that had abolished the death penalty long ago. Lynching, they argued, was not a substitute for the death penalty; rather, lynchings and executions rose and fell in tandem.[52] Recent students of the subject, armed with statistical techniques that were unknown in the early twentieth century, have generally concluded that both sides were wrong. Most of the time lynching rates and execution rates showed little or no correlation one way or the other.[53]

But the racial pattern of capital punishment in the South closely resembled that of lynching. Of the 771 people of identified race known to have been executed for rape between 1870 and 1950, 701 were black. (We lack data on the race of the victims.) For robbery during the period, 31 of 35 were black. For burglary, 18 of 21. Racial disparities were smaller but still noticeable for murder. In Virginia, blacks executed for murder outnumbered whites 217 to 57; in Texas, 301 to 135. Whether imposed inside or outside the official justice system, the death penalty was a means of racial control.[54]

Furman and After

It was the close relationship between race and the death penalty that led to the temporary abolition of capital punishment in 1972. In light of the emphasis people place today on the inequality with which capital punishment is administered, it is worth noting that inequality played almost no role in public debate over the death penalty before the twentieth century. To the extent that inequality was complained of at all, it was economic, not racial. "This is a d——d cold blooded selfish world," swore the murderer Amos Miner, awaiting his execution in Rhode Island in 1833. "If I but possessed some five hundred dollars I could find friends enough; but as it is, I suppose I must be abandoned!"[55] After Wisconsin abolished capital punishment in the 1850s, a local prosecutor explained to a jury that the "death penalty hangs poor, penniless men, guilty or innocent; and it sets free and turns at large the wealthy and the influential, whether they be guilty or innocent; and every good citizen should abhor and deprecate a law that works so alarmingly unequal."[56] But even this kind of commentary was unusual. The prevailing view may have been accurately summed up by the anonymous Massachusetts writer who explained:

> To the honour of this state be it said, that most of the felons, who have here died on the scaffold, have been vagrant foreigners—fugitives from jails and gibbets—the refuse and dregs of society, thrown off in the effervescence of that morbid mass which lies at the bottom of old and dense communities, and cleaves like leprosy to decaying governments. Such wretches we yield to the executioner without much more regret, than when we witness the extermination of a beast of prey.[57]

Before the twentieth century it appears to have been simply taken for granted, as an inescapable fact of life, that the poor were more likely to hang than the rich. Few—or rather few with the liberty to complain—seemed to notice whether blacks were more likely to hang than whites.

But of course times were changing. The idea of mounting a systemic constitutional challenge to the death penalty was an outgrowth of the civil rights movement. The litigation campaign to abolish capital punishment was led by civil rights organizations, first the National Association for the Advancement of Colored People, and later its legal affiliate, the Legal Defense and Educational Fund (LDF). It was a campaign based on race discrimination. And it was race that lurked beneath the Court's 1972 opinion in *Furman v. Georgia,* finding capital punishment unconstitutional. The pivotal opinions of Justices Stewart and White identified the flaw in the states' capital sentencing schemes as unguided jury discretion, and the nonsensical pattern of sentences the system produced. But the problem with discretion wasn't randomness—it was that black and white defendants were sentenced to death unequally, and everyone knew it.

After *Gregg v. Georgia* (1976), when the Supreme Court approved the sentencing schemes that are still in effect, the race-of-defendant disparity disappeared in many states, but the new sentencing schemes are only one cause of that change, and they are most likely not the most significant one. Two other developments around the same time were probably more important. First was the Court's holding in *Coker v. Georgia* (1977) that the Eighth Amendment bars capital punishment for rape. Rape had always been the crime for which the race of the defendant made the biggest difference, so *Coker* instantly wiped away more discrimination than any reform of murder sentencing could have. Second was the fact that after the civil rights movement of the 1960s blacks gained better representation on juries, especially in the South, where most of the death sentences were imposed. These developments would probably have reduced much of the race-of-defendant disparity even in the absence of *Furman*.

But the race-of-victim disparity has persisted, and the race-of-defendant disparity is still present in some states. Like so much in contemporary American race relations, they are distant traces of slavery. And it is the link to slavery and the associated history of race discrimination that accounts for the prominence of racial disparity in the death penalty debate.

The result is an odd reversal. In the 1960s and 1970s the fight to abolish the death penalty was led by the LDF, an organization whose purpose was to battle race discrimination. The LDF first got involved in capital cases in order to represent black defendants, just as it represented black students in school desegregation cases. Eventually the LDF expanded its campaign to urge the abolition of capital punishment regardless of the defendant's race, but still primarily as a means of achieving the LDF's larger goal, eliminating discrimination. As the campaign wore on, and the arguments explicitly based on race proved less successful in court than the arguments not explicitly based on race, the LDF increasingly found itself making non-race-based arguments for the purpose of advancing a race-based goal.

Today, by contrast, opponents of the death penalty often find themselves doing the opposite, making race-based arguments for the purpose of advancing a non-race-based goal, abolishing capital punishment. Many death penalty opponents would, if pressed, acknowledge that racial disparity is not their true target. If the race-of-defendant and race-of-victim disparities could be eliminated tomorrow, many would still urge that capital punishment be abolished, for reasons having little to do with the race of the defendant or the victim. The emphasis on racial disparity is often more a rhetorical tactic than a substantive criticism. But it is a rhetorical tactic that plays very well, probably better than the straightforward moral argument against capital punishment, because it can draw on our collective memory of three and a half centuries of American history.

NOTES

1. Laurie E. Ekstrand et al., *Death Penalty Sentencing: Research Indicates Pattern of Racial Disparities* (Washington, D.C.: General Accounting Office, 1990). The research published since the GAO study reveals the same pattern: statistically significant race-of-defendant disparities in some jurisdictions, and statistically significant race-of-victim disparities in all. See, e.g., David C. Baldus et al., "Racial Discrimination and the Death Penalty in the Post-Furman Era: An Empirical and Legal Overview, with Recent Findings from Philadelphia," *Cornell Law Review* 83 (1998): 1638–1770; Isaac Unah and Jack Boger, *Race and the Death Penalty in North Carolina: An Empirical Analysis: 1993–1997* (2001), www.deathpenaltyinfo.org/NCRaceRpt.html (visited 29 May 2002).

2. www.deathpenaltyinfo.org/topics.html (visited 28 June 2002).

3. Jesse L. Jackson, Sr., Jesse L. Jackson, Jr., and Bruce Shapiro, *Legal Lynching: The Death Penalty and America's Future* (New York: New Press, 2001); William S. McFeely, *Proximity to Death* (New York: W. W. Norton, 2000).

4. *The Federal Death Penalty System: A Statistical Survey (1988–2000)* (Washington, D.C.: United States Department of Justice, 2000).

5. David B. Mustard, "Racial, Ethnic, and Gender Disparities in Sentencing: Evidence from the U.S. Federal Courts," *Journal of Law & Economics* 44 (2001): 285–314; Shawn D. Bushway and Anne Morrison Piehl, "Judging Judicial Discretion: Legal Factors and Racial Discrimination in Sentencing," *Law & Society Review* 35 (2001): 733–64.

6. *The Colonial Laws of New York* (Albany: James B. Lyon, 1894), 1:761–67.

7. S.C. 1740, no. 695; Va. 1748, c. 38.

8. John D. Cushing, ed., *The Earliest Printed Laws of the Province of Georgia* (Wilmington, Del.: Michael Glazier, Inc., 1978), 19–23.

9. Md. 1737, p. 8.

10. Philip J. Schwarz, *Twice Condemned: Slaves and the Criminal Laws of Virginia, 1705–1865* (Baton Rouge: Louisiana State University Press, 1988), 17–18, 25.

11. Michael Stephen Hindus, *Prison and Plantation: Crime, Justice, and Authority in Massachusetts and South Carolina, 1767–1878* (Chapel Hill: University of North Carolina Press, 1980), 131–32.

12. Daniel J. Flanigan, "Criminal Procedure in Slave Trials in the Antebellum South," *Journal of Southern History* 40 (1974): 537–64.

13. Donna J. Spindel, *Crime and Society in North Carolina, 1663–1776* (Baton Rouge: Louisiana State University Press, 1989), 135, 125.

14. Tex. 1858, c. 121; Va. 1847–48, pp. 125–26; Fla. 1827, p. 109; La. 1818, p. 18; Miss. 1858, c. 98; S.C. 1843, p. 258; Tenn. 1835, c. 19.

15. George M. Stroud, *A Sketch of the Laws Relating to Slavery in the Several States of the United States of America*, 2d ed. (Philadelphia: Henry Longstreth, 1856), 75–87.

16. *New York Times*, 2 October 1858, 2:2.

17. Stuart Banner, *The Death Penalty: An American History* (Cambridge: Harvard University Press, 2002), 141.

18. Bertram Wyatt-Brown, *Honor and Violence in the Old South* (New York: Oxford University Press, 1986), 187–92.

19. Schwarz, *Twice Condemned*, 27–29.

20. Thomas D. Morris, *Southern Slavery and the Law, 1619–1860* (Chapel Hill: University of North Carolina Press, 1996), 253.

21. Tenn. 1837, c. 29; Ala. 1841, Jan. 9; La. 1846, no. 139; Ga. 1866, no. 208 (all capital crimes); Fla. 1872, c. 1877 (all capital crimes); Miss. 1872, c. 76 (all capital crimes); Tenn. 1865, c. 5 (horse-stealing, robbery, burglary, and arson); Tex. 1866, c. 137 (rape); Va. 1866, c. 14 (rape), c. 25 (burglary), c. 26 (robbery).

22. George W. Hays, "The Necessity for Capital Punishment," *Scribner's Magazine* 81 (1927): 581.

23. Richard Reifsnyder, "Capital Crimes in the States," *Journal of Criminal Law, Criminology and Police Science* 45 (1955): 691.

24. Dorothy Ripley, *An Account of Rose Butler* (New York: John C. Totten, 1819), 18 (emphasis in original).

25. *The Life, and Dying Speech of Arthur, a Negro Man* (Boston: s.n., 1768).

26. T. H. Breen, "Making History: The Force of Public Opinion and the Last Years of Slavery in Revolutionary Massachusetts," in Ronald Hoffman, Mechal Sobel, and Fredrika J. Teute, eds., *Through a Glass Darkly: Reflections on Personal Identity in Early America* (Chapel Hill: University of North Carolina Press, 1997), 77–92.

27. *The Life and Confession of Cato, a Slave of Elijah Mount* (Johnstown, N.Y.: Abraham Romyen, 1803), 3, 12.

28. *The Address of Abraham Johnstone, a Black Man* (Philadelphia: s.n., 1797), 6–7.

29. *Virginia Gazette*, 25 February 1736, 4:1.

30. Paul W. Keve, *The History of Corrections in Virginia* (Charlottesville: University Press of Virginia, 1986), 13.

31. Walter Clark, "Death Penalty by Burning at the Stake in North Carolina," *The Green Bag* 8 (1896): 149–50.

32. William Nelson et al., eds., *Documents Relating to the Colonial History of the State of New Jersey* (Paterson, N.J.: Press Printing and Publishing Co., 1880–1931), 19:233.

33. *Pennsylvania Gazette*, 23 January 1766.

34. Daniel Horsmanden, *The New-York Conspiracy* (New York: Southwick & Pelsue, 1810), appendix.

35. E. B. O'Callaghan, ed., *Documents Relative to the Colonial History of the State of New-York* (Albany: Weed, Parsons and Company, 1853–87), 5:39.

36. *Maryland Gazette*, 6 May 1746, 4:1.

37. John Demos, *A Little Commonwealth: Family Life in Plymouth Colony* (Oxford: Oxford University Press, 1970).

38. William Blackstone, *Commentaries on the Laws of England* (Oxford: Clarendon Press, 1765–69), 4:75.

39. Matthew Hale, *The History of the Pleas of the Crown* (1736) (London: Professional Books Limited, 1971), 1:382.

40. Thorsten Sellin, "The Philadelphia Gibbet Iron," *Journal of Criminal Law, Criminology and Police Science* 46 (1955): 11–25.

41. E.g., *Pennsylvania Gazette*, 9 January 1750, 4 June 1752; *Archives of Maryland*, 32:3. Sellin, "Philadelphia Gibbet Iron," provides many more examples.

42. A. J. F. Van Laer, ed., *Minutes of the Court of Albany, Rensselaerswyck and Schenectady* (Albany: University of the State of New York, 1926–32), 3:278.

43. Keve, *History of Corrections in Virginia*, 12, 13.

44. Md. 1729, p. 2.

45. Cushing, ed., *The Earliest Printed Laws of the Province of Georgia*, 17.

46. See, e.g., the accounts in the *New York Times* of 24 July 1871, 5:5; 9 April 1872, 5:3; 11 April 1874, 7:1; 27 November 1875, 1:3.

47. Ark. 1901, no. 58; Ark. 1906, no. 295; Ky. 1920, c. 163; *New York Times*, 20 April 1935, 28:2.

48. W. Fitzhugh Brundage, *Lynching in the New South: Georgia and Virginia, 1880–1930* (Urbana: University of Illinois Press, 1993), 8.

49. *Chicago Record-Herald*, 1 August 1906, 1:4; 23 November 1906, 7:2.

50. George C. Wright, *Racial Violence in Kentucky, 1865–1940: Lynchings, Mob Rule, and "Legal Lynchings"* (Baton Rouge: Louisiana State University Press, 1990), 71, 227.

51. J. E. Cutler, "Capital Punishment and Lynching," *Annals of the American Academy of Political and Social Science* 29 (1907): 622–25.

52. Raymond T. Bye, *Capital Punishment in the United States* (Philadelphia: Committee on Philanthropic Labor of Philadelphia, 1919), 70–71; "The Death

Penalty as a Preventive of Crime," *Annals of the American Academy of Political and Social Science* 17 (1901): 366–69; Andrew J. Palm, "Capital Punishment," *American Journal of Politics* 2 (1893): 326.

53. Stewart E. Tolnay and E. M. Beck, *A Festival of Violence: An Analysis of Southern Lynchings, 1882–1930* (Urbana: University of Illinois Press, 1995), 98–113; Charles David Phillips, "Exploring Relations Among Forms of Social Control: The Lynching and Execution of Blacks in North Carolina, 1889–1918," *Law & Society Review* 21 (1987): 361–74.

54. Banner, *The Death Penalty*, 230.

55. *Life and Confession of Amos Miner* (Providence: s.n., 1833), 15.

56. *Trial of David F. Mayberry* (Janesville, Wis.: Baker, Burnett & Hall, 1855), 37.

57. *Account of the Short Life and Ignominious Death of Stephen Merrill Clark* (Salem, Mass.: T. C. Cushing, 1821), 3.

Part II

Race and the Death Penalty Process

Chapter 4

The Role of Victim's Race and Geography on Death Sentencing

Some Recent Data from Illinois

Michael L. Radelet and Glenn L. Pierce

By any measure, the most significant date in the past three decades for death penalty abolitionists in the United States was January 11, 2003, when Illinois Governor George Ryan announced that he was commuting the death sentences of some 167 prisoners in Illinois. Almost all of these inmates had their sentences reduced to life imprisonment without parole; four had their terms reduced to forty years. In announcing the commutations in a nationally televised speech at Northwestern Law School, Governor Ryan stated:

> Our own study showed that juries were more likely to sentence to death if the victim were white than if the victim were black. . . . Our capital system is haunted by the demon of error—error in determining guilt, and error in determining who among the guilty deserves to die. Because of all of these reasons today I am commuting the sentences of all death row inmates.[1]

In this chapter, we will describe the research we conducted for Governor Ryan that, in part, led to his commutation decision. The study examined more than 5,300 cases involving a conviction for first-degree murder in Illinois over a ten-year period, 1988–1997.

I. Background to Our Involvement

By early 2000, there had been twelve executions in Illinois since 1972, and thirteen prisoners had been released from death row in the state because of evidence supporting their innocence. This led the legislative, judicial, and executive branches of the Illinois government to debate what reforms were necessary, if any, to reduce the occurrence of these and other problems. One idea was to impose a moratorium on executions (but not on death sentencing) in the state until various experts and the state's policy makers could study and debate possible reforms.

One source of concern was some sketchy data that suggested that death sentencing might be related to race (e.g., Gross and Mauro, 1989). During the past twenty-five years, each of us has been involved in several studies that have examined the role of race in contemporary death sentencing in the United States (e.g., Bowers and Pierce, 1980; Radelet, 1981; Radelet and Pierce, 1985; Radelet and Pierce, 1991). Because of this concern and our expertise, one of us (MLR), along with several other experts, was invited by Rep. Lauren Gash, Chair of the Illinois House Judiciary Committee on Crime, to appear before her committee in Springfield on January 27, 2000. Radelet spoke to the committee about research on innocence, public opinion, religious perspectives on the death penalty, and, most important, the research that had been conducted throughout the United States on race and death sentencing. Four days later, on January 31, Governor Ryan thwarted any legislative action on a moratorium by acting solely on his own initiative and imposing a moratorium on executions in Illinois (Armstrong and Mills, 2000).

In early March, Governor Ryan appointed a fourteen-member blue ribbon commission to study the death penalty. The Commission was chaired by Frank McGarr, a former federal judge who had spent five years as the Chief Judge of the Northern District of Illinois. Co-chairs were former Illinois U.S. Senator Paul Simon and former U.S. Attorney Thomas Sullivan. Commission members were truly diverse; included were several state attorneys and death penalty defense attorneys, including novelist Scott Turow (a former federal prosecutor who had represented one of the Illinois death row inmates who was exonerated).[2]

Governor Ryan quickly decided that one responsibility of the Commission would be to examine if the death sentence was being equitably applied in the state. For similar homicides committed by offenders with similar levels of culpability (e.g., similar records of prior convictions), were similar sentences imposed? Were death sentences imposed only for the most heinous and premeditated murders, or were they imposed in an arbitrary fashion that left observers unable to distinguish (with legally appropriate factors) who was sentenced to death and who was not?

On June 13, Radelet was invited to Chicago to meet with Matthew R. Bettenhausen, Deputy Governor for Public Safety and Executive Director of the Commission, and Jean M. Templeton, an attorney who had recently been appointed as Research Director for the Governor's Commission on Capital Punishment. Also attending the meeting was Leigh Bienen, Professor of Law at Northwestern University, who has conducted several major studies on race and death sentencing (Bienen et al., 1988, 1990; Bienen 1996). Our meeting, which took place in the governor's office in Chicago, lasted two hours, and covered four main issues:

- *Methodology:* How to conduct a race/proportionality study.
- *Data:* What data were needed, both on homicides committed in Illinois and on cases where the death penalty was imposed, and what sorts of data on both were available.
- *Funding:* What such a study would cost and what agencies might fund it.
- *Researchers:* Who are the researchers around the United States who have conducted such studies who might be available to do an Illinois study.

Because of numerous other commitments, both Radelet and Bienen made it clear that they themselves could not undertake the study.

On June 28, Radelet and Bienen returned to Chicago to meet with the full Commission on Capital Punishment and again discuss the above issues. At that time the Commission was having monthly meetings, private and informal, during which members organized themselves into working subgroups. The June meeting was the third time that the full Commission met. In our ninety minutes with the Commission, we focused on how a study of race and death sentencing should be conducted and what data would be needed. Again, both Bienen and Radelet stated that their other commitments prohibited them from being considered as possible researchers on the study.

In the two months that followed, Radelet supplied the Commission (through Jean Templeton) with copies of several studies that had been published on race and death sentencing and approached, on her behalf, several experienced researchers to see if they might be interested in conducting the study. Templeton also approached possible researchers, including Glenn Pierce. By early October, Pierce had decided to do the study, and soon thereafter, after additional conversations with both Pierce and Templeton, Radelet was on board.[3]

II. Generation of Hypotheses

Before our study began, two sources of data led to the suspicion that death sentencing in Illinois might be contaminated by racial biases. First, characteristics of cases in which the death penalty was imposed were inconsistent with demographic patterns in the larger population. Second, an analysis of homicides in Illinois from July 1, 1977, through December 31, 1980, found evidence of race-of-victim disparities (Gross and Mauro, 1989).

A comparison between those sentenced to death and the demographic characteristics of the state as a whole raised some interesting questions. Estimates by the U.S. Bureau of Census put the population of Illinois on April 1, 2000, at 12.42 million, of whom 75.1 percent were white or Hispanic and 15.6 percent black. On the other hand, between mid-1977, when the then-current Illinois death penalty statute took effect, and December 31, 2001, the state sentenced 289 people to death. Of these, 173 remained on death row at the end of 2001; the other 116 had been resentenced to prison terms, had died from natural causes, suicides, or executions, or had been otherwise removed from death row (Center for Wrongful Convictions, 2001). The data indicate that 169 of the 289 sentenced to death, or 58.5 percent, were blacks, which is approximately 3.75 times their representation in the state's population. Whites accounted for 75 percent of the Illinois population, but only 35 percent (101/289) of those sentenced to death. And, although 40.8 percent of the African-Americans sentenced to death had been convicted of killing whites (69/169), only 4 of the 101 whites sentenced to death had been convicted of killing blacks. Of the last 12 men executed in Illinois before Governor Ryan imposed the moratorium, 11 had been convicted of killing at least one white victim. By the end of 2001, some 63 percent of the 173 on death row in Illinois were black.

Such comparisons between census data and the racial characteristics of those sentenced to death or those on death row raise interesting questions.

However, because such comparisons do not control for differential involvement in, or victimization from, homicides (much less the most aggravated homicides), in and of themselves they do not, and cannot, prove racial disparities. Instead, they simply challenge the researcher to examine, or "control for," legally relevant factors that might explain the disparities. For example, to say that African-Americans are 15.6 percent of the population and 58.5 percent of those sentenced to death leads to no conclusions; it simply invites one to see if the disparity is "explained" by such factors as the possibility that African-Americans are more likely to be involved in highly aggravated homicides than are whites.

The same can be said about characteristics of homicide victims. As mentioned, between the time the Illinois death penalty statute took effect in 1977 and the end of 2001, 289 people were sentenced to death, of whom 173 remained on death row at the end of 2001. Table 1 displays the racial breakdowns of the homicide victims of the 289 death-sentenced defendants. Thus, among the 289 Illinois death sentences, 173, or 60 percent, were imposed on defendants who had been convicted of killing at least one white victim. As we began our study, we did not know if this pattern was because of the possibility that 60 percent of the homicide victims in Illinois were white, or, more important, because of the possibility that 60 percent of the victims of the death-penalty-"eligible" homicides were white. But if the death sentencing rate is higher for those who kill whites than for those who kill blacks, given similar homicides, evidence of racial bias would be uncovered.

A. The Gross-Mauro Study

The only post-*Furman* scholarly study to assess the possibility of racial disparities in death sentencing in Illinois was published by Samuel Gross

TABLE 1
Race of Victim among 289 Sentenced to Death in Illinois, 1977–2001

Victim|Race/Ethnicity	N	% of Total N
White	164	56.7
Black	97	33.6
Latino	13	4.5
Black & White	10	3.5
Asian & White	1	0.3
Other	4	1.4
Total	289	

and Robert Mauro (1989). Their study, which also examined seven other states, focused on the five-year period January 1, 1976, through December 31, 1980, or, as they note, "for that portion of that period during which the state in question had a capital sentencing statute in force" (Gross and Mauro, 1989:35). Because Illinois did not have an active death penalty statute until mid-1977, Gross and Mauro confined their attention to Illinois from July 1, 1977, through the end of 1980 (Gross and Mauro, 1989:233).

Gross and Mauro gave special attention to death sentencing in Florida, Georgia, and Illinois, the three states with the largest death row populations at the time. Of the three states, Illinois had the lowest death sentencing rate: 1.4 percent of all homicides with known offenders were sentenced to death, compared to 3.7 percent each in Georgia and Florida (Gross and Mauro, 1989:43). Their study included 45 death sentences in Illinois, approximately 15 percent of all death sentences imposed in Illinois between mid-1977 and the end of 2001. Their homicide data came from the Supplemental Homicide Reports (SHR), which are compiled by local police departments and filed with the Uniform Crime Reports program of the Federal Bureau of Investigation. The data cover the following:

1. sex, age, and race of the victim or victims;
2. sex, age, and race of the suspected killer or killers;
3. date and place of the homicide;
4. weapon used;
5. commission of any separate felony accompanying the homicide; and
6. relationship between the victim(s) and the suspected killer(s).

To determine which of the homicides resulted in a death sentence, Gross and Mauro used data on death penalty cases collected by the NAACP Legal Defense Fund. That death row data set also included data on such characteristics as the county of the crime, its month and year, and the sex, age, and race of defendant and victim. By comparing these items in both the Legal Defense Fund and the SHR data, it became possible to "match" cases and identify those that resulted in a death sentence.

According to the 1980 Census, the population of Illinois was 11.5 million, 80 percent of whom were white, 14.5 percent black, and 5.5 percent Hispanic (U.S. Bureau of the Census, 1981:33). Despite the fact that blacks were only 14.5 percent of the total population, Gross and Mauro note that some 58.6 percent of the homicides in Illinois during the three and a half year of the study period took the lives of blacks (Gross and Mauro, 1989:43). Thus, blacks were four times more likely to be victims of homicides than their representation in the population would suggest.

Gross and Mauro then demonstrated that race was clearly associated with the imposition of death sentences. Among those suspected of killing whites, 2.9 percent went to death row, compared to 0.5 percent of those suspected of killing blacks (Gross and Mauro, 1989:44). In cases where a black was suspected of killing a white, 7.5 percent were sentenced to death, compared to 1.9 percent of the whites killing whites and 0.6 percent of the blacks killing blacks. None of the 56 whites suspected of killing blacks during the study period were sentenced to death (Gross and Mauro, 1989:45).

What accounts for these racial disparities? One hypothesis might be that homicides that victimize whites are generally more serious or "death penalty eligible" than those that victimize blacks. But if it was found that among only those highly aggravated cases (such as rape murders or multiple murders) those who victimize whites are still more likely to be sentenced to death, then solid evidence of racial disparities—or even racial discrimination—would remain. After all, in Illinois only 27.1 percent of the homicides involved an accompanying felony, but 75 percent of the death penalty cases involved accompanying felonies (Gross and Mauro, 1989:45). If felony circumstances were more prevalent in white-victim cases, then a race-neutral and legally relevant explanation for the racial differences in death sentencing would be suggested.

Nonetheless, the presence of felony circumstances (i.e., a murder in the course of another felony) did not explain the racial disparities. In Illinois, 9.4 percent of the white victim cases with felony circumstances ended in a death sentence, compared to only 3.0 percent of similar cases with black victims (Gross and Mauro, 1989:47). Nor did the relationship between defendant and victim explain the racial disparities, where 22 percent of all homicides, but 70 percent of death penalty cases, involved strangers (Gross and Mauro, 1989:46). Here 5.8 percent of those suspected of killing white strangers were sentenced to death, compared to only 1.5 percent of those suspected of killing black strangers (Gross and Mauro, 1989:49). Similarly, 4 percent of all murders, but 44 percent of the death penalty cases, involved multiple murders (Gross and Mauro, 1989:48). But when the victims of those multiple murders included at least one white, 22.5 percent ended in a death sentence, compared to 6.8 percent of the cases where the victims were black (Gross and Mauro, 1989:51).

In the end, these "control variables" failed to explain the racial disparities in death sentencing. Among all homicides, those suspected of killing whites were 5.8 times more likely to be sentenced to death than those who kill blacks (2.9/0.5). Among those with accompanying felonies, the ratio was 3 to 1 (9.4/3.0). Among those suspected of killing strangers, the ratio was 3.9 (5.8/1.5). Among those suspected of multiple murders, the ratio was 3.3 (22.5/6.8).

To conclude their study, Gross and Mauro developed an Aggravation Scale by assigning each homicide one point for each of three factors: (1) it involved accompanying felonies; (2) the suspect and victim were strangers; (3) there were multiple victims. This aggravation scale does a good job in predicting who is sentenced to death. Only 0.1 percent of the homicides with a "0" on the scale ended in a death sentence, 1.0 percent of those coded "1"; 7.4 percent of those coded "2"; and 22.6 percent of those coded "3" (Gross and Mauro, 1989:59). However, within each level of aggravation, those suspected of killing whites were more likely than other homicide suspects to be sentenced to death. For example, among those with a "2" or "3" level of aggravation, 12.4 percent of those suspected of killing whites in Illinois and 4.4 percent of those suspected of killing blacks were sentenced to death. When all the variables were entered into a logistic regression model, it was found that "[i]n Illinois the overall odds of an offender receiving the death penalty for killing a white were 4.0 times greater than for killing a black" (Gross and Mauro, 1989:66).

We now turn our attention to the data we gathered to test whether the patterns found by Gross and Mauro remained after their study period ended at the end of 1980.

III. Methodology

A. Data Sources

The data we used in our study are a subset of conviction data from the cases of all defendants convicted of first-degree murder in Illinois who were formally sentenced during the ten-year period January 1, 1988, through December 31, 1997. The cases included are analyzed in terms of sentencing events. As used in this report, the term "sentencing event" refers to a judicial proceeding in which a sentence is imposed. A defendant may be sentenced in one judicial proceeding for the murders of multiple victims where those murders occurred as part of the same course of conduct. Or, where multiple murders occur in separate events, a defendant is more likely to be sentenced in separate judicial proceedings for each murder. As a result, defendants in the latter category appear in our data set on more than one occasion. A total of 5,310 cases or sentencing events in the study time frame were identified from Illinois Department of Corrections (IDOC) records, of which 115 ended with a death sentence. The subset of cases for which there are no missing data for any of the independent variables used in this analysis is 4,182 cases, which contain 76 death sentence cases.

As we will discuss later in this chapter, the focus on only those convicted of first-degree murder introduces a conservative bias into our results. Race or region, for example, might be correlated with which types of homicide cases (other factors constant) are most likely to result in a conviction for first-degree murder. Thus, race or region may correlate with the amount of effort made by the prosecutor to find mitigation sufficient to justify offering to reduce the penalty for first-degree charges. Or, once a prosecutor brings a defendant charged with first-degree murder before a jury, race may correlate with the probability the defendant is found guilty. Illinois is among several states that have been criticized for the unbridled discretion that prosecutors have in deciding in which cases the death penalty will be sought (Potratz, 1980).

However, the multitude of decisions made before a defendant is convicted of first-degree murder are not examined in this project, so any possible impact on these decisions by political and extralegal factors cannot be exposed. Again we refer to the "continuous chain" of decisions that are necessary before a person is executed, with police, prosecutors, jurors, judges, appellate courts, and governors all involved. The individual decisions may be invisible (that is, detailed data are not collected that would allow one to show consistency), but their effects are not. Therefore, if extralegal factors are shown to correlate with sentencing decisions among those convicted of first-degree murder, the results will be conservative because these earlier decision points are not studied, and whatever improper biases may or may not exist will not be spotted. In addition, our data measure only whether or not the death penalty was imposed. This sentence reflects decisions made not only by prosecutors but also by judges and juries. To pinpoint any political influences in prosecutors' decisions, the ideal research project would examine cases where the death penalty was sought, not only where it is imposed.

Several sources of official data were supplied to the researchers to develop the analytic database for this analysis. The final database for the analysis was based exclusively on data supplied and/or collected by the State of Illinois. The specific data used in this study are outlined below.

1. *Department of Corrections.* Our "master list" of cases was obtained from the Illinois Department of Corrections (IDOC). This is a confidential, nonpublic database that was made available to us solely for purposes of this study. That office maintains an "Offender Tracking System" (OTS) data file that contains a wide array of information about the offender and the offense/s for which she or he was convicted. Included in this study are only the cases where defendants were sentenced for first-degree murder, where the sentencing date occurred between January 1, 1988, and December 31, 1997.

In addition to providing the sample of events that are the basis for this study, IDOC data also allowed us to construct a broad range of variables that measure the potential seriousness of a homicide(s) associated with the first-degree homicide offenders in our sample. This is possible because IDOC data provide information on all previous and contemporaneous offenses for which a first-degree homicide offender has been convicted and incarcerated in the Illinois Department of Corrections. Two types of indicators of legally relevant factors were developed from IDOC data on offenses for which defendants were incarcerated: indicators of (1) death sentence eligibility and (2) aggravating facts for the death sentencing proceeding. Finally, IDOC data also provide information on the race and sex of offenders and on the county from which offenders in this study were sentenced.

Although the IDOC data provide detailed information on the offense, we turned to three additional sources of data to obtain information about the victims.

2. *Chicago Homicide Data.* Approximately three-quarters of Illinois homicides occur in Cook County, and almost all of those take place in the City of Chicago. Detailed data on Chicago homicides have been collected by the Chicago Police Department, on and off, for at least 130 years. Data from cases during the study period were obtained from the Illinois Criminal Justice Information Authority (ICJIA), a state agency responsible for research on the criminal justice system in Illinois. The data give important information about the circumstances of the crime and characteristics of the victim. Of special importance is that the Chicago Police data also contain a unique number that we used to link the case with the information

on the offender in the IDOC database.[4] Using the unique Chicago case number, we were able to link information on the victims of homicide to 2,898 (or 54.7 percent) of the offenders in the sample.

3. *Victim Data from Selected State and Local Records.* Information on the race, ethnicity, and sex of victims for non-Chicago first-degree murders in the study sample was obtained primarily by the Illinois Criminal Justice Information Authority. This information was gathered by ICJIA through a search of a variety of official records, both state and local, including some law enforcement records. Data were gathered on the race of victims for an additional 1,091 (or 20.6 percent) first-degree murder offenders in the sample.

4. *Supplemental Homicide Reports Data.* For offenders in the study for whom no victim information was available from the search of state records or from linking to Chicago police data, a final search for victim information was conducted through use of the Supplemental Homicide Report (SHR) data. SHRs represent homicide data gathered by local police departments and forwarded to the Uniform Crime Reporting Program of the Federal Bureau of Investigation for national tabulations. Although the data do not give the name of the victim or offender, or the specific date of the offense, they do contain information on the county, month, and year of the offense; the gender, race, and age of the defendant and victim; and information on (1) the victim-defendant relationship, (2) the method of killing, and (3) information on the type of felony (if any) that accompanied the homicide. There was sufficient SHR information on the race, age, and sex of offenders, as well as on the date and county of offense to "match" SHR victim data with comparable information from the Department of Corrections. Using SHR data, we were able to link homicide victim information to 263 additional offenders in the sample who did not already have victim data from the state or Chicago Police sources. Linking to SHR data added an additional 4.9 percent of offenders where the victim information was available. Overall race of victim information was matched to 80.1 percent of the offenders in our sample.

B. Variables Used for the Analysis

Two major categories of variables were developed for this analysis: legally relevant factors that could be expected to affect the likelihood of a first-degree murder offender's receiving a death sentence, and extralegal factors that should not affect whether an offender receives a death sentence. Among the legally relevant factors, two types of indicators were developed for the first-degree murder offenders in this study: (1) indicators of death sentence eligibility, and (2) indicators of aggravating facts. Below the specific variables used in the analysis are reviewed within their major substantive categories.

1. *Indicators of Death Sentence Eligibility*. Illinois has a bifurcated death-sentencing proceeding. The first part focuses on whether the defendant is *eligible for the death penalty*. Here the state must prove, beyond a reasonable doubt, that the defendant is at least age 18, and prove the existence of at least one of the twenty death penalty eligibility factors provided for under Illinois law. Using IDOC offender data, we developed indicators for two major classes of death penalty eligibility; specifically, indicators were developed for "multiple-murder factor" first-degree murders and "in the course of another felony" first-degree murders. Under the multiple-murder factor, a defendant may be eligible for the death penalty if she or he has been convicted of murdering two or more individuals. Case law indicates that these contemporaneous and/or prior convictions must be for intentional murder or for knowing murder (not for felony murder) to qualify as a multiple murder eligibility factor. Variables 1 and 2 in Table 2 present the indicators of contemporaneous and prior multiple murder eligibility factors used in this analysis (for more information, see Pierce and Radelet, 2002).

Under the "in the course of another felony" factor, a defendant is eligible for the death penalty where the murder has occurred in the course of any one of several statutorily specified felonies. Using IDOC data, a number of specific "in the course of another felony" eligibility indicators were developed, based on convictions for felonies that occurred within the same sentencing event as the first-degree murder for which the defendant was incarcerated. Variables 3 through 12 in Table 2 present the indicators of "in the course of another felony" eligibility factors used in this study. There is a requirement that, in addition to a contemporaneous felony offense,[5] there be some element of intentional or knowing conduct on the part of offender. This element cannot be measured with IDOC data.

Finally, three additional indicators of death penalty eligibility were developed from victim information that was obtained from the Chicago Police Department, state records, or SHR data sources. Specifically, indicators for the murder of an elderly person (over age 59), for the murder of a young person (under age 12), and for multiple-victim murders (contemporaneous murders, but not necessarily "intentional or knowing") were developed from victim data. For the age of the victim to qualify as a death penalty eligibility factor requires "brutal and heinous" conduct, which is a factor that we were unable to measure. Variables 13 through 15 in Table 2 present these indicators.

2. *Indicators of Aggravating Facts.* After the defendant is determined to be eligible for the death penalty, then proceedings move on to the "aggravation/mitigation" phase. At that point, the state provides evidence in aggravation (prior criminal history, etc.) and defendant provides mitigation evidence. In theory defendants with the worst set of aggravating facts (e.g., the worst criminal history) should be more likely to receive the death penalty (assuming level of culpability, and so on are constant).

IDOC data provide information on evidence in aggravation in the form of measures of contemporaneous or prior other serious murder convictions (e.g., solicitation for murder, conspiracy to murder, attempted murder, etc.) and in the form of measures of offender's prior criminal history that go beyond the offender's prior history of murder. In terms of prior criminal history, IDOC provides information on the number of prior IDOC incarcerations for all Class X, 1, 2, 3, and 4 offenses for the first-degree offenders in our sample (see variables 16 through 22 in Table 2 for the indicators of other serious murder convictions and prior criminal history).

3. *Indicators of Extra Legal Factors.* Information on the race, ethnicity, and sex of victims was provided from victim information that we acquired from the Chicago Police Department, selected state records, or SHR data sources (see variables 23 and 24). IDOC data provide information on the race and sex of offenders (see variables 25 and 26 in Table 2) and on the county from which offenders in this study were sentenced (see variable 27 in Table 2). Information on offender's trial court sentencing county allows us to investigate the possibility of geographic disparities in death penalty sentencing. The county of offender's sentencing was coded into four standard Illinois subregions used by the Illinois Criminal Justice Information Authority (ICJIA): Cook County, "collar" counties, other urban counties, and rural counties. Because of its size, Cook County is its own category. The collar counties are the five counties that border on Cook County (DuPage, Lake, Kane, McHenry, and Will). Urban and rural counties are defined by whether or not they lie within a Metropolitan Statistical Area (MSA). Based on this definition, there are 28 counties in Illinois that are part of an MSA (Cook, collar, and urban counties) and 74 counties that are not part of an MSA (in other words, rural).

A number of obvious potential extralegal factors are not included in the analysis, such as the social class of the victim, whether the victim was a member of the community, adequacy of legal counsel, and the quality of police/forensic investigative work on the case. In addition to the more obvious factors, this class of variables has the peculiar quality of containing information that may seemingly be far removed from the legal process of a given case but may nevertheless sometimes have a direct and significant effect on the imposition of a death sentence. Such factors may include events such as violent crime waves or spectacular media coverage of violent crime, and/or they may include organizational/political phenomena, such as political campaigns or local community pressures (Brooks and Raphael, 2002). Very little is known about the influence of

TABLE 2

Independent Variables for Death Sentence Analysis

1. MPMFM1
   Prior Intentional/Knowing Murder (no = 0; yes = 1)
2. MCMFACTR
   Contemporaneous Intentional/Knowing Murder (no = 0; yes = 1)
3. MCGRPA1
   Contemporaneous Armed Robbery (no = 0; yes = 1)
4. MCGRPB1
   Contemporaneous Aggravated Criminal Sexual Assault (no = 0; yes = 1)
5. MCGRPC1
   Contemporaneous Home Invasion (group 3c) (no = 0; yes = 1)
6. MCGRPD1
   Contemporaneous Aggravated Kidnapping (group 3d) (no = 0; yes = 1)
7. MCGRPE1
   Contemporaneous Arson (no = 0; yes = 1)
8. MCGRPF1
   Contemporaneous Simple Robbery (no = 0; yes = 1)
9. MCGRP3BR
   Contemporaneous Residential Robbery (no = 0; yes = 1)
10. MCGRP3CR
    Contemporaneous Armed Violence (no = 0; yes = 1)
11. MCGRP3DR
    Contemporaneous Vehicular Hijack (no = 0; yes = 1)
12. MCBFCTR1
    Contemporaneous Burglary (no = 0; yes = 1)
13. VCCNTT4
    Number of Additional Homicide Victims (0, 1, 2, 3+)
14. VICGT59D
    Homicide Victim/s Over Age 59 (no = 0; yes = 1)
15. VICLT12D
    Homicide Victim/s Under Age 12 (no = 0; yes = 1)
16. MCSM2
    Contemporaneous Other Serious Murder Convictions (0, 1, 2+)
17. MPSM2
    Prior Other Serious Murder Convictions (0, 1, 2+)

these types of factors on processes in the criminal justice system because they are very difficult to study. Nevertheless, they do provide some examples of types of extralegal factors that are potentially useful to examine in death penalty research and may be important in the monitoring of the death sentencing process.

C. Statistical Approach

The analysis first examines the bivariate relationships between sentencing and 22 indicators of legally relevant factors that are potential determinants of death sentencing in Illinois. These indicators include measures of death penalty eligibility factors (variables 2–15 in Table 2), and measures

TABLE 2 *(Continued)*
Independent Variables for Death Sentence Analysis

18. MPCLAS12
    Prior Class 1 Offenses (0, 1, 2+)
19. MPCLAS22
    Prior Class 2 Offenses (0, 1, 2+)
20. MPCLAS32
    Prior Class 3 Offenses (0, 1, 2+)
21. MPCLAS42
    Prior Class 4 Offenses (0, 1, 2+)
22. MPCLASX2
    Prior Class X Offenses (0, 1, 2+)
23. VICSEX_D
    One or more female victims (none = 0, 1+)
24. VICRACE
    Victim's Race (1 = only white, 2 = only black, 3 = only Hispanic, 4 = only other race, 5 = victims from more than one race)
24a. VICBLK_D
    At least one black victim (none = 0, 1+). This is a dichotomous version of variable 24.
25. MI_RSEX
    Offender's sex is female (0 = not female, 1 = female)
26. OFFRACE
    Offender's Race (1 = white, 2 = black, 3 = Hispanic, 4 = other race)
    26a. OFFBLACK (0 = not black, 1 = black). This is a dichotomous version of variable 26.
27. COUNTY
    County of Trial (1 = Cook County, 2 = Collar Counties, 3 = Other Urban Counties, 4 = Rural Counties)
27a. COOKOTH
    County of Trial (0 = Not Cook County, 1 = Cook County). This is a dichotomous version of variable 27.
27b. CNTYCOUR
    County of Trial (0 = Not Collar or Other Urban counties, 1 = Collar or Other Urban Counties). This is a dichotomous version of variable 27.

of facts of aggravation (variables 16–22 in Table 2). The analysis also examines the bivariate relationship between death sentencing and three potential extralegal factors, including the race and sex of victims, the race and sex of homicide offenders, and the county where the offenders were sentenced (variables 23–27 in Table 2).

After presenting the results of these cross-tabulations, we then assess the *unique* ability of each of the variables to explain who is and who is not sentenced to death. That is, we assess the potential impact of extralegal factors on death sentencing while statistically controlling for legally relevant factors. To do this, logistic regression analysis was employed. Logistic regression models estimate the average effect of each independent variable (predictor) on the odds that a convicted felon would receive a sentence of death. An odds ratio is simply the ratio of the probability of a death sentence to the probability of a sentence other than death. Thus, when one's likelihood of receiving a death sentence is .75 (P), then the probability of receiving a non-death sentence is .25 (1 – P). The odds ratio in this example is .75/.25 or 3 to 1. Simply put, the odds of getting the death sentence in this case are 3 to 1.

The dependent variable is the natural logarithm of the odds ratio, y, of having received the death penalty. Thus, $y = P / 1 - P$ and

$$(1) \ \ln(y) = â_0 + Xâ + ?_i$$

where $â_0$ is an intercept, $â_i$ are the i coefficients for the i independent variables, X is the matrix of observations on the independent variables, and $?_i$ is the error term.

Results for the logistic model are reported as odds ratios. Recall that when interpreting odds ratios, an odds ratio of 1 means that someone with that specific characteristic is just as likely to receive a capital sentence as not. Odds ratios of greater than 1 indicate a higher likelihood of the death penalty for offenders who have a positive value for that particular independent variable. When the independent variable is continuous, the odds ratio indicates the increase in the odds of receiving the death penalty for each unitary increase in the predictor.

IV. Findings

A total of 5,310 cases in the study time frame were identified from IDOC records, of which 115 ended with a death sentence. Of the 5,310 cases, there was county of trial information on 5,300. We were able to match 4,252 cases with race of victim information (80.1 percent). Of the total universe of cases, we were able to match to race of victim in 84.1 percent of the cases from Cook County, 60.8 percent of the cases from the collar county region, 72.9 percent of the cases in the urban county region, and 66.1 percent of the cases in the rural county region. The subset of cases for which there are no missing data for any of the 27 independent variables used in this analysis (see Table 2) includes 4,182 cases, of which 76 ended with a death sentence.

1. *Bivariate Analysis of Death Sentence Eligibility.* The first step in our analysis was to crosstabulate all of the variables used in our study with whether or not the defendant was sentenced to death (these tables are presented in Pierce and Radelet, 2002). The crosstabulations first examine the imposition of the death penalty by the indicators of death sentence eligibility. These include an indicator for "multiple murder factor" (i.e., conviction for a contemporaneous or prior "intentional or knowing murder" in addition to the offender's first-degree murder conviction), and for "in the course of another felony" murders. In addition, death sentence eligibility indicators were examined for the murder of an elderly person (over age 59), the murder of a young person (under age 12), and for multiple victim murders.[6]

Several factors were related to death sentencing. For example, death sentencing is correlated with convictions for prior and contemporaneous murders. Under the "in the course of another felony" factor, a defendant is eligible for the death penalty when the murder occurred in the course of any one of several statutorily specified felonies.

We constructed several crosstabulations to examine the imposition of the death penalty by our indicators of "in the course of another felony" eligibility factors. Of the ten accompanying felony indicators examined, nine showed a statistically significant relationship with imposition of the death sentence based on the Pearson chi-square test, and six showed a significant relation based on the Yates Continuity Correction for the chi-square test.[7] Some of these indicators may not have achieved a statistically significant relationship with death sentences due to the low frequency of their occurrence in the sample. In addition, the magnitude of the relationships between the "in the course of another felony" factors and imposition of a death sentence shows considerable variability across the ten indicators. Among the indicators showing a statistically significant effect on death sentencing, the percent of death sentences imposed where one of these eligibility factors is present varies from a low of 4.1 percent for the armed robbery indicator (Pierce and Radelet, 2002: Table 5) to a high of 15.7 percent for the aggravated kidnapping indicator (Pierce and Radelet, 2002: Table 8). Because these variables represent indicators of death penalty eligibility, the data indicate that the eligibility factors vary considerably in their overall importance in death penalty decisions.

We then constructed three crosstabulations to see if the imposition of the death penalty was related to the three indicators of death sentence eligibility derived from homicide victim data: the murder of an elderly person (over age 59), the murder of a young person (under age 12), and for multiple victim murders (Pierce and Radelet, 2002: Tables 15–17). As would be expected, each of these indicators showed a statistically significant correlation with imposition of the death sentence, with the multiple victims murder indicator showing the largest effect on death sentencing.

2. *Bivariate Analysis of Facts of Aggravation.* As noted, after a defendant is determined to be eligible for the death penalty, the judicial proceedings then move on to the "aggravation/mitigation" phase. At that point, the state provides evidence in aggravation (e.g., prior criminal history), and the defendant provides mitigation evidence. IDOC data provide information on evidence in aggravation in the form of measures of contemporaneous or prior "other serious murder convictions" (e.g., solicitation for murder, conspiracy to murder, attempted murder, etc.), and in the form of measures of offender's prior criminal history that go beyond the offender's prior history of murder.

We next presented two tables (Pierce and Radelet, 2002: Tables 18 and 19) that examined imposition of the death penalty by contemporaneous and prior "other serious murder convictions." Convictions for contemporaneous offenses are not statistically related to the imposition of a death sentence. Cases with one or more convictions for prior "other serious murder offenses" show a statistically significant relationship with imposition of the death sentence using only the Pearson Chi-square test, but not with the Continuity Correction.

In terms of prior criminal history, IDOC provides information on the number of prior IDOC incarcerations for all Class X, 1, 2, 3, and 4 offenses for the first-degree offenders in our sample. The next five tables (Pierce and Radelet, 2002: Tables 20–24) examined the relationship between offenders' prior criminal record and imposition of the death sentence. Of the five indicators of prior criminal record examined, three show a statistically significant relationship with death sentencing. The indicators not statistically related to the death sentence were (1) an offender's prior record of incarcerations of Class 1 offenses (Table 21), and (2) his or her prior record of Class 4 offenses (Table 24).

3. *Bivariate Analysis of Extralegal Factors.* Extralegal factors represent those factors that should not affect whether an offender receives a death sentence. A major objective of this study is to examine the potential impact of extralegal factors on death sentencing in Illinois. Factors we examined include geographic region of the state, the race and sex of the first-degree murder victims and offenders. These crossclassifications are reprinted as Tables 3–8 herein.

Geographic Region. Information on county of sentence allows us to investigate the possibility of geographic disparities in death penalty sentencing decisions. To this end, offender's county of trial was coded into the four standard Illinois subregions used by the Illinois Criminal Justice Information Authority: Cook County, Collar counties, other urban counties, and rural counties. Table 3 shows patterns of death sentencing in these four regions. In Cook County, 1.5 percent the first-degree murders ended with a death sentence, versus 3.3 percent of the cases in the Collar counties, 3.4 percent of the cases in other urban counties, and 8.4 percent of the cases in rural counties. The cross regional differences were statistically significant at < .001 level of significance.

Sex and Race of Victim. Table 4 displays the imposition of the death sentences by the sex of the homicide victims. Examination of Table 4 shows that the sex of murder victims is significantly related to imposition of the death sentence. Specifically, 4.3 percent of the offenders who were

TABLE 3
Death Sentence by Region

Sentence		Trial Court Region				
		Cook County	Collar Counties	Urban Counties	Rural Counties	Total
Other	N	3,948	348	659	230	5,185
	%	98.5	96.7	96.6	91.6	97.8
Death	N	59	12	23	21	115
	%	1.5	3.3	3.4	8.4	2.2
Total	N	4,007	360	682	251	5,300
	%	100.0	100.0	100.0	100.0	100.0

	Value	df	Significance
Pearson Chi-Square	61.528	3	.000
Continuity Correction	42.877	3	.000
Number of Cases	(5,300)		

TABLE 4
Death Sentence by Sex of Victim

Sentence		No Females	One + Females	Total
		Sex of Victim Is Female		
Other	N	3,235	973	4,208
	%	98.8	95.7	98.1
Death	N	38	44	82
	%	1.2	4.3	1.9
Total	N	3,273	1,017	4,290
	%	100.0	100.0	100.0

	Value	df	Significance
Pearson Chi-Square	41.467	1	.000
Continuity Correction	39.796	1	.000
Number of Cases	(4,290)		

TABLE 5
Death Sentence by Race of Victim

Sentence		Only White	Only Black	Only Hispanic	Only Other	One + Races	Total
		Race of Victim					
Other	N	996	2,656	464	33	24	4,173
	%	96.2	98.9	98.5	94.3	96.0	98.1
Death	N	39	30	7	2	1	79
	%	3.8	1.1	1.5	5.7	4.0	1.9
Total	N	1,035	2,686	471	35	25	4,252
	%	100.0	100.0	100.0	100.0	100.0	100.0

	Value	df	Significance
Pearson Chi-Square	36.640	4	.000
Continuity Correction	28.131	4	.000
Number of Cases	(4,252)		

TABLE 6
Death Sentence by Sex of Offender

Sentence		Male	Female	Total
		Sex of Offender		
Other	N	4,896	299	5,195
	%	97.8	98.7	97.8
Death	N	111	4	115
	%	2.2	1.3	2.2
Total	N	5,007	303	5,310
	%	100.0	100.0	100.0

	Value	df	Significance
Pearson Chi-Square	1.084	1	.298
Continuity Correction	.702	1	.402
Number of Cases	(5,310)		

convicted of killing one or more females received the death penalty, versus 1.2 percent of the offenders who were convicted of killing solely male victims.

Table 5 reveals statistically significant differences in the imposition of the death penalty by race of the victim(s). Specifically, 3.8 percent of the first-degree murder cases where the victim(s) was (were) white resulted in a death sentence, versus 1.1 percent of the cases where the murder victim(s) was (were) black, and 1.5 percent of the cases where the victim(s) was (were) Hispanic.[8] Where the victim was "other" race or was part of a mixed-race multiple homicide case, the death sentence was imposed 5.7 and 4.0 percent of the time, respectively. This disparity in the imposition of the death sentence was statistically significant at a < .001 level of significance.

Sex and Race of Offender. Table 6 examines the imposition of death sentences by the sex of the offender. This shows that 1.3% of the women and 2.2% of the men in our sample were sentenced to death. This difference, however, is not statistically significant.

Table 7 reveals statistically significant differences in the imposition of the death penalty by race of offender. Specifically, 4.5 percent of the first-degree murder cases where the offender was white resulted in a death sentence, versus 1.8 percent of the cases where the offender was black, and .7 percent of the cases where the offender was Hispanic.[9] None of the 23 cases where the offender's race was listed as "other" ended in a death sentence. This disparity in the imposition of the death sentence was statistically significant at a < .001 level of significance. However, as we will discuss below, focusing simply on the race of offender without also including race of victim is very misleading.

Race of Victim and Offender Combinations. Initial examination of Table 7 shows that black offenders are less likely than white offenders to receive the death penalty, given a conviction for first-degree murder. We also know, however, that most murders are *intraracial* incidents and that (as Table 8 shows) first-degree murders with black victims are the least likely to receive the death sentence. Thus, in order to examine the imposition of the death penalty by the race of offender, it is important to control also for the race of victim. In comparing white and black homicide offenders, we must control for the race of the victim because our data show that blacks are most likely to be convicted for killing other blacks and the murders of black victims are the least likely to receive a death sentence (regardless of race of offender).

Table 8 examines the imposition of the death sentence by race of victim and offender combinations for white and black victims and offenders. The table shows that when race of victim is taken into consideration, the offender race differences largely disappear. Thus, among offenders convicted of killing white victims, 4.5 percent of the black offenders received a death sentence, versus 4.8 percent of the white offenders. In contrast, only 1.1 percent of the black offenders who killed black victims were sentenced to death. Finally, 4.8 percent of the whites who were convicted of killing blacks received the death sentence, but this percent is based on only 62 cases in this category.

TABLE 7
Death Sentence by Race of Offender

Sentence		White	Black	Hispanic	Asian/ American Indian	Total
					Race of Offender	
Other	N	883	3,604	683	23	5,193
	%	95.5	98.2	99.3	100.0	97.9
Death	N	42	67	5		114
	%	4.5	1.8	.7		2.1
Total	N	925	3,671	688	23	5,307
	%	100.0	100.0	100.0	100.0	100.0

	Value	df	Significance
Pearson Chi-Square	34.128	3	.000
Continuity Correction	30.935	3	.000
Number of Cases	(5,307)		

TABLE 8
Death Sentence by Race of Victim/Offender Combination for Whites and Blacks

Sentence		Black kills White	White kills White	Black kills Black	White kills Black	Total
Other	N	363	458	2,526	59	3,406
	%	95.5	95.2	98.9	95.2	98.0
Death	N	17	23	27	3	70
	%	4.5	4.8	1.1	4.8	2.0
Total	N	380	481	2,553	62	3,476
	%	100.0	100.0	100.0	100.0	100.0

	Value	df	Significance
Pearson Chi-Square	44.665	3	.000
Continuity Correction	38.304	3	.000
Number of Cases	(3,476)		

4. *Multivariate Analysis of Indicators of Death Eligibility, Aggravating Facts, and Extralegal Factors.* In the final stage of our analysis, we assess the potential impact of extralegal factors on death sentencing while statistically controlling for legally relevant factors. To do this, as noted above, logistic regression analysis was employed. Logistic regression models estimate the effect of each independent variable (predictor) on the odds that a convicted felon would receive a sentence of death while controlling for the other variables in the equation.

Logistic regression is the preferred statistical approach for analysis of dichotomous dependent variables such as the dependent variable in this study that measures the presence or absence of a death sentence. Nevertheless, any multivariate statistical technique will be limited by the quality and scope of available data. As noted, despite extensive efforts to obtain data, there may be important legal and/or extralegal factors that have not been included in the present analysis. In addition, although most of the independent variables in the study have very little missing data, there are some missing data on race and sex of victims.

The level of missing data varied somewhat across variables in the analysis. For example, there was no missing information on the sex of the defendant (see Table 6), but on the sex of the victim(s) there was missing information on 19 percent of the cases. There are many techniques available to researchers that deal with the problem of missing data in multivariate analyses (see Little and Rubin 1987 for a full discussion). For the analysis conducted for the *Oregon Law Review* and the Governor's Commission on Capital Punishment, any case with missing data on one or more variables was excluded from the multivariate logistic analysis. This resulted in excluding 21.2 percent of the cases from the analysis. For the present analysis we used an approach that included dummy variables in the analysis to control for the missing information in variables with missing information (see Little and Rubin 1987). Dummy variables to control for missing data were included for victim's age, the number of victims, and victim's race. Since the dummy variables are used only to control for missing data, we do not include their coefficients in Table 9. Using the dummy variable approach for variables with at least modest levels of missing data, the number of missing cases in the logistic regression analysis is only 3 cases or .1 percent of the total number of cases (compared with 21.2 percent of the cases in the analysis presented in the *Oregon Law Review* and the Governor's Commission on Capital Punishment).

Table 9 presents the results of the logistic regression analysis. The logistic analysis shows that two important extralegal factors identified in the bivariate analysis—race of victim and sentencing county/region are statistically significant predictors of imposition of the death sentence after controlling for the 22 indicators of legally relevant factors developed for this study. Of the statutorily defined indicators of death penalty eligibility (variables 1–12 in Table 2 and in the logistic regression) introduced into the analysis, 7 of the 12 indicators remained statistically significant predictors of death sentencing when the effects of all the other variables were controlled. In addition, the number of additional homicide victims in the cases and two measures of an offender's prior criminal record (variables 19 and 20 in Table 2) remained statistically significant predictors of death sentencing when the effects of all the other variables were controlled.

TABLE 9
Logistic Regression of Legally Relevant and Extralegal Indicator with Death Sentence

	B	S.E.	Wald	Significance	Exp(B)
MPMFM1	1.772	.311	32.514	.000	5.880
MCMFACTR	2.966	1.277	5.394	.020	19.405
MCGRPA1	.786	.270	8.449	.004	2.194
MCGRPB1	1.626	.398	16.712	.000	5.085
MCGRPC1	1.078	.403	7.167	.007	2.938
MCGRPD1	1.696	.415	16.674	.000	5.451
MCGRPE1	1.220	.509	5.755	.016	3.388
MCGRPF1	.316	.703	.202	.653	1.372
MCBFCTR1	−.418	1.006	.172	.678	.659
MCGRP3BR	1.070	.662	2.609	.106	2.915
MCGRP3CR	.638	1.316	.235	.628	1.893
MCGRP3DR	1.341	1.295	1.072	.301	3.821
VICCNTT4	1.419	.206	47.495	.000	4.133
VICG59D	.187	.404	.213	.644	1.205
VICL12D	.153	.487	.099	.753	1.165
MCSM2	−.147	.367	.159	.690	.864
MPSM2	−.051	.520	.010	.921	.950
MPCLAS12	−.703	.364	3.733	.053	.495
MPCLAS22	.461	.186	6.161	.013	1.585
MPCLAS32	.550	.231	5.668	.017	1.733
MPCLAS42	.156	.308	.257	.612	1.169
MPCLASX2	.389	.222	3.059	.080	1.475
COOKOTH	−1.862	.328	32.262	.000	.155
CNTYCOUR	−.726	.326	4.952	.026	.484
VICSEX_D	.278	.290	.923	.337	1.321
MI_RSEX	−.245	.539	.207	.649	.782
VICBLK_D	−.753	.305	6.084	.014	.471
OFFBLACK	.146	.262	.312	.576	1.157
Constant	−3.268	.330	97.870	.000	.038

Comparison across all the variables in the logistic regression analysis shows that sentencing county/region (i.e., Cook County, variable 27.a, COOKOTH, in Table 2 and the Collar and other urban counties, variable 27.b, CNTYCOUR, in Table 2) and race of victim (one or more black victims versus all other race of victim categories, variable 24a, Table 2) are among the thirteen independent variables (not counting the dummy variables for missing data) that achieved a .05 level of statistical significance (see Table 9). To examine the estimated effect of an independent variable, controlling on the other variables, we use the exponentiated value of the Beta (B) coefficient, which is the logistic regression beta coefficient, Exp(B) (see the Table 9 for these coefficients). The Exp(B) coefficient is the B coefficient expressed as an odds ratio.

Examination of the Exp(B) coefficients in Table 9a shows that the odds of receiving a death sentence for killing a black victim(s) decrease by a factor of .471. As noted, .471 (the Exp(B) value for black victim), is the odds ratio of a first-degree murder offender who killed a black victim being sentenced to death. An odds ratio of exactly 1.0 would mean that the likelihood of receiving the death sentence changed by a factor of 1, or not at all. In this case, the results indicate that the odds of receiving a death sentence, if a first-degree murder offender kills a black victim, are on average 52.9 percent lower (i.e., 1 − .471 = .529 or 52.9%) controlling for the other variables in the analysis. These findings are very similar to the results obtained in the analysis based on the missing data approach used in the *Oregon Law Review*/Governor's Commission on Capital Punishment analysis.

Turning to the question of geographic region, Table 9 indicates that the odds of receiving a death sentence for killing a victim(s) in Cook County decrease by a factor of .155 (i.e., the Exp(B) value for COOKOTH in Table 9). Hence, the odds of receiving a death sentence in for killing a victim or victims in Cook County are on average 84.5 percent lower than for killing a victim(s) in the rural county region of Illinois controlling for the other variables in the analysis. In addition, Table 9 also indicates that the odds of receiving a death sentence for killing a victim or victims in the Collar or other urban counties decrease by a factor of .484 (i.e., the Exp(B) value for CNTYCOUR in Table 9). Hence, the odds of receiving a death sentence in for killing a victim or victims in Cook County are on average 51.6 percent lower than for killing a victim or victims in the rural county region of Illinois, controlling for the other variables in the analysis. The findings for Cook County are very similar to the results obtained in the analysis based on the missing data approach used in the *Oregon Law Review*/Governor's Commission on Capital Punishment analysis. Finally, in this analysis there is a statistically significant effect for the dummy variable identifying the Collar and other urban counties on death sentence decisions, and in the *Oregon Law Review*/Governor's Commission on Capital Punishment analysis, this same variable achieves near statistical significance (.059) (see Pierce and Radelet, 2002, Table 31.a).

Overall, the statistical analysis reveals some surprises about what factors correlate with death sentences in Illinois. Some of the predictor variables that would be expected to affect death sentencing do not show statistically significant relationships with sentence outcomes. For example, of the twelve indicators of statutorily defined death eligibility included in the analysis, only seven were significantly related to death sentencing, even though each of the twelve is legally relevant in identifying which first-degree murder cases are eligible for a death sentence. The twelve indicators represent two (i.e., the multiple murder factor and the "in the course of another felony" factor) of the twenty death eligibility factors identified in Illinois statues. Nonetheless, these two factors are the most commonly used factors in death sentence cases, and thus account for a high proportion of death eligible cases.

V. Conclusions and Policy Recommendations

The results of our study were included in a Technical Appendix to the Final Report of Governor Ryan's Commission on Capital Punishment and were released to the public on April 15, 2002.[10] In our report, we cautioned about the study's limits and included several policy recommendations.

A. Limits to This Study

The results of this study are limited by both scope and data. First, its goal was to examine only the cases that involved a conviction for first-degree murder, comparing cases that resulted in a death sentence with those that did not. Our study examines only sentencing decisions, not charging decisions or a wide array of other decisions involved in sending a defendant to death row. It is quite possible that disparities correlated with extralegal factors (e.g., race, social class, region, or gender) also exist, either at a greater or lesser strength, in decisions in the criminal justice system that are not examined in this research.

Critics of this study who point to its limited scope and limited number of variables should realize that the addition of more data could very well *increase* the power of nonlegal explanatory variables. Baldus et al., for example, point to nine states where both well-controlled and less-well-controlled studies of death sentencing have been conducted. In two-thirds of these states, the racial disparities were *stronger* in the well-controlled studies than in the less complex work (Baldus et al., 1998:1661–62). Certainly the data we have gathered for this research are strong enough to raise serious concerns in the minds of both those who support and oppose the death penalty about whether it is being equitably applied in Illinois.

A second limitation of this research is missing victim data on cases included in our analysis. As noted, we were able to match 4,252 cases with race of victim information (80.1 percent) to form the final sample for our analysis. However, missing data are a problem only if the cases excluded are somehow different from the cases for which we do have complete data. We see nothing to indicate that the cases with missing data in this study are significantly different from the cases for which there are data.

B. Summary of Major Conclusions

Indicators of three extralegal factors—the race of first-degree murder victims and two different geographic regions—were found to be statistically related to the imposition of the death sentence in Illinois controlling on the other variables in this study. Although there are limitations to the present study, these findings on race and geography are consistent with those reported in many other studies. This pattern of findings raises important concerns about how the death sentence is imposed in Illinois.

A major limitation of this study is the lack of high-quality data that are needed to measure additional factors that may affect death penalty decision making. A great deal of time and effort was expended to acquire data necessary for the present study, and despite these efforts, the study's data are limited in both scope and completeness. The data problems encountered in this study are not the responsibility of the Illinois state and local agencies that participated in the study. They provided extensive support and consultation (at no cost) to the project. The problem arises because present criminal justice information systems were designed primarily to support administrative functions of the agencies they assist. The systems were not designed to support research activities and, equally important, judicial monitoring activities. Thus the limitations of data and information encountered by this study directly mirror the limitations that any death sentencing monitoring system would encounter in Illinois. Indeed, properly conducted assessments of death sentences in Illinois would resemble smaller scale projects of the type conducted for this project. Critically, today's criminal justice information systems are entirely inadequate to collect, manage, and integrate the range and quality of information on criminal cases necessary to support a reliable criminal justice monitoring system. As a result, the quality of available criminal data will greatly limit the integrity of any death sentencing monitoring system for the foreseeable future.

C. Recommendations

The results of our analysis lead us to suggest two policy recommendations:

1. *Proportionality Review.* The data suggest the necessity for the Illinois Supreme Court, as the body responsible for reviewing death penalty cases, to pay special attention to issues of proportionality. As in New Jersey, they might consider a comparison between cases in which the death penalty was imposed and other death-eligible cases with equal levels of aggravation and mitigation in which the defendant was sentenced to a prison term.[11] This type of review, however, will be very limited if only cases that end with a death sentence are examined and information and cases from prior stages of the criminal justice system decision-making process are not available.[12]

2. *Monitoring.* To conduct a meaningful proportionality review, officials will need to construct, maintain, and use a database on Illinois homicides. As criminologists, one of the most important lessons we have learned from this research is that data on Illinois homicides are fragmented, difficult to obtain, and often of poor quality. It has been gathered not for purposes of ensuring evenhandedness in sentencing but, rather, for unique needs of individual state agencies (e.g., local police departments, the Illinois Department of Corrections). If the death penalty is to be continued, comprehensive high-quality data need to be gathered and made available to a diverse group of researchers so that issues of equity can be monitored.

A monitoring system built on a foundation of comprehensive high-quality data can be used both to help ensure that race and other inappropriate factors are not involved in death sentencing decisions, and that pure arbitrariness (inequities not attributable to either legal or not-legal factors) does not permeate sentencing. Although it is beyond the mandate given to the current authors to design a comprehensive monitoring system, it is clear that there must be an intensive effort by all parties involved in capital cases in Illinois to gather detailed data on all aspects of homicide cases. Here we are *not* suggesting data collection on decisions made from charging through sentencing but, rather, going back to the day of the homicide and beginning with measures of the quality of the investigation by the police. If the police devote more resources to the investigation of the murders of prominent white victims than to other cases, even if all other decision makers (e.g., prosecutors, judges, jurors, and governors) are fair, racial bias will still permeate the system. In addition, a database needs to be constructed to follow all cases from the time a death sentence is imposed to the time the person exits death row (via court or gubernatorial action, natural death, suicide, or execution). All links in the "continuous chain" of decision makers need to be involved in gathering data, which they can use to monitor their own performance.[13]

In some cases, data gathering itself may add an element of fairness in the system. For example, a study that examines charging decisions would most certainly remind prosecutors of their duty to be evenhanded. But even if they were, decisions made at earlier points (e.g., by police) would remain invisible. Gathering data at all decision points on the chain of decisions makes the decisions more transparent, more accountable, and reminds everyone that his or her work is no longer invisible.

Those designing such a database would need input from prosecutors, defense attorneys, judges, law enforcement investigators, forensic experts, and other criminal justice personnel, as well as from scholars and other more disinterested parties. To be sure, there will undoubtedly be differences in informed opinion between various parties in the debate, but if all cooperate in data gathering, the system will be made much more transparent.

Recent research has also shown the importance of gathering data on the racial characteristics of potential jurors in capital cases, and on how (and why) jurors are excused through peremptory challenges. The most thorough research to address this issue focused on 317 capital prosecutions in Philadelphia, 1981–1997. The authors found that "discrimination in the use of peremptory challenges on the basis of race and gender by both prosecutors and defense counsel is widespread" (Baldus et al., 2001:3; see also Bowers, Steiner, and Sandys, 2001). They found that prosecutors are more successful than defense attorneys in controlling jury composition, and that these biases tend to increase the number of death sentences and the degree of racial discrimination in death sentencing decisions. The opportunity for prosecutors and defense attorneys to interview jurors after they have completed their service and rendered their verdicts might reveal occasional acts of overt racism that may have infected their work.

D. A Final Note

In conclusion, the unique character of homicide in general and the death penalty in particular raises the distinct possibility of powerful political and psychological factors intruding on and interfering with the criminal justice and judicial decision process and with the goal of equity in administration of the death penalty. Hence the importance of vigilant monitoring. When a murder occurs, all who hear about it—citizens, prosecutors, jurors—feel a threat and a need to confront, to varying degrees, personal fears of death. One way to deal with the threat is to retreat to the comfort of people who are familiar to us. When the murder victim is a member of communities with which we are most familiar (and race and social class are part of the victim's social or human capital that can make him or her part of a familiar community) and the killer is more of an outsider (in both in a social and geographic sense), the fear and outrage grow.

And in the past thirty years, the potential for death penalty decisions to become more political has grown as never before. One reason for this is media pressure—the media can sensationalize homicides and prioritize them in terms of outrage and threat (not all murders are given equal media coverage), and they can put pressure on decision makers to accept those priorities. In addition, all of the reforms of the death penalty in the past three decades have made it an extremely costly and time consuming practice. Especially in these days when state budgets are constrained, prosecutors must make priority decisions. There may be pressure from one source to pursue death (e.g., from the media), but also pressure from the office accountant not to do so.

Rational and informed citizens will continue to disagree on the death penalty, but certainly one point on which all interested parties can agree is that if we are going to make these life and death decisions, we need to make them as carefully and equitably as possible.

NOTES

Portions of this paper were first published in *Oregon Law Review*, vol. 81, Spring 2002. These portions are reprinted by permission of *Oregon Law Review*.

1. The full text of Governor Ryan's speech is available at http://www.law.northwestern.edu/depts./clinic/wrongful/RyanSpeech.htm.

2. For a complete roster of members, see http://www.idoc.state.il.us/ccp/member_info.html.

3. Governor Ryan's office also supplied $20,000 for research expenses (primarily for a computer programmer; neither Pierce nor Radelet was paid for his participation).

4. The Chicago Police Department's unique identifying link, which the department provided to connect IDOC case numbers to victim information, was provided by the Chicago Police Department. These linking identifiers are generally not available to the public. They were obtained for this study pursuant to a confidentiality agreement.

5. An actual conviction for the contemporaneous felony is not required for an offense to serve as a death sentence eligibility factor. Because we can measure the cases only in which there was an actual conviction, our data are thereby rendered more conservative.

6. It should be noted that the multiple murder conviction factor and the multiple victim murder indicator are not duplicative; one depends almost entirely on prior murder convictions, and one relates to the number of victims in a single incident.

7. In using the chi-square as a test for statistical significance, care must be taken if in a given table some of the expected frequencies are very low (under 10). In such a case, the Yates continuity correction reduces the difference between the observed and expected frequencies by .5. This reduces the overall size of the chi-square and provides a more conservative estimate of statistical significance.

8. No information on ethnicity was available on the 263 cases that were matched to SHR for race of victim data. For these 263 cases, victims who were Hispanic would have been coded as white or possibly black victims depending on their race.

9. See *id.*

10. For full report, see http://sss.idoc.state.il/us/ccp/.

11. This proportionality review has the added advantage of alerting prosecutors and trial courts to the importance of issues of proportionality, which in turn

may affect decisions on when to seek a death sentence. The New Jersey Supreme Court, for example, has struck down only one death sentence because of issues of proportionality. *State v. Papasavvas,* 790 A.2d 798 (2002).

12. A further limitation on proportionality review is that it does not provide a mechanism for criminal defendants to address the racially discriminatory impact of the death penalty. In 1988, the U.S. Congress introduced the Racial Justice Act (RJA), which would have allowed all state and federal death penalty death row inmates to challenge their sentences retroactively in the face of discrimination. The act prohibited the imposition of the death penalty where there was an unacceptable risk of racial discrimination. Unlike the Supreme Court ruling in *McCleskey,* the RJA assumed that intentional discrimination could be proven by statistical evidence showing racial disparities. The act also provided for specific procedures to adjudicate racial claims, including the requirement that states designate a central agency to oversee the collection of data on capital sentencing. Further, the act required federal courts to provide counsel to indigent persons to research criminal justice statistics and other expert services to assist in developing a claim of racial disparity. The act failed to get enacted during the 100th Congress, although it was passed by the House of Representatives.

To date, only one state (Kentucky) has passed an RJA. Under the Kentucky law, courts may consider statistical evidence of racial discrimination relating to whether the decision to seek the death penalty was influenced by the race of the victim or defendant (Ky. Rev. Stat. Ann. § 532.300 (2001)). No other jurisdiction has enacted legislation to address the racially discriminatory impact of the death penalty.

13. The racial and ethnic backgrounds of these decision makers are one example of data needed (as well as continued efforts to bring more diversity into the decision-making circle).

REFERENCES

Armstrong, Ken, and Steve Mills. 2000. "Ryan Suspends Death Penalty." Chicago Tribune, Jan. 31, at 1.
Baldus, David C., George Woodworth, David Zuckerman, Neil Alan Weiner, and Barbara Broffitt. 1998. "Racial Discrimination and the Death Penalty in the Post-Furman Era: An Empirical and Legal Overview, with Recent Finds from Philadelphia." Cornell Law Review 83:1638–1770.
Baldus, David C., George Woodworth, David Zuckerman, Neil Alan Weiner, and Barbara Broffitt. 2001. "The Use of Peremptory Challenges in Capital Murder Trials: A Legal and Empirical Analysis." University of Pennsylvania Journal of Constitutional Law 3:3–172.
Bienen, Leigh B. 1996. "The Proportionality Review of Capital Cases by State High

Courts After Gregg: Only 'The Appearance of Justice'?" Journal of Criminal Law and Criminology 87:130–314.

Bienen, Leigh B., Neil Alan Weiner, Deborah W. Denno, Paul D. Allison, and Douglas Lane Mills. 1988. "The Reimposition of Capital Punishment in New Jersey: The Role of Prosecutorial Discretion." Rutgers Law Review 41: 27–372.

Bienen, Leigh B., Neil Alan Weiner, Deborah W. Denno, Paul D. Allison, and Douglas Lane Mills. 1990. "The Reimposition of Capital Punishment in New Jersey: Felony Murder Cases." Albany Law Review 54: 709–817.

Bowers, William J., and Glenn L. Pierce. 1980. "Arbitrariness and Discrimination Under Post-Furman Capital Statutes." Crime and Delinquency 26:563–635.

Bowers, William J., Benjamin D. Steiner, and Marla Sandys. 2001. "Death Sentencing in Black and White: An Empirical Analysis of the Role of Jurors' Race and Jury Racial Composition." University of Pennsylvania Journal of Constitutional Law 3:171–274.

Brooks, Richard R. W., and Steven Raphael. 2002. "Life Terms of Death Sentences: The Uneasy Relationship Between Judicial Elections and Capital Punishment." Journal of Criminal Law and Criminology 92:609–39.

Gross, Samuel R., and Robert Mauro. 1989. Death and Discrimination: Racial Disparities in Capital Sentencing. Boston: Northeastern University Press.

Little, R., and D. Rubin. 1987. Statistical Analysis with Missing Data. New York: John Wiley and Sons.

Pierce, Glenn L., and Michael L. Radelet. 2002. "Race, Region, and Death Sentencing in Illinois, 1988–1997." Oregon Law Review 81:39–96.

Potratz, William G. 1980. "The Prosecutor's Discretionary Power to Initiate the Death Sentencing Hearing." DePaul Law Review 29:1097–117.

Radelet, Michael L. 1981. "Racial Characteristics and the Imposition of the Death Penalty." American Sociological Review 46:918–27.

Radelet, Michael L., and Glenn L. Pierce. 1985. "Race and Prosecutorial Discretion in Homicide Cases." Law and Society Review 19:587–621.

Radelet, Michael L., and Glenn L. Pierce. 1991. "Choosing Those Who Will Die: Race and the Death Penalty in Florida." Florida Law Review 43:1–34.

U.S. Bureau of the Census. 1981. Statistical Abstract of the United States (102d edition). Washington, D.C.: U.S. Government Printing Office.

Chapter 5

Death in "Whiteface"
Modern Race Minstrels, Official Lynching, and the Culture of American Apartheid

Benjamin Fleury-Steiner

I. Introduction: Modern Race Minstrel as "Official Lynching"

The argument in this chapter is straightforward: To impose the death sentence as a capital juror in the contemporary United States one must don a "white face." Minstrelizing poor blacks, whites, and Latinos as *other* than white middle or upper class *does not,* however, necessarily mean that death penalty performers (jurors, victims, or defendants) themselves must have white skin. By "white face," I refer to the purchase of an ideology or broad belief system grounded in the idea that poor nonwhite or "white trash" others are innately prone to irresponsibility and immorality. Focusing on the stories of citizens who have recently served as jurors in United States death penalty cases elucidates the contours of white face in death penalty judgments. At the same time, former capital jurors' stories reveal a far broader indictment of America's death penalty in action. Indeed, jurors' stories reveal the decision to impose death as a practice inseparable from racial and class domination, what I call *official lynching.* While the courtroom and its formal procedures render official decisions to impose death a less visceral, graphic, and disturbing act than the extralegal lynchings that were especially common in the South in the middle part of the twentieth century, official lynchings by jury do reveal a dehumanization process that is eerily similar. As a recent essay by historian Leon F. Litwack in *Without Sanctuary,* a book that presents a collection of powerfully disturbing photographs of actual lynchings, demonstrates,

The men and women who tortured, dismembered, and murdered in this fashion understood perfectly well what they were doing and thought of themselves as perfectly normal human beings. Few had any ethical qualms about their actions. This was not the outburst of crazed men or uncontrolled barbarians but the triumph of a belief system that defined one people as less human than another. . . . What is most disturbing about these scenes is the discovery that the perpetrators of the crimes were ordinary people, not so different from ourselves—merchants, farmers, laborers, machine operators, teachers, doctors, lawyers, policemen, students; they were family men and women, good churchgoing folk. (Litwack 2000: 14)

Citizens enlisted by the state to impose the death sentence are also ordinary folk. However, by contrast to the festival-like atmosphere of vigilante lynchings, official lynching by jury is a far more sanitized affair. Hidden behind jury-room walls, twelve ordinary folk perform a kind of lethal minstrelizing of the other. Telling stories of "threatening blacks," "devious Latinos/as," and poor, "white trash," jurors perform the modern death penalty decision in *white face.* Cloaking themselves in the invisibility of white, middle-class or upper-class privilege, they condemn the other to die as everything they are *not.*

In this chapter, I begin with a detailed discussion of what I call the "cultural life of white suburban privilege." Arguing that inequality across dimensions of race and class identity endure as narrative, I next draw on the racial minstrel as a touchstone for elucidating three predominant minstrels in the post–Civil Rights era: The Criminal Black, Illegal Alien, and Primitive White minstrels. Next, I focus on jurors' stories of their sentencing decisions in capital cases. Demonstrating how the modern race and class minstrels infect jurors' decisions to impose the death sentence elucidates modern capital punishment in the United States as an apartheid institution. In conclusion, I argue that although all apartheid societies (e.g., the United States and South Africa) struggle to different degrees with the demons of their explicitly unequal pasts, an important step in rejecting the culture of apartheid in the United States begins with a sobering analysis of how the death penalty invests in what the United States has struggled for centuries to overcome.

II. The Cultural Life of White Suburban Privilege

Whiteness and class privilege as systems of economic, social, and political advantages have had long and pervasive *cultural* lives. In other words, possessing white skin color (and thus disproportionately possessing middle-class or upper-class status) has become a ubiquitous part of public understandings of, and expectations of what, for example, it means to be hardworking, law-abiding, and/or trustworthy. As markers of white suburban privilege, one's skin color and material or social capital (e.g., cars, clothing, and education) are, in effect, prerequisite for dominant group membership. From this perspective, transcending the cultural stigma of race and class disadvantage is, to borrow from popular parlance, quite literally "beating the odds" of sociocultural disadvantage. But "beating the odds" is particularly difficult, given the stubborn life of contemporary racist ideology:

> [W]hites' racial views are not mere erroneous ideas to be battled in the field of rational discourse. They constitute a racial ideology, a loosely organized set of ideas, phrases, and stories that help whites justify contemporary white supremacy; they are the collective representations whites have developed to explain, and ultimately justify, contemporary racial inequality. (Bonilla-Silva 2003: 178)

As a fabrication, as a culturally coded belief in an inherently superior "race" and "class," white suburban privilege has not surprisingly had devastating implications for those who are not white middle class or upper class (or heterosexual). Throughout history, the demonization of poor whites, typically unskilled and, today, increasingly service-sector workers often denied satisfactory employment benefits and strong union protection (e.g., Ehrenreich 2001) legitimized a belief in an inferior, innately primitive breed of "white trash."

The contemporary representation of the racialized other in the United States has been culturally rationalized away as a kind of ignorance and bias relegated to the pre–Civil Rights era. Injustices in the name of white supremacy, including genocidal atrocities committed against Native Americans, centuries of African-American chattel slavery and decades of Jim Crow laws, and the countless killings and forced subordination of Chicano/a Americans are remembered more as actions of a kind of pure racial and ethnic animus than a series of state actions in the name of white suburban privilege (e.g., Steiner & Argothy 2001). Even a cursory glance at the primary transmitters of United States culture elucidates the enduring life of inequality. Centuries of newspapers, books, theatrical performances, and popular songs are replete with images of Native Americans as savages, blacks as biologically inferior, Latino/as as violent aliens, and poor whites as patently immoral and irresponsible (for a comprehensive review, see Mann & Zatz 1998), images, that I argue, stubbornly endure in the contemporary United States today and have insidious consequences for what Austin Sarat (1998) aptly calls the "killing state."

III. Stories of the Other

The explicit acceptance of racialized images in pre–Civil Rights American culture live on today as narrative. As timeless, ready-made scripts for making sense of a whole slew of social problems, domination stories insidiously serve to powerfully frame (e.g., "racialize") public policy debates and thus lawmaking and legal behavior. Importantly the stories of the other rely on visuals of persons and places and, perhaps most importantly, coded language. A contemporary vernacular of the other that sociologist Eduardo Bonilla Silva cogently argues has far more insidious effects than simple racial stereotypes:

> Not surprisingly, then, since stories are a normal part of social life, they are a central component of color-blind racism. . . . They are often based on impersonal, generic arguments with little narrative content—they are the ideological "of course" racial narratives. . . . These racial narratives, therefore, do more than assist dominant (and subordinate) groups to make sense of the world in particular ways; they also justify and defend (or challenge, in the case of oppositional stories) current racial arrangements. (Bonilla-Silva 2003: 76)

Juxtaposing nonwhite faces plastered on the pages and screens of mainstream American media and/or non-middle-class spaces such as housing projects or trailer parks with politically charged stories of "irresponsible" others in need of harsh punishment, contemporary criminal justice, welfare, and immigration discourses are perhaps the most glaring examples of how race and class narratives become, often overlapping, catalysts for Draconian policy reforms and the widespread perpetuation of injustice. Writing about official policy discourse in the late 1980s debates over the 100-to-1 crack–powder cocaine sentencing disparity, Steiner observes:

> Drawing on the past and present, Senators in the federal crack cocaine debates of 1986, temporally blurred the contemporary tale (or lack thereof) of Civil Rights in America, by evoking an old White supremacy tale and making it appear "new." Such blurring of racist stories vividly displays the resilience of Whiteness as political narrative in America's contemporary inequality, and, hence, law and order marketplaces. (Steiner 2001: 203)

IV. "White-Facing" Crime, Immigration, and "White Trash"

We'd know no darks 'cept them dat had de dollars,
And dem dat wore fine clothes wid de largest kind ob
big shirt collars;
Read police reports and then we'd see
How many colored men there be
Sent by his honor for thirty days
At public expense to mend their ways
And then the telegraph reports we'd read of darkies
killed in showers,
And laugh to think what a happy fate was ours.
—"Claude Melnott," from Charles T. White's
Negro minstrel *The Hop of Fashion* (1856)

The racial minstrel, especially in the latter part of the twentieth century "Ethiopian skits,"[1] is found to be more about communicating stories of dominant-subordinate racial *identities* than about obviously demeaning portraits of blacks (Bean et al. 1996). Claude Melnott's dialogue in Charles T. White's black face minstrel *The Hop of Fashion*, a parody of Shakespeare's classic tragedy *Macbeth*, elucidates the race and class ideologies that give meaning to middle-class and upper-class white identities at the same time that Melnott's dialogue gives meaning to lower-class black identities in this era. In short, blacks are acceptable human beings only if they tout the material assets of class privilege (e.g., "We'd know no darks 'cept them dat had de dollars"). At the same time, Melnott's dialogue revels in the belief that blackness more broadly and lower-class blackness in particular are represented as inherently criminal and murderous. Furthermore, it is interesting that nowhere in Melnott's dialogue is whiteness explicitly mentioned. Rather, class privilege and blackness are the audible purchases in his dialogue for differentiating "us" (read white, middle class or upper class) from lower-class blacks.

Locating the invisibility of whiteness as the implied "everything that is not black or lower class" is thus not simply seeing the obviously racist imagery of the burnt cork on Melnott's face and hearing the obvious racist epithets in his dialogue. Indeed, it is what is left *unseen* and *unsaid* that elucidates white privilege and class advantage as *taken-for-granted* performance. In this way, whiteface minstrels are performances driven by *implied* ideological representations minus the blatantly racist, cork-painted face that was synonymous with Jim Crow era blackface minstrel performances.

V. Political Narrative as Whiteface Minstrel

Modern American politics as presented in the media serves as the premier public stage for the spectacle of the whiteface minstrel. Putting a black, Latino/a, or poor white face on America's contemporary social problems, politically televised minstrels such as "criminal blacks," "illegal aliens," and "primitive whites" are, in effect, the new Zip Coon, Jim Crow, and Sambo.

Although such early blackface minstrelsy was a profound representation of white fears of miscegenation (Lhamon 1996), the new minstrels represent the conservative and neoconservative backlash against Civil Rights. Draped in the rhetoric of "individual responsibility for crime," the white-facing of social policy in the United States mobilizes a discourse perniciously analogous to Claude Melnott's narrative: *Blacks, Latinos/as, and poor whites are wanting special privileges for their innately violent and immoral tendencies, and we middle-class and upper-class whites are fed up with their "excuses" and demand harsh punishment.*

VI. The Criminal Black Minstrel

You don't need any fancy theory to figure out what went on between the L.A. police and Rodney King. That's true. But the Rodney King events are also particularly illuminating for an approach that focuses on the ideological, because part of what was revealed in the Rodney King saga was the need for an account of how racial power continues to work, blatantly in the King case, decades after it has been outlawed as a matter of formal decree, cultural convention, and elite preference.

—Kimberlé Crenshaw and Gary Peller, "Reel Time/Real Justice" (1993)

The Rodney King video and other racialized spectacles like it (i.e., the infamous Willie Horton ads) typify the current story of death penalty law and society. While Civil Rights has dramatically improved the lives of communities of color, the media's and politicians' hyperfocus on blacks as criminals—that is to say, the new criminal black minstrel—reproduces the same pre–Civil Rights ideology: whites are law-abiding, and blacks are lawless. The new black minstrel of "criminal blacks" has insidious consequences for contemporary legal policy, including the administration of the death penalty.[2]

The criminal black minstrel is a cultural production; antiwelfare and punitive criminal justice policies continue to be the most effective technologies for defending it. Consider conservative attacks on "welfare queens"[3] and the unprecedented targeting of disproportionately poor African and Latin American "crack demons":

> Crack was a godsend to the Right. They used it and the drug issue as an ideological fig leaf to place over the unsightly urban ills that had increased markedly under Reagan administration social and economic policies. "The drug problem" served Conservative politicians as an all-purpose scapegoat. They could blame an array of problems on the deviant individuals and then expand the nets of social control to imprison those people for causing the problems. (Reinarman & Levine 1997: 38)

The end of Aid to Families with Dependent Children (AFDC) legitimized the view of poor black mothers and men as patently immoral, dangerous, and oversexualized. Targeting such aggrieved groups, political elites have made critical *investments* in suburban white privilege. As Frank Munger, writing about the making and remaking of the contemporary poor and unpoor, has cogently observed,

> Stereotyping the poor creates values for and reinforces the identity of the nonpoor by justifying avoidance of the "dangers" posed by the poor, by making the nonpoor feel superior as possessors of traits that are distinct from

the traits of the poor, by reinforcing the moral values of the nonpoor, by creating a class of popular-culture villains from which moral lessons (and commercial sales) can be derived, by contributing to spatial stigmatization that justifies patterns of exclusion and social control. (Munger 1998: 959–960)

As I have stated in previous research (e.g., Fleury-Steiner 2004), the argument I advance in this chapter proceeds as follows:

The targeting of poor blacks by the criminal justice system also invests in white suburban privilege. As a long standing means for controlling such groups perceived as economic threats to Whites, seek and destroy tactics that arrest, incarcerate, and disenfranchise racial and ethnic minorities, in a word, *eliminates the competition* faced by a predominantly White labor market (e.g., Musto 1973).[4] . . . [B]y erroneously reinforcing blacks as "criminal" suburban white identities are erroneously reinforced as "law-abiding" and "innocent." That is to say, although class, race and ethnic status are social and cultural constructions—as opposed to being biological determinants— they speciously become proxies for who is moral and who is immoral. (Steiner & Argothy 2001: 450).

When considering the criminal black minstrel as represented in the remorseless glare of Willie Horton or the racialized violence of the Rodney King spectacle, a deeper, taken-for-granted hegemonic becomes clearer— a tale that serves to legitimize America's excessively punitive war on economically and racially marginalized outsiders. Thus, while intended at the time as a progressive call to rescue the so-called black underclass, the infamous "Moynihan Report" can be seen as perhaps the most enduring public exposition of the story of middle-upper-class white moral identity and poor, black immoral identity:

A community that allows large numbers of young men to grow up in broken families, dominated by women, never acquiring any stable relationships to male authority, never acquiring any set of rational expectations about the future—that community asks for and gets chaos. Crime, violence, unrest, disorder, are not only to be expected, but they are very near to inevitable. And they are richly deserved. (Moynihan 1973)

The Moynihan Report's narrative, however, is now distorted by the political establishment, viewed by most contemporary policy makers as commonsensical. The politics of black crime ignores the devastating effects of social and economic exclusion and alienation; political elites tacitly tell a story of "richly deserved" disorder and the need for harsh punitive response. As principal architect of America's contemporary crime war, President George Bush stated,

> We must raise our voices to correct an insidious tendency—the tendency to blame crime on society rather than the criminal. . . . I, like most Americans, believe that we can start building a safer society by first agreeing that society itself doesn't cause the crime—criminals cause crime. (Bush 1989)

As an obvious allusion to color-blind racism, the use of the criminal black minstrel has thus been an indispensable way for political elites to justify the "dangers" of crime.

VII. The Illegal Alien Minstrel[5]

> It is my contention that the "border experience" should occupy a central role in any conceptualization of the Latino experience, for there is a sense in which Latinos, try as they may, cannot divorce themselves from their Mexican roots. Despite efforts to merge into the melting pot by establishing themselves as "Mexican Americans," "Americans of Mexican descent," or just plain "Americans," the United States has been reluctant to incorporate them. . . . [T]o many Americans they somehow remained "Mexican" or "foreign."
> —Alfredo Mirandé, 1987

> Because inhabitants of the Americas were depicted as savages and cannibals, people without morals, culture, or religion, stereotypes could easily be constructed and later effortlessly reconstructed to accommodate a different time period. Thus, contemporary racial stereotypes that depict Latinos as deviant, inferior, violent, lazy, and uncultured (to name but a few) had their foundation established long ago by the imagination of earlier writers who knew little or nothing of what or who they wrote about.
> —Diego O. Castro, 1998

To explicate the lasting impact of the stereotypes described above, one must first understand how the forced subordination of Latinos/as in the United States occurred. After the United States and Mexican war, America was legally bound by the Treaty of Guadalupe Hidalgo to both protect Chicanos/as' property rights on annexed territories and to grant all Latinos/as United States citizenship. In a word, the United States never lived up to its end of the bargain. Congressional actions, such as the California Land Act of 1851, reclaimed much of this territory and violated the treaty by using "law as a weapon, and joining with extra-legal methods, forced alienation" (Luna 1999: 701) and, indeed, racism. As Guadalupe T. Luna observes,

> Chicanas/os confronted a hierarchy of laws that sought to exclude them from assimilating within the mainstream culture. Stereotypes targeted them on the basis of their race by those seeking to benefit from that forced exclusion. Building from these myths, facilitated a legal culture that directly disallowed them the full attributes of citizenship status. (Luna 1999: 701)

Moreover, media coverage of the bloody aftermath of the California Land Act of 1851 was replete with images of "violent Mexican bandits" and "dangerous land robbers" (Muñoz et al. 1998).

The contemporary American media serve as a disciplinary mechanism for keeping racialized ideology alive. Newspapers, television, and cinema have been "principal purveyors of racist images, constructing and institutionalizing stereotypes that have preserved the status quo whereby members of the dominant group stay on top while all others have been forced to linger at the bottom" (Castro 1998: 141). In the context of crime, the media have created the illusion of black and Latino/a criminality at the same time that they have created the illusion of white innocence.[6]

The evidence of racial and ethnic bias in the media is well documented, but such stereotypical overrepresentations tell us less about how they are made hegemonic. Beyond simple racial binaries, I argue that a historically situated set of narratives represented chiefly by the "threatening alien" elucidates the taken-for-granted character of jurors' stories of their death sentencing decisions. In other words, jurors' narratives may "work as a form of shorthand, functioning effectively even when their content was and is not explicitly spelled out" (Lubiano 1992: 331).

The ethnic shorthand of the "threatening alien" closely paralleled an ever-more-hostile anti-immigration rhetoric in United States border states in the late twentieth century. The representation of Latinos as "alien" is manifested in the acts of hate-induced violence by private citizens (e.g., Moran 1997) and through the passage of federal and state laws that have a discriminatory impact on all immigrants. Despite the fact that the vast majority of Latinos/as in the United States are *legal* immigrants (e.g., Moran 1997), recent laws such as California's Proposition 187

> require providers of public social services to deny services to anyone whom
> the service provider determines or "reasonably suspects" is "an alien in the
> United States in violation of the federal law." . . . Finally, Proposition 187
> aims to exclude undocumented children from both public elementary and
> secondary schools as well as public postsecondary institutions. (Garcia 1995:
> 131)

Moreover, in 1996 anti-immigrant legislation was passed at the federal level in the form of the Welfare Reform Act, which goes beyond Proposition 187 in that it excludes *legal* immigrants from most public assistance programs.

Politicians such as former California governor Pete Wilson capitalized on Proposition 187 to mobilize white racialized fears of crime during the 1994 gubernatorial campaign. In one such televised advertisement used by the Wilson campaign, immigrants were shown grouped along the California-Mexico border, with the voice-over "They keep coming." Representing Latinos/as as criminal aliens and thus whites as law-abiding and innocent, Proposition 187 was yet another powerful example of United States lawmaking as part of a broader "White Supremacy Story" (Steiner 2001; Steiner & Argothy 2001).[7]

VII. The Primitive White Minstrel

> Today nearly one couple in ten lives in a mobile home—one of those trailers you see bunched up in cozy camps near every sizable town. Some critics argue that in such surroundings love tends to become casual. Feverish affairs take place right out in the open. Social codes take strange and shocking twists.
>
> —"Trailer Park Woman," 1954

The primitive white minstrel serves and has served as a potent means for blaming the poor for their impoverishment. How it serves as a critical ideological investment in middle-class and upper-class cultural privilege is perhaps less obvious.

The term "white trash" goes back at least to the latter part of the nineteenth century:

[C]urrent stereotypes of white trash can be traced to a series of studies produced around the turn of the century by the United States Eugenics Records Office (ERO). From 1880 to 1020, the ERO and affiliated researchers produced fifteen different "Eugenic Family Studies," wherein the researchers sought to demonstrate scientifically that a large numbers of rural poor whites were "genetic defectives." (Wray and Newitz 1997: 2)

Throughout the 1930s and 1940s, politicians depicted rural poor whites as, for example, "sexually promiscuous," "violent," "lazy," and "stupid." Calling for the end of all forms of welfare, predominantly conservative policy makers of this period legitimized the use of involuntary sterilization and the forced institutionalization of poor whites.

White trash ideology pervades American popular culture. Representations of white trash in books and film have a protracted history in the United States. In the 1950s, the proliferation of "trash" paperbacks such as "Trailer Park Woman" portrayed

trailer parks as trashy slums for white transients—single men drifting from job to job, mothers on welfare, children with no adult supervision. Their inhabitants supposedly engaged in prostitution and extramarital sex, drank a lot, used drugs, and were the perpetrators or victims of domestic violence. (Bérubé 1997: 19)

Contemporary popular films in the United States are replete with portrayals of poor rural whites as "white trash." Making white trash visible in film involves making them not simply poor but poor and violent or hypersexualized. J. W. Williamson's (1995) insightful *Hillbillyland*, for example, demonstrates how films from *Deliverance* to *Evil Dead 2* represent poor white trash culture as "uncivilized" and separate, especially when juxtaposed with middle-class whites:

When middle-class whites encounter lower-class whites, we find that often their class differences are represented as the difference between civilized folks and primitive ones. Lower-class whites get racialized, and demeaned, because they fit into the primitive/civilized binary as primitives. (Newitz 1997: 134)

The stubborn cultural life of the primitive white minstrel has oppressive consequences for poor whites; trailer park dwellers are segregated from suburban privilege under zoning laws (Bérubé 1997: 19), and biological determinism has reemerged in public discourse. Regarding the latter, conservative policy intellectuals led chiefly by Charles Murray promulgate pseudoscientific eugenic theory to call for the evisceration of the welfare state. *New York Times Magazine* columnist Jason DeParle describes his interview with Murray in October of 1994:

> [In the past] people were poor because of bad luck or social barriers. "Now," [Murray] says, "what is holding them back is that they're not bright enough to be a physician." In Murray's words, the white kids who drop out of school are low-IQ, low-income "White Trash." (DeParle 1994)

VIII. White Face Minstrels and the Official Lynching of Black and Hispanic Defendants[8]

Previous scholarship has documented in vivid detail the racialized narratives of capital jurors in both black and Hispanic defendant death cases (Fleury-Steiner 2004; Fleury-Steiner & Argothy 2004).[9] For economy of presentation, I draw selectively from this previous published work to illustrate the ways jurors minstrelize such defendants. The minstrels that constitute official lynching in black and Hispanic defendant cases

> provide the aura of authenticity and emotionality that only "firsthand" narratives can furnish ("I know this for a fact since I have worked all my life with blacks"). Therefore, these stories help narrators in gaining sympathy from listeners or in persuading them about points they want to convey.... [M]any of the testimonies whites tell serve rhetorical functions with regard to racial issues, such as saving face, signifying nonracialism, or bolstering their arguments on controversial racial matters. (Bonilla-Silva 2003: 76–77)

It goes without saying that when death-qualified whites decide whether or not a nonwhite defendant will live or die that the issue is often fraught with controversial racial matters. These include but are not limited to the crime problem both in a particular community and in society in general; matters of race and poverty both particular and general; immigration and non-English-speaking populations living in America; and in some instances blatantly racist beliefs about the inferiority of nonwhites. In the pages that follow, I present the testimonies of several such jurors.

Robert Waingrow, a white, high-school-educated, 43-year-old construction worker, served on a case involving the defendant Ivan Strayhorn, a black man who murdered his stepmother. He begins by telling the "tragically familiar" story of "The Blacks are killing the Blacks." Here, Waingrow offers his reactions to murder of Strayhorn's mother:

> [I]t's a shame, a woman that lived a good life, you know? And it's just a shame to see the way she went. I'm not going to be racial about it, but you have to state the facts: The Blacks are killing the Blacks. And you don't punish gently. It's just brutal. You think that he would do that to somebody who put her hand out to help him?

Waingrow's story of the "all too familiar" escalating black-on-black violence is a matrix for understanding Strayhorn's responsibility for the crime. Indeed, it helps him to make sense of the defendant's senselessness. Trying to save face (e.g., "I'm not going to be racial about it"), Waingrow "knows the facts." However, he is far less subtle in his representation of Strayhorn's altercation with the courtroom deputies during the trial:

> During the trial we determined he was a very violent person, because he jumped up and grabbed a deputy and tried to get the pistol out of his holster in the court, in front of everybody. It took six guys to subdue him. One of the detectives went over, and Strayhorn damn near got his gun and probably would have shot him. And the judge is yelling, "get the jury out, get the jury out!" And everybody is going "oh my god, oh my god!" People scattered like you wouldn't believe. This guy was big, you know. And these big deputies are jumping all over him, and he's just dragging them along. Just like a gorilla. Like Rodney King, you know the same situation.

Waingrow's narrative speaks for itself. The black body is but a racist caricature in his story—a minstrel of inherently "criminal blacks." Drawing on the Rodney King spectacle, he presents Strayhorn as an inhuman beast, a chained gorilla. If "black-on-black" violence helped him to broadly locate the defendant's murder of his stepmother, than seeing Strayhorn in this courtroom altercation only confirms for Waingrow *what he already knew* about blacks "like" Rodney King. Waingrow knows from the beginning "who" Ivan Strayhorn "is" and "how" he will vote on punishment. Employing the ideology of "black crime," Waingrow dehumanizes Strayhorn as a chained "gorilla. . . . Like Rodney King."

Older, less educated, white jurors' stories convey an even more explicit contempt for blacks. Such jurors weave racial epithets into their stories; they, as in Jim Crow–era minstrel shows, explicitly represent blacks as inferior. Marking the defendant with a racial identity rooted in a hopeless and savagely violent black group, they express an utter lack of surprise over his actions.

Ralph Lewis is a 62-year-old white retired farmer born and raised in Alabama who is, in a word, *proud* of his Southern heritage. Indeed, throughout his interview, he seemed to take great pride in "how thick my accent is." While there were some audio problems and hence difficulties transcribing his three-hour interview, Lewis's description of Alfred Watson, a black man convicted of shooting a black victim in an apparently failed drug deal, was captured by the tape recorder:

> Anybody that was born and raised in the South when I was born and raised in the South and says they're not prejudice[d] is a liar. I try very, very hard to get over it. Every time . . . I meet a nigger, and I don't like White ones anymore than I do Black ones. That's the way it is. And what difference [there] [is] between me and anybody else is that I admit it . . . I mean, like when I heard about the killing, I thought, well, they're just wiping each other out again. You know, if they'd been White people, I would've had a different attitude.

Obviously, Ralph Lewis's overt racism elucidates his underlying contempt toward blacks such as Alfred Watson. While only one other juror in the sample referred to the defendant as a "nigger," such contempt stories, albeit more explicitly than Robert Waingrow's story, convey a very similar point: This defendant's violence is indicative of a racially inferior group. However, "they're just wiping each other out again" and "if they'd been White people, I would've had a different attitude" are more than just obvious racist blather. Viewed through the lens of punishment at the hands of the state, Lewis's story reveals how sentencing the other has as much to do with constructing black identities as it has to do with *confirming* whiteness.

Next, Ralph Lewis is asked to describe the defendant. Employing a tale of his religious community's concern of a growing "black" violence problem, he observes:

We were discussing it in church last Sunday. We were talking about race and class. . . . And one of our parishioners says he wasn't prejudiced, but he was pragmatic about how many murders were in the city. You know, "Let's say there were forty six." [And I responded], "How many would there have been if they'd been committed by Whites?" [Answer] Four (laughs)!

Joking about the community's racial fears of murder, Lewis attempts to make his racial inferiority story more palpable. He evokes a "laughing racism" that recalls the "comedy" of the black-faced minstrel shows of the Jim Crow South (e.g., Woodward 2001). Lewis's story legitimizes his fellow parishioner's "pragmatism" concerning the white community's "Black" murder problem. Failing to appreciate the reality that most murders go unreported, Lewis asks, "How many would there have been if they'd been White?" In addition to the obvious linking of blackness with murderous threat, his rhetorical question is part of his own blackface "routine." Indeed, Lewis's reply "Four!" can be heard in the tape recording of his interview as if he were delivering the punch line to an obvious or old joke.

Fred Dawson, a 38-year-old business executive, served on the capital jury that sentenced to death Ray Floyd Cornish, a 20-year-old black male convicted of shooting a white male convenience store clerk. While Dawson described sentencing deliberations as "challenging" and was full of sympathy for a black juror who struggled to join the majority, he was anything but sympathetic towards the defendant and what he describes the defendant as representing. Consider Dawson's responses to the following questions concerning his impressions of the defendant, his family, and the crime:

Interviewer: Did you have the following thoughts or feelings about the defendant, "You felt anger or rage toward him?"

Dawson: I was angry because hundreds of thousands of people are like this throughout the country who cause all this aggravation and money to be spent on the court system. It's just ridiculous! It's wasting my time.

Interviewer: Did you feel contempt or hatred for the defendant's family?

Dawson: I don't hate anyone. It's the same bullshit that never stops. There's too much of it. Our welfare system makes these people. Our dollars we give them. It's terrible and awful.

Interviewer: In your mind how well do the following words describe the killing, "It made you sick to think about it?"

> *Dawson*: No, because that is a personal thing. I don't get upset about people like that. I just want to put him away from society. Hang them if they have to be hung, or the death penalty, whatever. I am sick and tired of this. It's a fairly universal attitude of people today. There is so much stupid crime! It's ridiculous, you know? We have so many liberal "do wells" —those bleeding heart liberals. This is nonsense. The guy knew what he was doing when he pumped four shots into the guy.

The nexus of white, middle-class, male identity, and conservative, tough-on-crime rhetoric is audible in each of Dawson's responses. Replete with racially coded phrases such as "these people" and "the same bullshit that never stops," his angry responses stem not only from the defendant's actions but from *whom* Cornish and his family represent. Thus, Dawson's individual responsibility story has little to do with an "individualized" assessment of the defendant's conduct. Rather, Dawson's identity is one of a "conservative avenger"—he sees himself as "evening the score" against the prowelfare, liberal establishment he blames for producing "the Ray Floyd Cornish's of America"—a racialized discourse heavily employed during the Reagan and first Bush presidencies (Omi and Winant 1993).

Dawson focuses his contempt for Cornish's crime on the liberal "do wells." In effect, he reconciles the contradiction in fellow juror Sheila Brooks's assessment of the defendant as *both* responsible for his actions and as a product of his tragic "Black" environment. Indeed, in Dawson's story, antiliberal rhetoric is a justification in and of itself—it is taken for granted as the *way things are* (e.g., "a fairly universal attitude"). And it enables Dawson to make Cornish's crime *personal* (e.g., "Our dollars we give them") at the same time that it obscures his own racist stereotypes of a dangerous, black welfare class.

The racialization of Latino/a Americans as "threatening aliens" is reproduced in and by the penal process, including in death penalty trials.[10] Jurors speak in ways reflecting a sense of ethnic superiority and thus Latino/a American inferiority. In other words, "[I]f racism is reproduced through discourse and communication we may expect this also to be the case for stories and storytelling—in informal everyday conversation, in institutional storytelling, in the stories of novels and movies, as well as in the special "stories" communicated by the mass media in the form of news reports" (van Dijk 1988: 123). And we might also expect racism to be reproduced in the stories of jurors in death penalty cases involving Latino defendants.

When the defendant is Latino, gestures and nonverbal exchanges between jurors, judges, and perhaps even the Latino defendant's family may be described. Consider a Texas juror's description of the predominantly Latino courtroom's reaction to a case in which she sentenced a Latino defendant to death for murdering a white victim:

> I think the Hispanics were really, really together. And I don't know if they were relatives of his, I don't know, but they looked hard. None of them got up and witnessed on his behalf except his mother pled for us not to give the death sentence. When it happened, I mean, all the big husky people that were in the audience stared towards him and stared towards us.

What is interesting in the above story is how this juror finds it necessary to mention ethnicity. Calling attention to those "hard looking Hispanics" reveals a pervasive racialized representation of Latino/a identity. By denying the defendant his individuality—indeed, by locating the defendant among the "hard looking Hispanic" group—this juror makes sense of "who" she was dealing with. Lastly, calling attention to ethnic solidarity, "the Hispanics were really, really together," seems useful to this juror as a discursive device for distancing herself from "them." In other words, it seems to be an attempt on her part at minimizing the jury's responsibility for the decision to impose the death sentence on "one of them."

Next, the respondent goes on to describe in more detail the defendant's reactions to receiving the death sentence: "I think he did break down when he saw his mom. Right down by, I mean, he tried to get to her. But how do you read this? Do you read it because he felt bad for his mother? Or he realized what he had done?" This juror's questioning reveals an acute sensitivity she has towards the Latino defendant's manner and appearance in court. Indeed, if her questioning is suggestive of such a visual fixation on "the other" by white jurors, then it is not surprising that she concludes her story by recalling a sequence of events that provide further justification for her death sentencing decision:

> I felt definitely, if he could threaten a guy that was on the stand in front of everybody, and I know *they* (emphasis added) look like that. The lady that was the judge, I know she saw it because she was like looking at us and looking back at him. And you can read it in her eyes, "Did you all see that?"

The above account speaks for itself. Describing both images of racial threat and feelings of paternalism, this white respondent's phrase "I know *they* look like that," while obvious as a racialized stereotype, suggests a form of discursive backpedaling on this respondent's part. Indeed, such a phrase is similar to the claim "I'm not racist, I have many friends who are black," heard in contemporary white racial discourse of African-Americans (e.g., Feagin 2000). Finally, and perhaps most interestingly, is this juror's justification for her interpretation of the "dangerous Hispanic" by recalling the judge's reaction and, indeed, speaking through the judge's voice: "Did you all see that?" The "that" may be interpreted as "the threatening Hispanic who should be executed." Indeed, if he isn't, he may put "respectable" people in danger.

Moreover, some jurors' stories describe language barriers as reinforcing "the border" between "us" and "them." As a white juror from a fourth Texas case illustrates when responding to the question "[D]id any member of defendant's family remind you of someone or make you think about anyone?" bluntly stated, "No, it was in Spanish, I couldn't understand any of it anyway." Thus, not "understanding any of it" as an answer to whether or not the defendant's family reminded this juror of anyone is revealing. Indeed, it illustrates why some whites may see Latinos as other, indeed, "those" who can't speak *our* language.

The language border in a second California case was critical to a juror's sense making of "who" the defendant is. In other words, he racializes the Latino defendant as an "untrustworthy" and "lazy"—as a "Hispanic" who "spoke Spanish" to try to "pull one over on *us*." Perhaps eerily reminiscent of the divisive and degrading rhetoric of California's Proposition 187 (e.g., Mata 1998), this juror candidly recounts the following:

> You got the impression he was trying to get you to believe that he wasn't even around or even remotely involved. He was just a guy, generally nice guy who just happened to get unfairly picked on. Yeah, I remember right when they were getting ready to, you know, he was on the stand, the prosecutor was kinda leading him into, he got him right where he was supposed to. You know, he was supposed to go over to the bank machine and rob the guy, and I think right about then we took a break for lunch and he happened to get sick for the rest of the afternoon. [It] seemed kind of suspicious. . . . And then . . . every time they got into some kind of a tricky spot he'd start speaking in Spanish instead of English, and we'd have to go to an

interpreter. We knew he could speak English well enough he was just trying to make more of a hassle or something.

The story of "the deceitful Latino" is clearly audible in this respondent's story. The phrase "happened to get sick," although of little interpretive significance on its own, seems to enable this juror to foreshadow the defendant's "otherness." Indeed, this "suspicious" "guy" when in "a tricky spot" would *then* "start speaking Spanish instead of English." Conjuring a rising tension in this story is thus very useful to this respondent for articulating *both* "suspiciousness" and "speaking Spanish" in the construction of the Latino defendant as other. Moreover, this respondent states, in addition to being suspicious, the defendant was a "hassle or something." "Something," indeed "not speaking English," more than the defendant's happening "to get sick" suggests in the end that this defendant—like the immigrants in Governor Pete Wilson's campaign advertisement—had "crossed" the majority's "border" of "white" *English only* supremacy.

IX. A Poor, White Defendant: The Case of Donald Carson

For most of their childhood, Donald Carson and his brother Rupert were physically abused by their alcoholic father.[11] They lived in abject poverty most of their lives. Their mother, a prostitute and drug addict, had abandoned the brothers very early. After their father had died of a heart attack when they were thirteen and nine, both were placed in an orphanage, an orphanage where children were often subjected to corporal punishment. In and out of youth detention facilities and prison thereafter, Donald and Rupert were incarcerated in a state penitentiary for separate violent felonies in their early thirties.

In May 1989, Donald, Rupert, and a black friend, Homer Edwards, escaped in a stolen getaway car. On the afternoon of May 14, almost out of gas, they spotted what seemed to be a gas pump behind a rural mobile home and stopped to investigate. There was no pump, but they noticed that no one was inside the trailer and decided to burglarize it. The brothers entered the trailer, and Homer Edwards waited in the car.

The home belonged to a white middle-aged couple, Dwight and Emma Davis. Unaware that their trailer was being burglarized, Dwight and his father, John, pulled in behind it. Meeting them at gunpoint, Donald Carson followed them inside. After their pockets were emptied, Dwight was taken into the south bedroom of the trailer, and John was taken to the north bedroom. Donald shot and killed Dwight, and then he and Rupert shot and killed the elder Davis.

Soon after, Dwight's brother, James Davis, drove up on a tractor, walked to the back door and knocked. Rupert answered the knock and ordered James inside at gunpoint. James Davis was forced to lie on the sofa in the living room, where Donald shot and killed him.

After Donald went out to move the tractor, which was parked in front of the Carsons' stolen car, Dwight Davis's wife, Emma, drove up. Donald entered the trailer behind her and accosted her. Meanwhile, John Davis's uncles, Everett and Thomas, arrived in a pickup truck. Leaving Homer Edwards to watch Emma, Donald and Rupert confronted the two Davises and forced them at gunpoint into the trailer. Thomas was taken to the south bedroom, where Donald shot and killed him; Everett was taken to the north bedroom, where Rupert killed him.

Homer Edwards and Donald Carson raped Emma Davis on a kitchen table, then they drove several miles to a heavily wooded area, where Emma was raped again, and then shot and killed by Homer. Homer and Donald abandoned their car in the woods and then took Emma's car, which they later abandoned. They stole another car there and were arrested a few days later, in possession of guns later identified as the murder weapons, and of property belonging to the victims.

Each defendant was tried separately. By agreeing to testify against Donald, Edwards and Rupert were spared capital murder charges. Donald Carson was convicted in approximately two days; the penalty phase lasted a full week. A key issue of contention for jurors involved the importance of mitigating evidence concerning Donald's abusive childhood. Interviews were conducted with jurors Margaret Wentworth and Candace Ballard.

Margaret Wentworth, a 51-year-old, college-educated high school teacher describes the scene inside the jury room during the penalty phase. She is convinced that Donald Carson deserved the death sentence after the guilt phase. In this story, she describes the majority's struggle to convince a black female holdout:

> One Black lady went bonkers. She was hysterical, and just wanted out of there. She was talking about how he was abused as a child and everything— that the child abuse caused him to do all this. But that's no excuse! I'm sorry

I felt very bad that he had no life, but that's no reason to do what he did and enjoy it, you know? She really thought she could get out of it: She was banging on the door yelling! And another person shared that she had been abused her whole childhood, and she did not go out and commit crimes like these. That she had pulled herself up by her bootstraps and worked hard and made herself a productive member of society. But the holdout was crawling up the walls yelling and screaming, and they were trying to calm her down by saying, "Nobody's threatening you and you have a right to your opinion."

The confounding of identity and punishment is powerfully revealed in Wentworth's story of individual responsibility. "Pull yourself up by the bootstraps," a timeless American axiom made famous in the classic nineteenth-century novels of Horatio Alger, is a dominant theme in how she accomplishes identity.

Writing about a similar dynamic in neighborhood-watch members' discussions of community crime problems, Theodore Sasson cogently observes:

The bit of wisdom that says "everyone's the same"—that from a moral standpoint the poor are no different from the nonpoor—derives from individualism (i.e., the belief that people ought to be regarded first and foremost as individuals and not as members of groups). And the notion that people freely "choose" crime derives, in part, from the notion that people are responsible for their own welfare (self reliance), and in part from the veneration people attach to the act of choosing (individualism). (Sasson 1995: 150)

Holding the marginalized defendant "responsible" for his actions is taken-for-granted in Wentworth's story. Describing her self-reliant counterpart who "had been abused her whole childhood," she quickly dispenses with the defendant's social history. Despite Donald Carson's prolonged abuse, and economic and social marginalization, his life experiences are ideologically wiped away by Wentworth as empty excuses—indeed, as implicit evidence that he must be inherently prone to violence. In this way, the story of individual responsibility invests in her belief in "primitive whites" and thus denies the frequency with which capital defendants such as Donald Carson are brutalized and neglected as children, pushed to the social and economic margins of our society, and often mistreated by the very institutions we had entrusted with the task of helping them. . . . Study after study has confirmed the cycles of desperation, hopelessness, and violence; cycles in which many capital defendants have become enmeshed. (Haney 1998: 376)

X. A Final Whiteface Minstrel: The Immoral Homosexual

A victim's homosexual may identity may pose a threat to heterosexual male jurors (See Fleury-Steiner, 2004). Consider the story of 52-year-old Bernadette Garvin, a white, college-educated housewife who sentenced to life without parole Lawrence Kendrick, a white man convicted of beating a homosexual man with AIDS, Thomas Winter, to death with a hammer in an apparent hate-related crime:

> The victim, Thomas Winter, was dying of AIDS. So during deliberations we had a whole gamut of things come out about sex, homosexuals, how men feel about homosexuals, and how women feel about homosexuals. That was one of the major things that happened. We could have gone in there if the man had not been a homosexual and got it done. It would have been a much easier decision. But the minute homosexuality came in, and the fact that the man had AIDS came in, all the men went to this side and all the women went to [the] other. It was a pretty typical situation. . . . The men just couldn't understand that a murder is a murder regardless of whether or not the victim is gay and has AIDS.

The heterosexual male jurors' revulsion towards the AIDS-infected, gay victim is "typical" to Bernadette Garvin; homophobia late-twentieth-century-style makes its way into jury decision making and has consequences for how state law is accomplished. Separating themselves from the more sympathetic female jurors, the heterosexual male jurors' behavior is expressly political. To them, the gay victim, Thomas Winter, who has AIDS, is worth inherently *less* than a "normal," noninfected heterosexual. Deciding the fate of a gay victim in death cases in a historical period of growing homophobia,[12] capital jurors, like many in the judiciary, send "a message that the courts inten[d] to be vigilant in controlling the spread of the epidemic to the mainstream of America, consistent with historical responses of the courts to enable repression of already stigmatized populations as an effective symbolic response to lethal epidemics" (Drass, Greg-ware, and Musheno 1997: 295). For the male jurors, people with AIDS (PWA) are inherently less human and make their decision to impose the death sentence "difficult." Bernadette Garvin's description of the jury's decision as "not easy" elucidates how morality and identity, including sexual orientation, combine in the jury's decision to impose punishment.

XI. Conclusion: Official Lynching as Apartheid Practice

Between 1882 and 1968, an estimated 4,742 blacks met their deaths at the hands of lynch mobs. As many if not more blacks were victims of legal lynchings (speedy trial and executions).

—Leon J. Litwack, 2000

The legacy of such legal, or what I have termed "official," lynchings lives on in the American criminal justice system today. Official lynchings are *realized* in death penalty jurors' performances of the "criminal black," "illegal alien," and "white trash" minstrels. The 985 lives lost to official lynchings in the United States since the practice resumed in 1976 symbolize a much broader and enduring culture of American apartheid. A culture that continues to be met by legislators and their public constituencies with a deafening silence, or worse, outright denials of the inhumanity of inequality in the United States altogether.

The stubborn life of economic marginality in both rural (e.g., Tick-amyer and Duncan 1990) and urban (e.g., Wilson 1987) areas and persistent racial segregation (e.g., Massey 1995) are the most vivid examples of how persistent policies of denial and obfuscation—and the media and political establishment that celebrate them—continue to bear their ugly fruit today. Thus, as long as the *lived* reality of inequality endures in the United States, such a reality must be weighed against the *consequences* its legal system evokes in its people's name.[13] That capital punishment is a qualitatively unique policy goes without saying. If America continues to embrace its use in the name of retributive or utilitarian values, then inequality remains not just a "tolerable" American value. Inequality remains a value that is *acted upon* and thus preserved inextricably through the state's persistent willingness to use the punishment of death. Thus, from this perspective, Sarat's "killing state" may more aptly be called the "*raced/classed* killing state" or the "*privileged* killing state"—the state through its insistence that the citizenry participate in legal life taking *legitimizes* the "white-faced" minstrels jurors perform in its name.

So, what is the United States to do? An honest accounting of the utter failure of the so-called modern death penalty by the political and legal elites would be a meaningful start. One need go only as far as the recent developments in postapartheid South Africa. The human rights narrative by South Africa's Constitutional Court in its recent landmark decision to abolish the death penalty presents a grammar of justice—a grammar that Justice Stevens recently employed in the United States Supreme Court's landmark and, indeed surprising, decision to set aside the death sentence for mentally retarded offenders in *Atkins v. Virginia*. And most recently, the Court by a 5–4 majority struck down the death penalty for juveniles in *Roper v. Simmons*.[14]

To be sure, this is not to suggest that if the United States Supreme Court were to declare the death penalty unconstitutional that decision *in and of itself* would bring about widespread social change. Indeed, one need look only to the continuing struggles and recent public clamor for the reinstatement of the death penalty in contemporary South Africa (e.g., Braid 1996). Even so, the abolition of official lynching by the United States Supreme Court would be a powerful statement in the name of racial and class equality and thus social justice. Such a decision would stand for equity in the criminal justice system in a way analogous to the Court's *Brown* decision stood for equality of opportunity. By recognizing the dignity in the lives of the disadvantaged and dysfunctional individuals who are being put to death, the Court could send a powerful message to the nation and the world. Such an action would demonstrate to the nation and the world that the Court is not afraid of "too much justice" as the late Justice William Brennan famously stated in his classic *McCleskey* dissent. The abolition of the death penalty in the United States is an inescapable next step if state legislatures and the Supreme Court are seriously committed to social justice and human rights, as both institutions demonstrated in their decisive decisions to strike down provisions that allowed for the execution of the mentally retarded and juveniles.

Beyond the current pragmatic but ultimately futile rhetoric of "death penalty reform,"[15] state legislatures and the United States Supreme Court must recognize that the culture of American apartheid, and the contemporary raced, classed, and sexualized minstrels that reinforce and constitute capital punishment as *official lynching*. By contrast, the abolition of the death penalty in the name of human dignity, embraces a broader human rights narrative[16] that *enforces* social justice and creates the potential to reinvigorate a national dialogue about the widespread injustices that continue to befall racial, ethnic, class, and sexualized minorities trapped in America's overly aggressive criminal justice system. Perhaps out of the glaringly bad, something good will eventually arise. The recent devastation of Hurricane Katrina revealed the entrenched racial apartheid in America's cities. But in its wake a new civil rights dialogue has emerged (Miller 2005: A3). Similarly, as Katrina exposed the stark racial inequalities in housing and other indicators of the American dream denied (e.g., adequate health care), one can only hope that exposing how the death penalty actually operates in practice will likewise shame into action a nation that professes to be concerned with human rights and social equality. One can only, in the timelessly relevant words of Dr. Martin Luther King, Jr., *keep hope alive.*

NOTES

1. For a fascinating history of the "Ethiopian skits" or "Coon shows," see Mahar 1998.

2. Rejecting the Baldus study's compelling evidence of racial discrimination in death sentencing outcomes, the Supreme Court in *McCleskey* disturbingly demonstrated this new orthodoxy: *Vengeance over equality under law.* From this perspective, America's death penalty protocol is implicitly driven by an ideology of the other. A belief system implicated in the political reproduction of the "black criminal."

3. As Franklin D. Gilliam observes, "During the election Reagan often recited the story of a woman from Chicago's South Side who was arrested for welfare fraud:

> She has 80 names, 30 addresses, 12 Social Security cards and is collecting veteran's benefits on four non-existing deceased husbands. And she is collecting Social Security on her cards. She's got Medicaid, getting food stamps, and she is collecting welfare under each of her names.

The implicit racial coding is readily apparent. The woman Reagan was talking about was African-American. Veiled references to African-American women, and African-Americans in general, were equally transparent. In other words, poor women of all races get blamed for their impoverished condition, but African-American women commit the most egregious violations of American values. This story line taps into stereotypes about both women (uncontrolled sexuality) and African-Americans (laziness) (Gilliam 1999).

4. "White workers found themselves competing with low-paid Chinese work-

ers for scarce jobs and viewed the Chinese as an economic threat. The campaign against *smoking* [emphasis in original] opium (but not against other, non-Chinese uses of opiates) included lurid, fictional newspaper accusations of Chinese men drugging white women into sexual slavery" (Reinarman and Levine 1997: 6–7). Additionally, historian David Musto (1973) in his insightful analysis of early American "drug wars," demonstrates that cocaine policies targeting blacks were less concerned with health issues and more concerned with the subordination and control of such racially defined groups.

5. A more recent and fuller exposition of this research appears in Fleury-Steiner & Argothy 2004.

6. Thus, Robert Elias (1994), in his analysis of more than thirty-five years of crime coverage in American newsmagazines, observes:

Blacks and other non white minorities were described and pictured in the newsweeklies crime coverage most frequently even though these groups *do not* commit the majority of crimes. . . . In contrast, the newsweeklies described and pictured victims mostly as white people. What emerges from my study is a pattern of discrimination in which criminals are conceptualized as [people of color] and crime as the violence they do to whites. (Elias 1994: 5)

7. Proposition 187 served also as a powerful catalyst for a revitalized assimilationism in California and the United States more broadly. Both former Ku Klux Klan leader David Duke and presidential candidate Patrick Buchanan were two high-profile voices in the media. "There is nothing wrong with us sitting down and arguing that we are a European country" (Hing 1993: 904) has become the rallying cry for English-Only and other anti-immigration initiatives in the United States ever since:

The calls for curbing undocumented immigration are concurrent with the rhetoric that programs and services such as bilingual education result in the Balkanization of America. Many who espouse this position also support an end or a severe cutback to legal immigration as well. These groups are strong proponents of an assimilationist perspective, which would effectively eliminate any display of the immigrant's culture once in the United States. (Garcia 1997: 138)

8. My analysis of black defendant death penalty cases involved close readings of thirty-three jurors' responses to open-ended questions concerning their punishment decisions and their impressions of the defendant. (For a more detailed analysis of black defendant death cases, see Fleury-Steiner 2002a).

9. See Fleury-Steiner 2004 for a detailed description of the data and methods employed for collecting the material presented in this chapter.

10. The present analysis draws on thirty-five jurors' stories from some fourteen capital cases in Texas and California in which a Latino defendant was sentenced to death. I focus on Texas because it has executed more Latino defendants than any other United States state (Death Penalty Information Center April 2002). On the

other hand, I focus also on California because it has more Latinos currently awaiting execution ($n = 119$) than any other United States state, including Texas (Death
Penalty Information Center 2002). (For a more detailed analysis of Latino defendant death cases, see Fleury-Steiner 2004; Fleury-Steiner & Argothy 2004.)

11. To preserve the defendant's confidentiality, a pseudonym is used. (For more
information on the Carson case, see Fleury-Steiner 2004.)

12.

The site of revenge has increasingly become the law in an attempt to pry courts
and legal doctrines loose from the demands of lesbians and gays and from the
sovereign imaginary across a broad spectrum of issues. Service in the military,
criminal regulation of same-sex conduct, employment protections against discriminatory treatment and same-sex harassment, public speech and the right to
parade, domestic partnership and same-sex marriage have all been sites of
intense anti-gay-rights politics. (Goldberg-Hiller 2002: 17)

13. I have made a similar argument against the contemporary war on drugs in
the United States (see Steiner 2001; Steiner and Argothy 2001).

14. The Court's *Atkins* decision explicitly legitimized a global commitment to
human rights as important for assessing the death penalty's efficacy in cases
involving mentally retarded offenders. This was most clearly illustrated in Justice
Stevens's reference to the European Union's call for the "approval" of the "world
community."

15. The rhetoric of "death penalty reform" focuses on "fixing" the capital punishment protocol, especially greater access to DNA testing for convicted capital
offenders. While mistaken identification is the most common way an individual is
wrongfully convicted (Scheck et al. 2000), DNA has been presented as a "silver
bullet" in reformist arguments. Indeed, even death penalty proponents have
recently used DNA as grounds *for strengthening* death penalty support. Consider a
St. Louis Post-Dispatch article by Alexander Tabbarok, the director of the Independent Foundation, a policy think tank that, perhaps not surprisingly, is heavily supported by the biogenetic industry:

More often than not, genetic testing proves beyond a shadow of a doubt that a
prisoner is guilty. . . . As time wears on there will be fewer and fewer "old" cases
that can benefit from DNA technology. . . . In the long run, the real impact of
genetic testing will surely be to increase, not decrease, support for the death
penalty. (Tabbarok and Helland 2000: B7)

16.

The language of international human rights not only captured the prior repression but also offered a means to inspire and galvanize a liberal opposition as
well as an image of hope. Here the language of rights shapes that of political discourse. The claim of right convergent with that of politics demand promises
mediating differences of culture, and building such discourse promises solidarity among diverse peoples. Ultimately, deliberations are thought to enable grad-

ual consensus. At the very least, the rights practices instantiate those of democracy. (Teitel 1999: 317)

REFERENCES

Barkan, Steven E., and Steven F. Cohn. 1994. "Prejudice and Support for the Death Penalty by Whites." *Journal of Research in Crime and Delinquency* 31: 202–209.

Bean, Annemarie, James V. Hatch, and Brooks McNamara. 1996. *Inside the Minstrel Mask: Readings in Nineteenth-Century Blackface Minstrelsy.* Middletown, CT: Wesleyan University Press.

Bérubé, Allan. 1997. "Sunset Trailer Park." In *White Trash: Race and Class in America,* edited by Matt Wray and Annalee Newitz. New York: Routledge.

Bonilla-Silva, Eduardo. 2003. *Racism Without Racists: Color-Blind Racism and the Persistence of Racial Inequality in the United States.* Lanham, MD: Rowman & Littlefield.

Bowers, William J., Marla Sandys, and Benjamin D. Steiner. 2001. "Death Sentencing in Black and White: An Empirical Examination of Juror Race and Jury Racial Composition in Capital Sentencing." *Pennsylvania Journal of Constitutional Law* 3: 171–274.

Braid, Mary. 1996. "ANC Considers Death Penalty to Fight Rising Crime." *Vancouver Sun,* September 3, p. A7.

Bush, George. 1989. "Remarks at the Acres Homes War on Drugs Rally in Houston, Texas," *Public Papers of the Presidents 1989, volume 2.* Washington, D.C.: United States Government Printing Office.

Castro, Diego O. 1998. "Hot Blood and Easy Virtue: Mass Media and the Making of Latino/a Stereotypes." In *Images of Color, Images of Crime,* edited by Coramae Richey Mann and Marjorie S. Zatz. Los Angeles: Roxbury Publishing Company.

Crenshaw, Kimberlé, and Gary Peller. "Reel Time/Real Justice." In *Reading Rodney King, Reading Urban Uprising,* edited by Robert Gooding-Williams. New York: Routledge, 1993.

Death Penalty Information Center. 2002. "Execution Update: As of April 1, 2002." http://www.deathpenaltyinfo.org/.

DeParle, Jason. 1994. "The Most Dangerous Conservative." *New York Times Magazine,* October 9, pp. 48–78.

Drass, Kris A., Peter R. Gregware, and Michael Musheno. 1997. "Social, Cultural, and Temporal Dynamics of the AIDS Case Congregation: Early Years of the Epidemic." *Law & Society Review* 31: 267–300.

Ehrenreich, Barbara. 2001. *Nickel and Dimed: On (Not) Getting by in America.* New York: Henry Holt and Company.

Elias, Robert. 1994. *Victims Still: The Political Manipulation of Crime Victims.* Newbury Park, CA: Sage.

Feagin, Joe R. 2000. *Racist America.* New York: Routledge.

Fleury-Steiner, Benjamin. 2002. "Narratives of the Death Sentence: Towards a Theory of Legal Narrativity." *Law & Society Review* 36: 549–574.

Fleury-Steiner, Benjamin. 2004. *Jurors' Stories of Death: How America's Death Penalty Invests in Inequality.* Ann Arbor: University of Michigan Press.

Fleury-Steiner, Benjamin, and Victor Argothy. 2004. "Lethal "Borders": How Latin Americans and the Death Sentence Are Racialized." *Punishment & Society* 6: 67–83.

Garcia, Ruben J. 1997. "Critical Race Theory and Proposition 187: The Racial Politics of Immigration Law." *Chicano-Latino Law Review* 17: 118–154.

Gilliam, Franklin D., Jr. 1999. "The 'Welfare Queen' Experiment." *The Nieman Reports* 53.2. http://www.nieman.harvard.edu/reports/992NRsummer99/Gilliam.html.

Goffman, Erving. 1963. *Stigma: Notes on the Management of Spoiled Identity.* New York: Simon & Schuster.

Goldberg-Hiller, Jonathan. 2002. *The Limits to Union.* Ann Arbor: University of Michigan Press.

Haney, Craig. 1998. "Mitigation and the Study of Lives." In *America's Experiment with Capital Punishment,* edited by James R. Acker, Robert M. Bohm, and Charles S. Lanier. Durham, NC: Carolina Academic Press.

Hing, Bill Ong. 1993. "Beyond the Rhetoric of Assimilation and Cultural Pluralism: Addressing the Tension of Separatism and Conflict in an Immigration-Driven Multiracial Society." *Cal. L. Rev.* 81.

Lhamon, W. T., Jr. 1996. " 'Ebery Time I Wheel About I Jump Jim Crow': Cycles of Minstrel Transgression from Cool White to Vanilla Ice." In *Inside the Minstrel Mask: Readings in Nineteenth-Century Blackface Minstrelsy,* edited by Annemarie Bean, James V. Hatch, and Brooks McNamara. Middletown, CT: Wesleyan University Press.

Litwack, Leon. 2000. "Hell Hounds." In *Without Sanctuary: Lynching Photography in America,* edited by James Allen. Santa Fe, NM: Twin Palms Press.

Lubiano, Wahneema. 1992. "Black Ladies, Welfare Queens, and State Minstrels: Ideological War by Narrative Means." In *Race-ing Justice, En-Gendering Power,* edited by Toni Morrison. New York: Pantheon Books.

Luna, Gadalupe T. 1999. "Beyond/Between Colors: On the Complexities of Race: The Treaty of Guadalupe Hidalgo and Dred Scott v. Sandford." *University of Miami Law Review* 53: 691–716.

Mahar, William J. 1998. *Behind the Burnt Cork Mask: Early Blackface Minstrelsy and Antebellum American Popular Culture.* Champaign: University of Illinois Press.

Massey, Douglas S. 1995. "Getting Away with Murder: Segregation and Violent

Crime in Urban America." *University of Pennsylvania Law Review* 143: 1203–1232.

Mata, Alberto G., Jr. 1998. "Immigrant Bashing and Nativist Political Movements." In *Images of Color, Images of Crime,* edited by Coramae Richey Mann and Marjorie S. Zatz. Los Angeles: Roxbury Publishing Company.

Mirandé, Alfredo. 1987. *Gringo Justice.* Notre Dame, IN: Notre Dame University Press.

Moran, Rachel F. 1997. "What If Latinos Really Mattered in the Public Policy Debate?" *California Law Review* 85: 1315–1345.

Morrison, Toni, and Claudia Brodsky Lacour. 1997. *Birth of a Nation 'hood: Gaze, Script, and Spectacle in the O. J. Simpson Case.* New York: Pantheon Books.

Moynihan, Daniel Patrick. 1973. *The Politics of a Guaranteed Income: The Nixon Administration and the Family Assistance Plan.* New York: Random House.

Munger, Frank. 1998. "Immanence and Identity: Understanding Poverty through Law and Society Research. *Law & Society Review* 32: 931–968.

Muñoz, E. A., David A. Lopez, and Eric Stewart. 1998. "Misdemeanor Sentencing Decisions: The Cumulative Disadvantage Effect of 'Gringo Justice.' " *Hispanic Journal of Behavioral Sciences* 20 (3): 298–319.

Musto, David, 1973. *The American Disease: Origins of Narcotic Control.* New Haven, CT: Yale University Press.

Newitz, Annalee. 1997. "White Savagery and Humiliation, or A New Racial Consciousness in the Media." In *White Trash: Race and Class in America,* edited by Matt Wray and Annalee Newitz. New York: Routledge.

Omi, Michael, and Howard Winant. 1986. *Racial Formation in the United States: From the 1960s to the 1980s.* New York: Routledge and Kegan Paul.

Reinarman, C., and H. G. Levine. 1997. *Crack in America.* Berkeley: University of California Press.

Riessman, Catherine Kohler. 1993. *Narrative Analysis.* Newbury Park, CA: Sage.

Sarat, Austin. 1998. *The Killing State: Capital Punishment in Law Politics and Culture.* New York: Oxford University Press.

Sasson, Theodore. 1995. *Crime Talk: How Citizens Construct a Social Problem.* Hawthorne, NY: Aldine de Gruyter.

Scheck, Barry, Peter Neufeld, and Jim Dwyer. 2000. *Actual Innocence: Five Days to Execution and Other Dispatches from the Wrongly Convicted.* New York: Doubleday.

Steiner, Benjamin D. 1999. "Race, Ideology, and Legal Action: The Case of Capital Sentencing Jurors." Ph.D. dissertation, Northeastern University, Boston; reprinted by Bell & Howell Dissertation Services.

Steiner, Benjamin D. 2001. "The Consciousness of Crime and Punishment: Reflections on Identity Politics and Law-Making in the War on Drugs." *Studies in Law, Politics, and Society.*

Steiner, Benjamin D., and Victor Argothy. 2001. "White Addiction: Race Inequality,

Racial Ideology, and the War on Drugs." *Temple Political & Civil Rights Law Review* 10: 443–475.

Sunnafrank, Michael, and Norman E. Fontes. 1983. "General and Crime Related Racial Stereotypes and Influence on Juridic Decisions." *Cornell Journal of Social Relations* 17: 1–15.

Sweeney, Laura T., and Craig Haney. 1992. "The Influence of Race on Sentencing: A Meta-Analytic Review of Experimental Studies." *Behavioral Sciences and the Law* 10: 179–195.

Tabbarok, Alexander, and Eric Helland. 2000. "DNA Should Boost Support for the Death Penalty." *St. Louis Post-Dispatch*, September 26, p. B7.

Teitel, Ruti. 1999. "The Universal and the Particular in International Criminal Justice." *Columbia Human Rights Law Review* 30: 285–303.

Thompson, William C. 1989. "Death Qualification after *Wainwright v. Witt* and *Lockhart v. McCree*." *Law & Human Behavior* 13: 185–207.

Tickamyer, Ann R., and Cynthia M. Duncan. 1990. "Poverty and Opportunity Structure in Rural America." *Annual Review of Sociology* 16: 67–86.

van Dijk, Teun A. 1993. "Stories and Racism." In *Narrative and Social Control: Critical Perspectives,* edited by Dennis K. Mumby. Thousand Oaks, CA: Sage.

Williamson, J. W. 1995. *Hillbillyland: What the Movies Did to the Mountains and What the Mountains Did to the Movies.* Chapel Hill: University of North Carolina Press.

Wilson, William Julius. 1987. *The Truly Disadvantaged: The Inner City, the Underclass, and Public Policy.* Chicago: University of Chicago Press.

Woodward, C. Vann. 2001. *The Strange Career of Jim Crow.* New York: Oxford University Press.

Wray, Matt, and Annalee Newitz, eds. 1997. *White Trash: Race and Class in America.* New York: Routledge.

Chapter 6

Stereotypes, Prejudice, and Life-and-Death Decision Making

Lessons from Laypersons in an Experimental Setting

Mona Lynch

Introduction

In the famous and controversial U.S. Supreme Court case *McCleskey v. Kemp* (1987), the Court was presented with compelling empirical evidence indicating that the racial characteristics of defendants and victims continued to influence capital case outcomes in Georgia despite the procedural remedies in place designed to eliminate such problems. The majority Justices rejected the data's significance as to the question of whether Georgia's capital system was "impermissibly tainted" by racism (Justice Powell in *McCleskey v. Kemp*, 1987, 315) by setting a standard that requires "proof that decision-makers in *his* case acted with discriminatory purpose" (292, emphasis in original) in order to prevail on the equal protection challenge. The logic underlying the decision points up the shortcomings of this kind of proof requirement in that contemporary racism, for the most part, is not manifested in a straightforward and overt manner to allow for such a showing. Indeed, what we know about why race still matters and will likely always matter in our system of capital punishment (as well as in a number of other settings) suggests a covert, subtle, and diffuse process whereby an easily identified racist action or utterance performed by a biased judge, juror, witness, or prosecutor is not likely to be found.

Yet despite the difficulty of pinpointing a "smoking gun" of racist behavior within any given capital case, a variety of empirical data indicate that the race of defendants, victims, capital jurors, and other legal actors appears to influence capital case outcomes in a variety of ways (see, e.g., Government Accounting Office, 1990). At each step of the capital case process, from initial prosecutorial assessment and filing decisions in homicide cases (Baldus, Woodworth, and Pulaski, 1990; Bowers and Pierce, 1980; Paternoster, 1983) through the discretionary granting of clemency to death row inmates (Radelet and Vandiver, 1983) there exists evidence of disparate case outcomes as a function of race in the modern era of the American death penalty. These works suggest that racially biased death penalty practices appear to flow from a wide range of contextual influences and causal factors, from capital punishment's unique American historical roots (Banner, 2002) to its symbolic political role (Haney, 1997a), and from social psychological factors shaping microlevel decision making (Lynch and Haney, 2000) to the structural context in which crime and its prosecution exist (Sarat, 2001; Haney, 1995). It is clear from the bulk of this research, however, that the discriminatory outcomes are not simply a product of deliberately motivated acts of racism by individuals; rather, they are best understood as a function of more "modern" forms of racism as situated within the social structural context of American inter-group relations.

In this chapter I focus on one particular stage of the modern capital punishment machinery—capital jury sentencing—to examine the various social psychological mechanisms that help to account for persistent patterns of racially biased death sentencing by capital juries in the United States. In doing so, I apply much of the theoretical work done by psychologists and sociologists on contemporary forms of prejudice and racism, which I describe below. Drawing largely on research Craig Haney and I have conducted in recent years, I will illustrate some of the underlying psychological processes and dynamics that are in play when jurors sit in judgment of capital defendants, particularly of those of a race different from their own.

The psychological processes I examine include (1) the role of cultural stereotypes and other cognitive heuristics that appear to contribute to jurors' differential construction of capital defendants; (2) the aspects of typical capital trial narratives that activate those stereotypes in the case of a racially different defendant; (3) the method by which modern forms of prejudice and racism may be activated in the jury trial situation and how aspects of the capital trial process itself amplify differences and increase psychological distance between capital jury members and the defendant; and (4) the role of empathy as a mediating psychological process that helps to account for the unwillingness or inability of jurors to identify with and appreciate the mitigating aspects of the life of a defendant whose racial background is different from their own. I conclude by discussing the implications of the social psychological understanding of capital jury decision making, including what they suggest about potential procedural remedies and the limits to remedial efforts aimed at neutralizing the problematic mechanisms.

Differentiating Stereotypes and Prejudice as Social Psychological Concepts

Several lines of basic sociological and social psychological research provide a theoretical basis for understanding how individuals and groups think and feel about racial and ethnic differences. On the cognitive side, ample research has demonstrated the strong human tendency to categorize and stereotype all kinds of information about people in such a way that both simplifies complex input and that exaggerates differences between categorical attributes in order to aid in the categorization process. This kind of cognitive shortcut allows for more efficient information processing, memory, and retrieval of the multitude of stimuli that we face in our daily lives (Fiske and Taylor, 1991). Nonetheless, this mental process, by design, results in an overgeneralized and often inaccurate body of knowledge about stereotyped people and objects (Krieger, 1995).

Stereotyping, then, is a form of heuristic that is cognitive and somewhat automatic in nature rather than affective and motivational, yet it has the potential to contribute to biased assessments and, consequently, discriminatory behavior on the part of the categorizer. This process is generally understood to be below the level of consciousness and to be particularly influential in situations where persons do not have adequate time or cognitive resources to fully process information (Devine, 1989; Kawakami, Dion, and Dovidio, 1998). Further, social-group stereotyping in particular is also shaped by sociohistorical factors; thus, there tend to exist widely known (if not widely accepted) culturally specific stereotypes about different groups in any given society (Devine, 1989; Devine and Elliot, 1995). As a result, racial and cultural stereotypes are generally highly accessible to most members of a given culture, so have the potential to shape views and perceptions about different groups in a subtle yet pervasive manner.

As a social psychological concept, prejudice is generally seen as "an unfair negative attitude toward a social group or a person perceived to be a member of that group" (Dovidio, 2001: 829), so prejudice is distinguished from racial stereotyping by its negative affective component. Although historically prejudice was seen as a manifestation of individual personality or pathology (Adorno, Frenkel-Brunswick, Levinson, and Sanford, 1950), over the past several decades this conception has dramatically shifted. Prejudice is now generally conceived of as being shaped by social norms and situational contingencies, group identities, and intergroup relations; thus, it is a social phenomenon occurring at both the individual and group levels (Bobo, 1999).

Further, theoretical work distinguishes between "old-fashioned" prejudice, which is overt and motivational, and modern prejudice, which has been described as "cool, distant, and indirect" (Meertens and Pettigrew, 1997: 54). The contemporary forms of prejudice tend to be manifested covertly through the expression of ostensibly nonprejudicial values and opinions that are, in practice, detrimental to out-group members (e.g., endorsing immigration restrictions; affirmative action bans; tough-on-crime measures) and may rely upon cultural stereotypes as justification. This kind of racial animosity—which has been conceptualized in similar terms by various theorists as modern racism (McConahay, 1986; Pettigrew, 1989), symbolic racism (Sears, 1988), subtle prejudice (Pettigrew and Meertens, 1995; Meertens and Pettigrew, 1997), and aversive racism (Gaertner and Dovidio, 1986)—is not necessarily manifested through the amplification of negative attributions directed at out-groups but through the assignment of more positive attributes for in-group members (Dovidio, Mann, and Gaertner, 1989), in-group favoritism (Tajfel, 1982), and through the withholding of empathy or positive affect for out-group members (Pettigrew and Meertens, 1995).

The link between racial stereotyping and other forms of cognitive biases, and racial prejudice has been explicated in recent work that seeks to understand the nature of contemporary racism. Stereotypes distort perceptions of out-groups, create social distance between in-group and out-group members, and may help justify negative feelings toward out-groups. Thus, recent work suggests that Whites who measure high in prejudice more easily access and rely upon racial stereotypes in their assessments of minority-group members (Kawakami, Dion, and Dovidio, 1998). Indeed, the linkage between White support for ostensibly nonracial yet harshly punitive crime measures and the use of cultural stereotypes about Black criminality exemplifies the nature of contemporary prejudice (Mendelberg, 1997).

Gaertner and Dovidio's (1986) conceptualization of aversive racism explicitly links cognitive explanations of bias and the affective elements of White prejudice against minority groups. They argue that because blatant, intentional racism has become less socially acceptable in the post-civil-rights period, a more subtle, unconscious form of prejudice has become more prevalent. Aversive racists espouse egalitarian beliefs yet will—often unintentionally—engage in forms of prejudiced or discriminatory behavior when their behavior is justifiable on nonracial grounds (Dovidio, 2001). Such expressions are especially likely in situations where social norms are conflicting and ambiguous, and where racial stereotypes are likely to be accessed.

Finally, these intra- and interpersonal processes must be understood as situated in a structural setting that plays a central role in their perpetuation. Bonilla-Silva (1997) argues that to understand racial phenomena— the instances, attitudes, or ideologies that we refer to as racism—we must examine the social systems that are structured in part by racial hierarchies and that then shape social relations among differently situated groups. In the case of Black-White relations in the United States, there exists a constant of White domination over Blacks such that neither opportunities nor costs are equitably distributed, yet the methods by which such inequality is maintained have changed shape over our history. Thus, racial hierarchies and their attendant inequalities as they have developed over time are produced and reproduced at a systemic level and spawn as by-products such phenomena as racial strife resulting from conflict interests, racial stereotypes, prejudice, and discrimination.

In a similar vein, Bobo (1997) suggests that to fully understand contemporary racism, group position must be taken into account. His extension of Blumer's group-position model of prejudice is structural in nature, in that it takes into account the historical development of racial group positioning in a given society, and the resulting inequalities that emerge across time. Self-interest on the part of dominant groups in the face of competitive threat by subordinated racial groups thus shapes the very structure of social institutions to ensure continued dominance. Further, dominant-group ideology concomitantly develops and transforms itself in order to legitimate racial inequality in socially acceptable terms. So, in the case of Black-White relations in the United States, while inequalities persist, dominant racial ideology has shifted from Jim Crow racism to a "laissez-faire" racist ideology (Bobo, 1997).

In sum, contemporary research on stereotypes and prejudice indicates that human cognitive tendencies, embedded within a set of social and cultural contingencies, work together in such a manner that modern forms of racism are subtler, more covert, and in many ways more intractable than were previous, more blatant, and motivational forms (Krieger, 1995; Pettigrew and Meertens, 1995; Quillian and Pager, 2001). These processes are both the product of a social structure that perpetuates racial inequalities through its various social institutions, including criminal law, and are made less visible in our contemporary world by being masked within the dominant, ostensibly nonracial ideologies about fairness, entitlement, and other social values.

The Capital Jury and Racial Bias

Several elements of the capital jury process converge to make the situation ripe for a modern form of racism to manifest itself. First, as a consequence of the capital jury selection process, those who come to sit on capital juries are demographically skewed such that a higher proportion are likely to hold racial stereotypes and biased attitudes about people of color. Because those who are opposed to the death penalty to such a degree that their views would interfere with their ability to follow the law are excluded from serving on capital juries,[1] the death-qualified jury pool ends up disproportionately White, male, older, and more religiously and politically conservative than the broader jury pool from which it was selected (Filkins, Smith, and Tindale, 1998; Gross, 1998; Haney, Hurtado, and Vega, 1994; Lynch and Haney, 2000), and such demographic characteristics tend to correlate with measures of subtle racism and stereotyped thinking (Barnes, 1997; Emerson, Smith, and Sikkink 1999; Meertens and Pettigrew, 1997; Sidanius and Pratto, 1992; Sidanius, Pratto, and Mitchell, 1993).

Generally, potential jurors who are "death qualified" tend to hold attitudes that differ in important ways from the general population, and those differences become exacerbated by the capital jury selection process (Haney, 1984; Hans, 1988). This cluster of attitudes appears to affect how death eligible citizens evaluate evidence, particularly mitigating evidence (Luginbuhl and Middendorf, 1988). Death penalty proponents' attitudes toward minorities and toward punishment issues may also play a role in biased decision making, according to some theorists (Russell, 1994). Several tests of this association have indicated that measures of White racial prejudice are associated with support for the death penalty (Barkan and Cohn, 1994; Stinchcombe, Adams, Heimer, Scheppele, Smith, and Taylor, 1980; Young, 1991), and some researchers have suggested that death penalty support among Whites is a form of "symbolic racism" toward Blacks (Aguirre and Baker, 1993).

Second, the very nature of the capital case, which always involves violence and often other forms of serious criminal behavior, feeds into cultural stereotypes about several ethnic and racial groups. Quillan and Pager (2001) argue that the stereotype of African-Americans as violent and criminally inclined is one of the most pervasive, well-known, and persistent stereotypes in American culture. Where other negative cultural stereotypes about Blacks have significantly diminished, this one has remained strong and influential, particularly among Whites (see also Devine and Elliot, 1995).

Indeed, Hurwitz and Peffley (1997) have illustrated through a series of survey experiments that White Americans are willing to be particularly punitive when presented with stereotypical images of African-American violent felons as the object of punishment policies, in contrast to their endorsement of harsh policies for identically situated White felons. In the case of those who are convicted of the most violent murders in our society, as capital defendants generally are, the possibility is quite strong that this kind of disparity is magnified as a function of the race of the capital defendant by the pervasive stereotypes about race, criminality, and violence, especially under the decision-making conditions faced by capital jurors. Evidence from the large-scale examination of how jurors decide life or death in actual capital cases, the Capital Jury Project, indicates such a phenomenon among the jurors interviewed (Bowers, Steiner, and Sandys, 2001), in that when Whites, especially White men, sit on a jury in a Black-defendant/White-victim case, they often relied upon racial stereotypes to come to a death decision. Most significantly, Fleury-Steiner's (2004) contextual analysis of the interviews with capital jurors has powerfully revealed how racialized cultural stereotypes, particularly about the propensity to do violence, shape White jurors' narratives about minority defendants, their culpability, and ultimately their death-worthiness.

Third, because jurors are put into a decision-making situation that is ambiguous, and where the appropriate norms are unclear, aversive racism may be more readily activated in this setting than in one where norms are clearer (as in a guilt determination). In the context of death sentencing, the key elements of the decision—determinations of moral culpability, heinousness, and blameworthiness, weighing acts of violence against the value in a defendant's life—are inherently subjective. There are no obvious or widely shared standards upon which lay jurors can rely in selecting between the life and death options.

Coupled with this situational ambiguity, a large body of work has demonstrated that laypersons face significant difficulties in understanding and applying capital jury instructions (Diamond, 1993; Eisenberg and Wells, 1993; Haney and Lynch, 1994, 1997; Luginbuhl and Burkhead, 1994; Lynch and Haney, 2000; Tiersma, 1995; Wiener, Pritchard, and Weston, 1995). By receiving incomprehensible sentencing instructions as their sole guideline, jurors are likely to feel uncertain and confused about the appropriate protocol, thus allowing them to fall back on their own set of cognitive heuristics and enabling any racial hostility or bias they may hold to come into play. The fact that the instructions seem to provide a neutral, legitimate framework for decision making may even further facilitate the operation of these racial biases.

Empirical evidence supports this possibility. Race of defendant has been noted to be particularly influential in ambiguous mock jury decision-making settings, such as in the absence of clear-cut and definitive decision-making guidelines (Hill and Pfeifer, 1992; Pfeifer and Ogloff, 1991; Rector, Bagby, and Nicholson, 1993) and when the evidence in the case was neither overwhelmingly weak nor strong (Applegate, Wright, Dunaway, Cullen, and Wooldredge, 1993). The influence of race in capital jury decision making may stem in part from complexities of the information-processing task faced by capital jurors, where stereotypes and biases are more likely to come into play. Social psychologist Galen Bodenhausen and his colleagues (Bodenhausen, 1988; Bodenhausen and Lichtenstein, 1987; Bodenhausen and Wyer, 1985) have provided empirical support for this hypothesis, finding that when information processing demands are high and complex in nature, ethnic stereotypes will exert a relatively stronger influence on the decision-making process, in contrast to a simple task situation.

Finally, empathy undoubtedly plays a part in capital sentencing judgments. Because in general the guilt phase of the trial that precedes the penalty phase exclusively focuses upon the violent acts of the defendant with little or no "humanizing" information emerging in this stage, jurors entering the penalty phase are apt to have defined the defendant primarily by his criminal behavior, which may make death an acceptable choice for jurors (Haney, 1997b). Interviews of capital jurors in a variety of jurisdictions indicate that a substantial number of these fact finders have already decided that death is an appropriate sentence before the penalty trial even has begun (Sandys, 1995). Data from juror interviews also suggest that a death verdict functions as the default sentence for many capital jurors, despite the proof requirements (Eisenberg and Wells, 1993). Thus, crucial to obtaining a life verdict is getting jurors to rehumanize the defendant in their minds, understand his acts in the context of his life experience, and empathize with him enough to spare his life.

Because creating empathy for the defendant in the penalty phase through a mitigation narrative is key to overcoming a death verdict, the willingness and/or ability of jurors to empathize with the defendant will influence outcome. And to the extent that empathy is influenced by race of target as well as of perceiver, as subtle prejudice theorists suggest, sentence outcomes will be influenced by race of defendant and race of victim, particularly where (as in most cases in this country) the jury is numerically dominated by Whites (Eisenberg, Garvey, and Wells, 2001). As Gross and Mauro (1989) have suggested, among the most plausible explanations for the consistent finding in archival analyses that killers of Whites are more likely to receive death sentences than killers of Blacks is that White jurors, who end up being the majority in most capital juries, feel more empathy for White victims.

The influence of empathy is likely magnified in cases where a White is victimized by a non-White—where, all other things being equal, the highest relative percentage of death sentences are found—when jurors may extend feelings of empathy for the victim but not for the defendant. Quantitative analyses of Capital Jury Project data indicate that this is indeed the case. In Black-defendant/White-victim cases, Black jurors were able to identify with the defendant and/or his family at a significantly higher rate than were White jurors (there were no juror differences in the other racial categories or cases), and were consequently eight times more likely to extend mercy to the defendant in those cases (Bowers, Steiner, and Sandys, 2001).

Lessons from Our Experimental Work
on Race and the Death Penalty

Craig Haney and I have been examining the way that race appears to play a role in capital jury decision making through a program of experimental research that uses a mock juror/jury paradigm. Our theoretical approach is primarily informed by contemporary social psychological explanations for individual and group discrimination; in particular, Gaertner and Dovidio's (1986) aversive racism conceptualization and Pettigrew and Meerten's (1997) theoretical work on subtle prejudice. We have conceived of this body of work as a complement to the many other important research endeavors in this area that take different methodological approaches; most significantly the body of work that conducts archival analyses of actual capital case outcomes in various jurisdictions (i.e., Baldus et al., 1990; Gross and Mauro, 1989) and the work coming out of the Capital Jury Project and similar efforts that use postcase interviews with actual capital jurors as a source of data, as described above.

We have conducted two experiments, the first using 402 jury-eligible nonstudent adults who went through a mock penalty phase procedure and made judgments individually, and the second using 539 nonstudent jury-eligible adults who served on one of one hundred small-group mock juries, to examine whether race of defendant and/or race of victim influences sentence outcome in a mock penalty phase trial, and if so, what factors seem to contribute to racial disparities. In both studies our participants were overwhelmingly White (86% in the first study; and 82% in the second).

Employing a 2x2 experimental design, both studies used a realistic videotaped simulation of a capital penalty trial that included the presentation of evidence and testimony of witnesses, opening statements and final arguments from the defense and prosecution, and the judge's reading of the set of California-pattern instructions to be used in sentence determination. The four versions of the tape were identical in all aspects, except that the race of the defendant (Black or White) and the race of the victim (Black or White) were varied to create the four experimental conditions. Participants were randomly assigned to view one of the versions about which they would render a decision. Very briefly, the case presented was as follows: A scrolling narrative at the beginning of the tape indicated that defendant Mitchell Hall was convicted of first-degree murder with two special circumstances: the murder was committed during the commission of a felony (robbery), and the defendant intentionally killed while lying in wait. Hall was found to have staked out a Domino's pizza establishment in San José, and once the store was clear of everyone but the cashier, he entered, held a pistol to the employee/victim—20-year-old John Emerson—and led him to a back storage room, where he bound his hands, gagged his mouth with a pair of dirty socks, and shot him point blank in the temple. Hall then removed all the cash from the register, $167, and left the store.

During the penalty phase of the trial—which was shown on the tape—the prosecutor put on three witnesses: (1) a paramedic from Ohio who testified about a similar robbery and nonfatal shooting alleged to have been committed by Hall a week before the capital offense, and before he fled to California. The paramedic had responded to the shooting incident and the victim had identified his former co-worker Hall as the shooter. (2) The arresting police officer in the San José case who had interviewed Hall. She testified that Hall told her he wanted to eliminate the victim to avoid getting caught. She indicated that he laughed about shooting two Domino's workers and showed no remorse for the crimes. (3) The victim's mother, who testified that her son was her only family, that he was a 4.0 student at San José State, and that he volunteered at Juvenile Hall to help kids in trouble. She also described her feelings of guilt about his death since she had convinced him to work in the store rather than as a delivery driver because she felt it was safer.

The defense put on four penalty phase witnesses: (1) Hall's mother testified about physical, psychological, and sexual abuse committed by her husband upon his stepchildren, including the defendant. She described the severe beatings Hall suffered as a young boy and adolescent at the hands of his stepfather, Hall's witnessing his sisters being raped by his stepfather, and other family traumas. (2) His half brother testified about how Hall took care of him when they were younger, and how he was a powerful role model as they grew up. He also testified about how Hall's stepfather hated Hall and attempted to smother him with a pillow on several occasions when the boys were in bed at night. (3) Hall's wife testified about his psychological troubles in adulthood, including a suicide attempt, his difficulties seeking professional help, and his feelings of guilt over his sister's psychological troubles. She also described how she and their three children still loved Hall and needed him in their lives. (4) A psychiatrist testified that Hall suffered from chronic depression, low self-esteem, and had a serious substance abuse problem (alcohol, marijuana, and cocaine). She described suicidal and self-mutilating behavior that Hall had engaged in prior to the offense, and linked his mental problems to the family abuse history.

The prosecutor argued in his closing that Hall was a cold, remorseless killer and that the facts of the crime alone called for the death penalty. He further argued that Hall's mental and substance abuse problems were not significantly mitigating, and his background of abuse, however horrible, had no connection to his criminal acts, which occurred years later. Hall's defense attorney argued that Hall had led a crime-free life up until these incidents happened in his midtwenties, when the devastating consequences of his abusive childhood took over. He linked the brutal lessons of Hall's childhood to his psychological problems and violent explosion in this crime. He further argued that justice would be served with life without the possibility of parole and that such a punishment is extremely harsh.

In both studies, participants were told that the video was taken from an actual trial and that the defendant had been found guilty of first-degree murder with special circumstances and that their task as jurors was to reach a sentencing decision. After viewing the videotape, participants were given a copy of the instructions for reference, then were asked to render a sentence for the defendant—a dichotomous choice of either life without the possibility of parole or death. In the first study, participants viewed the tape and rendered their decision individually; in the second, small groups of four to seven participants viewed the tape and rendered a sentencing verdict together. When this task was completed, verdict forms were collected, and each participant completed a series of questionnaires that included open-ended questions about their decision-making process and forced-choice questions in which they rated the defendant on several dimensions, the impact of the witnesses who testified, the evidence presented, and the arguments offered. Participants were also assessed on how well they understood the instructions.

We tested two sets of hypotheses in the experiments. First, that in this complex, yet ambiguous, decision-making task, race of defendant and race of victim would have an impact on penalty determination. Within that, we predicted that the ways in which both the aggravating and mitigating circumstances were interpreted and applied by the mock jurors would be influenced by the racial characteristics of the case. We expected that race would have an interactive influence, as predicted by prior research on this issue, so condition cell differences should reflect the relative punitiveness toward Black defendants, and in cases in which the victim was White. Second, we hypothesized that juror instructional incomprehension would contribute to racial bias in sentencing. The influence of race on sentencing was expected to be greatest for those subjects who had the most difficulty understanding and applying the instructions they were to follow in rendering the decision.

The results from our first study have provided key insights into the way race may play a role in laypersons assessments of culpability, especially as it relates to mitigating evidence. And although we are still in the midst of data analysis in the second study, our preliminary analyses indicate that the data replicate many of the original findings as reported in Lynch and Haney (2000) and, in addition, that they reveal how race plays out in the group deliberation process in such a way to magnify its influence on outcomes.

Let me first briefly outline the findings of the original study. First, even though race of victim as a *main* effect had no significant influence on sentencing, race of defendant did play role in sentencing, in that 52% of the subjects who viewed the case with a Black defendant assigned a death sentence, whereas 43% of the subjects with the White defendant meted out the same punishment (see Lynch and Haney, 2000, for detailed statistical analyses). Race of victim did amplify the effect such that those who viewed the tape with the White defendant and Black victim were the least likely to impose a death sentence on the defendant (40%); those who viewed the Black defendant/White victim case were the most likely to impose death (54%).

We also sought to uncover what it was about the participants' interpretation of the case that might account for the racial differences. What we discovered was that, consistent with theoretical work on modern forms of racism, the differences were rooted in how the participants viewed the mitigation evidence, which was offered as positive, sympathetic, and humanizing evidence, rather than in how they viewed the aggravating evidence. When assessed by condition, comparisons revealed significant differences for the weight given to all of the individual pieces of mitigating evidence,[2] based on the racial characteristics of the conditions. In the condition where the White defendant kills a Black victim, significantly more weight was given in favor of life on all of the mitigation compared to the other conditions. Jurors' assessments of three of the four mitigating circumstances—the defendant's history of child-abuse victimization, the psychiatric impairment, and the substance-abuse impairment—revealed the influence of race in that those pieces of evidence or testimony were weighted significantly more in favor of life for the White defendant.

There were also significant differences between *how* the mitigating evidence was used (weighing toward life, not weighing in the decision at all, or weighing toward death) based on race of defendant for all items of assessed mitigation. For example, twice the percentage of all the subjects (18%) who viewed the trial of the Black defendant improperly used the psychiatric impairment evidence in favor of death than did those subjects who saw the White defendant version (9%); a similarly troublesome pattern of use was evident in the case of the childhood-abuse evidence and the "loved by family" evidence. In contrast, the aggravating evidence was generally not differentially used as a function of the racial characteristics of the case. When considering either race of victim or race of defendant, none of the individual pieces of aggravating evidence was weighed differentially to a statistically significant level, either in terms of the relative strength of its weight or in terms of how it was used.

As would be predicted by the theories that link racial bias to the cognitive demands of a judgment situation, our mock jurors' inability to understand the guidelines appeared to significantly contribute to the race effect obtained. We conducted several analyses to assess the interactions between how well our participants understood the jury instructions, the racial characteristics of the case, and verdict choice. Specifically, low comprehension among the participants was related to a higher percentage of *life* verdicts for the White defendant when compared to high-comprehension subjects; whereas the opposite pattern was evident for Black defendants—low comprehension was associated with a larger percentage of *death* verdicts than high comprehension.[3] In terms of differences between conditions, similar relationships emerged between the White-defendant/Black-victim condition and the Black-defendant/White-victim condition, such that in the first, low comprehension among the subjects was again related to a lower percentage (36%) of death verdicts when compared to high-comprehension subjects; whereas in the second, the opposite pattern was evident—low comprehension was associated with a larger percentage (68%) of death verdicts than high comprehension. In both sets of analyses, the differential outcomes almost disappeared among those who scored high on the jury instruction comprehension test.

Thus, the results indicated that racial bias likely becomes particularly influential when the sentencing guidelines are poorly understood, and the way that the bias plays out is that the White defendant benefits from the incomprehension, and the Black defendant is punished for it. But our findings also indicated that the bias cannot be completely eliminated by increasing jurors' comprehension of the instructions. In tests where we controlled for subject comprehension and tested for race effects in the evaluation of mitigation, the differences in evaluating the mitigation depending on defendant race remained significant. The results also indicated that the evaluation of mitigation is an important key to understanding jurors' decision-making process, particularly as it is shaped by racial stereotypes and biases.

In the second study, where we added the component of group deliberation and verdict rendering, we were able to measure how individuals changed their views about the appropriate sentence as a consequence of the deliberation process in addition to all of the measures we used in the original study. We asked each individual to cast a confidential "straw" vote immediately after presentation of the case but before deliberations commenced, then recorded each participant's postdeliberation verdict vote (not all juries were unanimous). There were two rather striking findings about this process. First, overall, the deliberation process shifted a significant number of participants toward death across conditions. Videotapes of the actual deliberations revealed that those in favor of death tended to be vocal, dominating, and at times aggressive in their interactions with life leaners, whereas those in favor of life tended not to be as assertive with their peers in the deliberation process.

Second, and particularly relevant to this discussion, those life straw voters who viewed a tape with the Black defendant were significantly more likely to switch to death after the deliberation process than were those life straw voters who viewed the White defendant. Specifically, before deliberations, 52% of those in the White defendant conditions voted for death, and 61% voted for death after deliberations. In the Black defendant conditions, 57% of the participants voted for death before deliberations, and 71% were for death after deliberations. This resulted in significant differences in sentence outcome by defendant race when jurors' final votes were analyzed individually.

As in the first study, we found that the participants' assessments of the individual pieces of mitigating evidence were also influenced by defendant race in the case of the evidence about his history of child-abuse victimization, his psychiatric problems, and his substance-abuse impairment. In this study, we also found that the facts of the murder, which were perceived by our participants as the primary aggravator in this case, but which under California law can be weighed as either aggravation or mitigation, were weighed significantly more heavily toward death in the case of the Black defendant than the White defendant. Again, we found no race of victim effect for the weighing of evidence in this study. And again, consistent with what we know about how aversive racism can be activated where ambiguous or confusing decision-making conditions exist, we found that low comprehension of the sentencing instructions among our participants played a significant role in racially disparate outcomes such that the incomprehension benefited the White defendant and disadvantaged the Black defendant.

We have also looked at some of the qualitative data collected in both studies to see what they reveal about the differences in assessments of mitigating evidence by our participants, depending upon the racial characteristics of the case they viewed. In both studies we asked participants to name the piece of evidence, witness, or argument that had the *most* impact on their decision and to explain why it was so important, and to name the piece of evidence, witness, or argument that had the *least* impact on their decision and why that was the case. Again, race of defendant appeared to have shaped these perceptions. Generally, across conditions, those who voted for death found that facts related to the capital offense were the most important in their penalty decisions, and among those who voted for life, the testimony about the defendant's history of child abuse and the psychiatric problems he faced as a result of his upbringing was the most compelling evidence in favor of life.

Nonetheless, the relative frequency and the way this mitigating testimony was used was influenced by defendant race. In the first study, the child-abuse testimony was mentioned as the most important piece of evidence by 106 of the 184 total life voters; however 68% of those mentions were from those who viewed the White defendant. Conversely, 11 of the death voters who improperly used this evidence in favor of a death sentence ranked it as the most important evidence in making their decision, and of the 11, 8 (73%) had viewed the Black defendant. And of the 27 death voters who reported that this mitigating evidence had the *least* impact on their decision, 59% had viewed the Black defendant.

In the second study, the mitigation evidence about the defendant's abusive background and its psychological consequences was also mentioned frequently as both the most important and least important evidence, and again its differential impact appeared to be a function of defendant race.

Thus, 94 of the life voters described this as the most important factor in their decision, and of the 94, 62% (58) had viewed the White defendant. In this study, a much larger number of death voters—58—inappropriately weighed this evidence as the most important element in favor of death, and of those 58% had viewed the Black defendant. To see the impact of this evidence from another angle, of those who viewed the Black defendant *and* who listed this evidence as most important to their decision, almost half were death voters (48%, or 33 of 69), whereas only 30% of those who viewed the White defendant and who listed this evidence as the most impactful on their decision were death voters (25 of 82). And, similar to the findings in the first study, 55% (93 of 170) of the death voters in the second study who mentioned this as the *least* impactful had viewed the Black defendant.

The way these sentiments were expressed by some of our participants in the second study illustrate its emotionally laden content as shaped by race of defendant. For instance, one of the participants who viewed the Black defendant and who voted for death contradictorily mentioned elements of this testimony as both the most and least impactful. It is clear that this mock juror used the evidence about the childhood beatings against the defendant when he described as the most important testimony justifying his death vote as "That his childhood was to blame. In that case, why didn't he go after his stepfather instead of someone who had nothing to do with his poor, miserable upbringing?" He went on to express his anger about this mitigating evidence when he listed the defendant's mother's testimony as the least impactful on his decision. He explained: "Where was she when her children were being molested and beaten? She should have defended them. She too was guilty of child neglect as far as I'm concerned." Another participant who viewed the Black defendant and who ranked the mother's testimony as most impactful on the decision for a death verdict justified it by arguing, in essence, the indelible nature of his violence: "It shows that Mitchell knows no other way of doing things except the way his father did—violence and alcohol. He followed his footsteps."

Among those who ranked this testimony as the least impactful on their decisions the common dismissal was that it had no bearing on the case; however, the level of antipathy toward this evidence tended to be greater among those who viewed the Black defendant. For instance, one such participant expressed anger about this testimony, ranked as the least impactful evidence, as follows: "Telling about his background! I HATE THE

VICTIM ACT WHERE IT'S OK TO KILL BECAUSE OF ABUSE!" Such testimony was frequently referred to as the "abuse excuse" which, in the words of one mock juror who viewed the Black defendant, "didn't work for sympathy" and in another was viewed as a failed attempt at "seeking pity."

In contrast, several participants who viewed the White defendant/Black victim tape were able to articulate how that same evidence, as presented by the defendant's mother, impacted their votes for a life verdict:

> Her testimony made me feel like this kid was on his own when he experienced torture at the hands of his father. Therefore, he had to put up "walls" to defend/protect his ego. I decided that this man's life was such a tragedy, it didn't exactly excuse what he did, but it did explain how a person could have such rage to commit the murder.

> I learned of what a horrible life he had had, not that that's an excuse for what he did but with a normal childhood I am certain this would not have happened. I felt that the abuse in his childhood was so bad that that outweighed the shooting of the pizza man. His only male role model was an extremely abusive drunk. Although killing the pizza man was horrible, it might not have happened if Mitchell had had a better childhood.

> I was influenced by his childhood experiences and the fact that he had no prior criminal activities before the two shootings that occurred with in 1 week of each other. It seems everything just got to be too much for him and he snapped even though there is no clinical diagnosis that satisfied the manual mentioned. In a way it let you understand why he snapped and was not making rational decisions. At the same time, it showed that he was not a career criminal or one who enjoyed the crimes he committed.

Not a single one of the 36 life voters who viewed the Black defendant and who mentioned this evidence as the most important factor in their decision articulated this level of empathy and understanding of its impact. Rather, the responses were briefer and more curt; for example: "His mother, his life [was most impactful]. Informing us of what he experienced as a child." And "Mother. The way she raised him." Some were even dismissive. For instance, one participant voted for life and listed the testimony about his psychiatric problems as impactful on her decision but described the testimony as "sterile, bland, self-serving, twisting of his behavior to show it wasn't his fault" and reported that she voted for life in part because death was "almost too easy a way out [and] costs way too much for [the] state."

Thus, although there were very few overt mentions of race in these qualitative data,[4] there is a quality to the responses that clearly reflected the nature of modern racism, most notably, the withholding of empathy for the Black defendant, and indeed some resentment that such a sentiment was sought for him. Further, as illustrated in Fleury-Steiner's (2004) work with actual capital jurors, racialized stereotypes about the propensity of violence among Blacks appeared to shape several of our mock jury participants' assessments of the defendant's life history.

Finally, the apparent lack of main effect for victim race in these studies, which seems to contradict the findings of the archival research (as in Baldus et al., 1990), needs to be addressed. First, race of victim clearly amplifies the effects found such that the *greatest* differences between groups were consistently evident in the two cross-racial condition comparisons. Consistent with the bulk of research on racial disparities in case outcomes (e.g., Baldus et al., 1990; Bowers, Steiner, and Sandys, 2001; Government Accounting Office, 1990), in our work, those judging a case where a Black defendant has killed a White victim are the least empathetic and most prone toward a death sentence in comparison to all other racial combinations. Further, the race of victim effect might have been attenuated due to our approach, in which we manipulated only race, and no other variables, resulting in a suppression of the correlates to race that exist in the real world. Because race, class, and social status are intertwined in ways that are not reflected in this study, those other variables are likely to covary with race in actual cases even when the analysts have attempted to control for them, independent of race. Because victims' social and economic status will predict level of "justice" achieved in courtroom settings (Black, 1989), the extent to which race and status are inexorably intertwined in our society will limit the ability to untangle those variables out in archival studies. By design, this research eliminated these covariates for both the victim and the defendant. As a result, our data would not be expected to reveal the effects of the correlates to race, which may account for the lack of victim-based disparities in the results.

Implications of Our Research for the Contemporary Administration of the Death Penalty

There are, of course, several major limitations to this kind of research, but nonetheless these findings contribute to the case against the death penalty as a racially biased process. One drawback of our work, if viewed in a vacuum, is that the analysis is truncated in terms of both narrow theoretical scope and procedural focus, thus can tell only a partial story about how and why race matters in the American death penalty machinery; even so, it does provide evidence of the microlevel processes at work in such decision-making contexts. A second significant drawback to our approach is that simulated trials cannot capture all of the subtle information that is conveyed in actual trial settings, and are not as emotionally involving as real-life trials; a particularly compelling problem in the case of deciding on life or death, as in this program of research. Yet, simulated jury experiments—especially those that are more rigorously designed—do reproduce patterns of racially discriminatory sentencing similar to those obtained in archival studies of the same issues (Sweeney and Haney, 1992). In addition, because we cannot systematically manipulate the race variables and hold constant all other variables in actual trials, this approach provides a source of information that would be otherwise inaccessible. In short, these findings are not equivalent to the kind of data that would be obtained from studying actual capital trials, but this research endeavor is just one piece in a larger body of ongoing multidisciplinary, multimethodological work on understanding how capital jurors carry out the life-and-death task they are asked to undertake.

Our findings, then, appear to echo what a number of other researchers have found about how and why race influences capital case outcomes (see, e.g., Fleury-Steiner, 2004). Further, the research suggests that although the influence of the defendant's race on how jurors "read" the penalty evidence—specifically the case for mitigation—might be attenuated by improving the guidelines that laypersons are to follow when deciding on punishment, the pervasive influence of cultural stereotypes about race in this context is not likely to disappear even with such remedies.

And indeed, capital jury instructions can and should be revised to make them more accessible and comprehensible to laypersons, but the underlying task that jurors are asked to undertake—deciding whether or not to sentence a fellow human to death—may be ultimately unguidable, thus ripe for the influence of all kinds of values, biases, and beliefs that differentially impact defendants depending upon their color and/or other status characteristics. And with the pretense of guidance, jurors and juries are left to their own resources to reach a decision with few limits on their discretion. In the end, capital jurors are for the most part unguided in their decision, all the while being able to rationalize that the law and the guidelines have led them to the outcome they have chosen.

The second major insight these data provide has to do with the insidiousness of modern forms of racial bias, and the resulting difficulty in remediating the problem and legally challenging its negative impact. As several commentators have pointed out about the nature of modern prejudice, because it is generally cloaked in nonracial terms, its impact on all kinds of social policy and other social relations is likely to remain for some time (Emerson, Smith, and Sikkink, 1999; Krieger, 1995; Quillian and Pager, 2001). Krieger (1995) has commented at length on the misfit between the social psychological realities of intergroup bias and the law's conception of discrimination in the context of Title VII's disparate treatment model of discrimination. Her assessment is somewhat grave in terms of its implications for challenging discrimination in the workplace. She points out that the law clings to a model of discrimination as overt, conscious acts perpetrated by individuals who are driven by discriminatory motives, whereas what we know about bias suggests a very different, more subtle process.

The legal prognosis for challenging the death penalty as racially biased is even more grave. Under the standard of proof articulated in *McCleskey v. Kemp* (1987), not even disparate outcome would be enough to demonstrate a potential problem; rather, the expectation is that discriminatory behavior looks like old-fashioned racism where bigots express open, racist antipathy toward persons of color and then act upon those negative feelings to disadvantage their targets. Clearly, our data, congruent with a huge body of work on contemporary prejudice, do not reflect such a model. Yet this does not negate the significance of their meaning and the attendant implications for achieving a fair and just system of capital punishment.

NOTES

1. Those who feel so strongly in favor of the death penalty that their ability would be so hampered are also excluded, yet research indicates that such individu-

als are not nearly as well screened and excluded as are opponents. See Sandys, 1995.

2. These are that the defendant was impaired by psychological problems; that he had a substance-abuse problem and was under the influence at the time of the crime; that he had been brutally abused as a child by his stepfather; and that his family still loved and needed him in their lives.

3. In the case of the subjects who saw the Black defendant, 60% of the low-comprehension subjects gave a death verdict, whereas 45% of the high-comprehension subjects gave death. For the White defendant subjects, 39% of the low-comprehension subjects gave a death sentence, whereas 46% of the high-comprehension subjects gave death.

4. There were two: one death voter actually stated that the fact that the victim was White was influential; the other death voter mentioned that the fact that the defendant was Black did not influence his decision.

REFERENCES

Adorno, Theodore, Else Frenkel-Brunswick, Daniel Levinson, and R. Nevitt Sanford (1950). *The Authoritarian Personality*. New York: Norton.

Aguirre, Adalberto, and David Baker (1993). Racial prejudice and the death penalty: A research note. *Social Justice*, 20, 150–155.

Applegate, Brandon, John Wright, R. Gregory Dunaway, Francis Cullen, and John Wooldredge (1993). Victim-offender race and support for capital punishment: A factorial design approach. *American Journal of Criminal Justice*, 18, 95–115.

Baldus, David, George Woodworth, and Charles Pulaski (1990). *Equal Justice and the Death Penalty: A Legal Empirical Analysis*. Boston: Northeastern University Press.

Banner, Stuart (2002). *The Death Penalty: An American History*. Cambridge, MA: Harvard University Press.

Barkan, Steven, and Steven Cohn (1994). Racial prejudice and support for the death penalty by whites. *Journal of Research in Crime and Delinquency*, 31, 202–209.

Barnes, Sandra (1997). Practicing what you preach: An analysis of racial attitudes of two Christian churches. *Western Journal of Black Studies*, 21, 1–12.

Black, Donald (1989). *Sociological Justice*. New York: Oxford University Press.

Bobo, Lawrence (1999). Prejudice as group position: Microfoundations of a sociological approach to racism and race relations. *Journal of Social Issues*, 55, 445–472.

Bodenhausen, Galen (1988). Stereotypic biases in social decision making and memory: Testing process models of stereotypic use. *Journal of Personality and Social Psychology*, 55, 726–737.

Bodenhausen, Galen, and Meryl Lichtenstein (1987). Social stereotypes and information processing strategies: The impact of task complexity. *Journal of Personality and Social Psychology*, 52, 871–880.

Bodenhausen, Galen, and Robert Wyer (1985). Effects of stereotypes on decision-making and information-processing strategies. *Journal of Personality and Social Psychology*, 48, 267–282.

Bonilla-Silva, Eduardo (1997). Rethinking racism: Toward a structural interpretation. *American Sociological Review*, 62, 465–480.

Bowers, William, and Glenn Pierce (1980). Arbitrariness and discrimination under post-*Furman* capital statutes. *Crime and Delinquency* 26, 563–635.

Bowers, William, Benjamin Steiner, and Marla Sandys (2001). Death sentencing in black and white: An empirical analysis of the role of jurors' race and jury racial composition. *Journal of Constitutional Law*, 3, 171–274.

Devine, Patricia (1989). Stereotypes and prejudice: Their automatic and controlled components. *Journal of Personality and Social Psychology*, 56, 5–18.

Devine, Patricia, and Andrew Elliot (1995). Are racial stereotypes really fading? The Princeton trilogy revisited. *Personality and Social Psychology Bulletin*, 21, 1139–1150.

Dovidio, John (2001). On the nature of contemporary prejudice: The third wave. *Journal of Social Issues*, 57, 821–850.

Dovidio, John, Jeffrey Mann, and Samuel Gaertner (1989). Resistance to affirmative action: The implication of aversive racism. In F. Blanchard and F. Crosby (eds.), *Affirmative Action in Perspective*. New York: Springer-Verlag.

Eisenberg, Theodore, Stephen Garvey, and Martin Wells (2001). Forecasting life and death: Juror race, religion, and attitude toward the death penalty. *Journal of Legal Studies*, 30, 277–311.

Eisenberg, Theodore, and Martin Wells (1993). Deadly confusion: Juror instructions in capital cases. *Cornell Law Review*, 79, 1–52.

Emerson, Michael, Christian Smith, and David Sikkink (1999). Equal in Christ, but not in the world: White conservative Protestants and explanations of Black-White inequality. *Social Problems*, 46, 398–417.

Filkins, Joseph, Christine Smith, and R. Scott Tindale (1998). An evaluation of the biasing effects of death qualification: A meta-analytic/computer simulation approach. In Tindale, R. Scott and Heath, Linda (eds.), *Theory and Research on Small Groups: Social Psychological Applications to Social Issues, Vol. 4*. New York: Plenum Press.

Fiske, Susan, and Shelley Taylor (1991). *Social Cognition, 2d ed.* New York: McGraw-Hill.

Fleury-Steiner, Benjamin (2004). *Jurors' Stories of Death: How America's Death Penalty Invests in Inequality*. Ann Arbor: University of Michigan Press.

Gaertner, Samuel, and John Dovidio (1986). The aversive form of racism. In J. F.

Dovidio and S. L. Gaertner (eds.), *Prejudice, Discrimination, and Racism*. San Diego: Academic Press.

Government Accounting Office (1990). *Death Penalty Sentencing: Research Indicates Pattern of Racial Disparities (Report to Senate and House Committee on the Judiciary, 101st Congress, 2d Session)*. Washington, DC: Author.

Gross, Samuel (1998). Update: American Public Opinion on the Death Penalty—It's Getting Personal. *Cornell Law Review*, 83, 1448–1475.

Gross, Samuel, and Robert Mauro (1989). *Death and Discrimination: Racial Disparities in Capital Sentencing*. Boston: Northeastern University Press.

Haney, Craig (1984). On the selection of capital juries: The biasing effects of the death qualification process. *Law and Human Behavior*, 8, 121–132.

Haney, Craig (1995). The social context of capital murder: Social histories and the logic of mitigation. *Santa Clara Law Review*, 35, 547–609.

Haney, Craig (1997a). Commonsense justice and capital punishment: Problematizing the "will of the people." *Psychology, Public Policy and Law*, 3, 303–337.

Haney, Craig (1997b). Violence and the capital jury: Mechanisms of moral disengagement and the impulse to condemn to death. *Stanford Law Review*, 49, 1447–1486.

Haney, Craig, Aida Hurtado, and Luis Vega (1994). "Modern" death qualification: New data on its biasing effects. *Law and Human Behavior*, 18, 619–633.

Haney, Craig, and Mona Lynch (1994). Comprehending life and death matters: A preliminary study of California's capital penalty instructions. *Law and Human Behavior*, 18, 411–436.

Haney, Craig, and Mona Lynch (1997). Debating life and death: An analysis of instructional comprehension and penalty phase arguments. *Law and Human Behavior*, 20, 575–595.

Hans, Valerie (1988). Death by jury. In Kenneth Haas and James Inciardi (eds.), *Challenging Capital Punishment: Legal and Social Science Approaches*. Thousand Oaks, CA: Sage Publications.

Hill, Erick, and Jeffrey Pfeifer (1992). Nullification instructions and juror guilt ratings: An examination of modern racism. *Contemporary Social Psychology*, 16, 6–10.

Hurwitz, Jon, and Mark Peffley (1997). Public perceptions of race and crime: The role of racial stereotypes. *American Journal of Political Science*, 41, 375–401.

Kawakami, Kerry, Kenneth Dion, and John Dovidio (1998). Racial prejudice and stereotype activation. *Personality and Social Psychology Bulletin*, 24, 407–416.

Krieger, Linda (1995). The content of our categories: A cognitive bias approach to discrimination and equal employment opportunity. *Stanford Law Review*, 47, 1161–1248.

Luginbuhl, James, and Michael Burkhead (1994). Sources of bias and arbitrariness in the capital trial. *Journal of Social Issues*, 50, 103–124.

Luginbuhl, James, and Kathi Middendorf (1988). Death penalty beliefs and jurors' responses to aggravating and mitigating circumstances in capital trials. *Law and Human Behavior*, 12, 263–281.

Lynch, Mona, and Craig Haney (2000). Discrimination and instructional comprehension: Guided discretion, racial bias, and the death penalty. *Law and Human Behavior* 24, 337–358.

McCleskey v. Kemp, 481 U.S. 279 (1987).

McConahay, John (1986). Modern racism, ambivalence, and the Modern Racism Scale. In J. F. Dovidio and S. L. Gaertner (eds.), *Prejudice, Discrimination, and Racism*. San Diego: Academic Press.

Meertens, Robert, and Thomas Pettigrew (1997). Is subtle prejudice really prejudice? *Public Opinion Quarterly*, 61, 54–71.

Mendelberg, Tali (1997). Executing Hortons: Racial crime in the 1988 presidential campaign. *Public Opinion Quarterly*, 61, 134–158.

Paternoster, Raymond (1983). Race of victim and location of crime: The decision to seek the death penalty in South Carolina. *Journal of Criminal Law and Criminology*, 74, 754–785.

Pettigrew, Thomas (1989). The nature of modern racism in the U.S. *Revue Internationale de Psychologie Sociale*, 2, 291–303.

Pettigrew, Thomas, and Robert Meertens (1995). Subtle and blatant prejudice in western Europe. *European Journal of Social Psychology*, 25, 57–75.

Pfeifer, Jeffrey, and James Ogloff (1991). Ambiguity and guilt determinations: A modern racism perspective. *Journal of Applied Social Psychology*, 21, 1713–1725.

Quillian, Lincoln, and Devah Pager (2001). Black neighbors, higher crime? The role of racial stereotypes in evaluations of neighborhood crime. *American Journal of Sociology*, 107, 717–769.

Radelet, Michael, and Margaret Vandiver (1983). Symposium on current death penalty issues: The Florida Supreme Court and death penalty appeals. *Journal of Criminal Law and Criminology*, 74, 913–926.

Rector, Neil, R. Michael Bagby, and R. Nicholson (1993). The effect of prejudice and judicial ambiguity on defendant guilt ratings. *Journal of Social Psychology*, 133, 651–659.

Russell, Gregory (1996). *The Death Penalty and Racial Bias*. Westport, CT: Greenwood Press.

Sandys, Marla (1995). Crossovers—Capital jurors who change their minds about the punishment: A litmus test for sentencing guidelines. *Indiana Law Journal*, 70, 1183–1221.

Sarat, Austin (2001). *When the State Kills: Capital Punishment and the American Condition*. Princeton, NJ: Princeton University Press.

Sears, David (1988). Symbolic racism. In P. Katz and D. Taylor (eds.), *Eliminating Racism: Profiles in Controversy*. New York: Plenum Press.

Sidanius, Jim, and Felicia Pratto (1993). The inevitability of oppression and the dynamics of social dominance. In P. Sniderman and P. Tetlock (eds.), *Prejudice, Politics, and the American Dilemma*. Stanford, CA: Stanford University Press.

Sidanius, Jim, Felicia Pratto, and Michael Mitchell (1994). In-group identification, social dominance orientation, and differential intergroup social allocation. *Journal of Social Psychology*, 134, 151–168.

Stinchcombe, Arthur, Rebecca Adams, Carol Heimer, Kim Scheppele, Tom Smith, and D. Garth Taylor (1980). *Crime and Punishment—Changing Attitudes in America*. San Francisco: Jossey-Bass Publishers.

Sweeney, Laura, and Craig Haney (1992). The influence of race on sentencing: A meta-analytic review of experimental studies. *Behavioral Science and Law*, 10, 179–195.

Tajfel, Henri (1982). Social psychology of intergroup relations. *Annual Review of Psychology*, 33, 1–39.

Tiersma, Peter (1995). Dictionaries and death: Do capital jurors understand mitigation? *Utah Law Review*, 1995, 1–49.

Wiener, Richard, Christine Pritchard, and Minda Weston (1995). Comprehensibility of approved jury instructions in capital murder cases. *Journal of Applied Psychology*, 80, 455–467.

Wittenbrink, Bernd, Charles Judd, and Bernadette Park (1997). Evidence for racial prejudice at the implicit level and its relationship with questionnaire measures. *Journal of Personality and Social Psychology*, 72, 262–275.

Young, Robert (1991). Race, conceptions of crime and justice, support for the death penalty. *Social Psychology Quarterly*, 54, 67–75.

Part III

Race, Politics, and the Death Penalty

Chapter 7

Discrimination, Death, and Denial
The Tolerance of Racial Discrimination in Infliction of the Death Penalty

Stephen B. Bright

I. Introduction

Capital punishment, one of the nation's most prominent vestiges of slavery and racial violence, is flourishing once again in the United States. After a moratorium on executions in the 1960s and '70s, the execution of human beings by the state has become "routine." More than three thousand men and women are on death rows throughout the nation and over one thousand have been executed in the last 30 years.[1]

Those awaiting their deaths are no different from those selected for execution in the past: virtually all are poor; about half are members of racial minorities; and the overwhelming majority were sentenced to death for crimes against white victims.[2] Many suffer from severe mental impairments or limitations, and many others were the victims of the most brutal physical, sexual, and psychological abuse during their childhoods.[3]

The death penalty was declared unconstitutional in 1972 because of its arbitrariness and discrimination against racial minorities and the poor.[4] New capital punishment laws, supposedly designed to prevent arbitrariness and discrimination, were upheld by the Supreme Court in 1976.[5] But race and poverty continue to determine who dies. The poor are frequently represented by inept court-appointed lawyers who often fail to protect the rights of their clients and fail to provide juries with critical information needed for the sentencing decision, leaving the accused virtually defenseless.[6] Prosecutors are given wide discretion in deciding whether to seek the death penalty, and juries are given great discretion in deciding whether to impose it This discretion provides ample room for racial prejudice to influence whether the accused lives or dies.

Although African-Americans are the victims in half of the murders that occur each year in the United States,[7] 85 percent of the condemned were sentenced to death for murders of white persons.[8] An analysis of twenty-eight studies by the U.S. General Accounting Office found a "remarkably consistent" pattern of racial disparities in capital sentencing throughout the country.[9] A study in 1994 of death sentences in Harris County, Texas, which has carried out more executions and sentenced more people to death than most states,[10] found that "Harris County has sent blacks to death row nearly twice as often as whites during the last ten years, a growing imbalance that eclipses the pre-civil rights days of 'Old Sparky' the notorious Texas electric chair."[11] In Florida, which has the nation's third-largest death row,[12] the Racial and Ethnic Bias Commission of the Florida Supreme Court found that "the application of the death penalty in Florida is not colorblind."[13] A congressional study found stark disparities in the use of the federal death penalty.[14] Racial disparities have been documented by other observers.[15]

Few people familiar with the state of race relations in the United States today would deny that there is a risk of racial prejudice influencing the sentencing decision in the typical capital case: an African-American facing the death penalty for the murder of a prominent white person who is prosecuted by a white prosecutor before a white judge and an all-white or predominantly white jury. The likelihood of racial prejudice influencing whether the death penalty is sought by the prosecutor or imposed by the jury is even greater if other factors are present, such as the rape of a white woman.[16]

The United States Supreme Court has observed, "[A] juror who believes that blacks are violence prone or morally inferior might well be influenced by that belief in deciding whether [the] crime involved aggravating factors."[17] In addition, a juror's racial biases might prevent him or her from considering evidence about the life and background of the accused in mitigation. The Court pointed out, for example, that "[s]uch a juror might also be less favorably inclined toward [the defendant's] evidence of mental disturbance as a mitigating circumstance."[18]

The Supreme Court also observed that "[m]ore subtle, less consciously held racial attitudes"—unconscious racism—"could also influence a juror's decision in [the] case."[19] For example, "Fear of blacks, which could easily be stirred up by the violent facts of [the] crime, might incline a juror to favor the death penalty."[20]

Although the Supreme Court spoke of jurors, racial prejudice is not limited to jurors. Law enforcement officials, prosecutors, judges, defense lawyers, and court officials may have racial biases that influence their attitudes toward crimes and those accused, as well as their exercise of discretion in the process leading to imposition of a death sentence.

A prosecutor who believes that "blacks are violence prone or morally inferior"[21] may be less likely to seek the death penalty in cases involving African-American victims and more likely to seek the death penalty in cases involving African-American defendants. A prosecutor's unconscious racism, his or her fear or misunderstanding of people of a different race or culture, may well be "stirred up" in a case involving an interracial crime and influence the prosecutor to seek the death penalty in that case but not in similar cases that are not interracial.

A judge with similar attitudes may fail to recognize or correct racial discrimination by prosecutors in selecting juries, in seeking the death penalty, or in presenting evidence or argument. A defense lawyer who has racial biases may not spend enough time with the client or the client's family to discover mitigating evidence. An African-American client may be seen as "arrogant" or "uncooperative" due to the lawyer's racial stereotypes.[22] A lawyer may not diligently try to save the life of one believed to be inferior.

Racial discrimination influences the capital sentencing decision in other ways as well. Members of racial minorities continue to be excluded as judges, jurors, prosecutors, lawyers, and law enforcement officials in the criminal justice system. A member of a racial minority who is also poor faces the disadvantage in a capital prosecution of being represented by a court-appointed lawyer. In many states, defense lawyers are appointed by elected trial judges, many of whom are former prosecutors who won positions on the bench after prosecuting high-publicity capital cases. Often, court-appointed lawyers lack the knowledge, skill, resources, sensitivity, and inclination to handle the case.[23] These lawyers may fail to recognize and challenge the role that race plays in determining who dies.[24]

It is difficult to measure precisely the extent to which race influences decision making in any particular capital case, but only those oblivious to the brutal history of racial discrimination in American law[25] would deny the danger of racial prejudice entering the decisions that lead to the imposition of a death sentence. However, instead of undertaking the challenge of minimizing or eliminating the potential for racial prejudice in these highly subjective and emotional decisions, courts and legislatures have been largely indifferent to the influence of race in the infliction of the death penalty. Despite pronounced racial disparities in the infliction of the death penalty in both state and federal capital cases, Congress and state legislatures have failed to limit application of the penalty or provide remedies for racial discrimination, such as the Racial Justice Act.[26]

Instead of acknowledging the risk of racial discrimination and attempting to identify and eliminate it, both federal and state courts frequently dodge the inquiry. They deny the existence of racial discrimination that is apparent to everyone; employ legal fictions that have no relation to the reality of race relations in America today; set legal standards or burdens of proof that are impossible to meet; or provide wholly inadequate remedies for discrimination that is undeniable. All this may be done while the courts are issuing sweeping pronouncements decrying the evil of racial discrimination and proclaiming their "unceasing efforts" to cure it.[27] One prominent federal appellate judge observed that the failure of the courts to remedy instances of racial discrimination has sent the message that federal courts, which once offered the greatest hope to the nation's minorities, are "no longer interested in protecting the rights of minorities."[28]

This chapter examines the historic relationship between racial violence and the death penalty, describes some of the ways in which racial prejudice continues to influence capital sentencing decisions, and discusses the failure of the courts to confront the racial bias that infects the criminal justice system.

II. "Legal Lynchings"

The death penalty is a direct descendant of lynching and other forms of racial violence and racial oppression in America. From colonial times until the Civil War, the criminal law in many states expressly differentiated between crimes committed by and against blacks and whites.[29] For example, Georgia law provided that the rape of a white female by a black man "shall be" punishable by death, yet the rape of a white female by anyone else was punishable by a prison term not less than two nor more than twenty years.[30] The rape of a black woman was punishable "by fine and imprisonment, at the discretion of the court."[31]

Disparate punishments—exacted by the courts and by the mob—based upon both the race of the victim and the race of the defendant continued in practice after the abolition of slavery. At least 4,743 people were killed by lynch mobs.[32] More than 90 percent of the lynchings took place in the South, and three-fourths of the victims were African-Americans.[33] The likelihood that Congress would pass an antilynching statute in the early 1920s led southern states to "replace lynchings with a more '[humane] . . . method of racial control'—the judgment and imposition of capital sentences by all-white juries."[34] As one historian observed,

> Southerners . . . discovered that lynchings were untidy and created a bad press. . . . [L]ynchings were increasingly replaced by situations in which the Southern legal system prostituted itself to the mob's demand. Responsible officials begged would-be lynchers to "let the law take its course," thus tacitly promising that there would be a quick trial and the death penalty. . . . [S]uch proceedings "retained the essence of mob murder, shedding only its outward forms."[35]

The process of "legal lynchings" was so successful that in the 1930s, two-thirds of those executed were black.[36]

Powell v. Alabama,[37] decided by the Supreme Court in 1932, involved nine young African-Americans who were charged in Scottsboro, Alabama, with the rape of two white women, the classic case for a lynching or the death penalty.[38] The youths were tried in groups in three trials while mobs outside the courtroom demanded the death penalty.[39] The accused were represented by two lawyers; one was a drunk and the other was senile.[40] All-white, all-male juries sentenced the accused to death.[41] When there was a national outcry about the injustice of such summary trials with only perfunctory legal representation, the people of Scottsboro did not understand the reaction. After all, they did not lynch the accused; they gave them a trial.[42]

In one of many examples of legal lynchings, a man was hung immediately after a trial in Kentucky that lasted less than an hour.[43] The *Louisville Courier-Journal* "tried to put the best light on the execution," saying that although it was a little hasty, at least there was not a lynching.[44] The paper also observed that because a Negro had raped a white woman, "no other result could have been reached, however prolonged the trial."[45] As racial violence was being achieved increasingly through the criminal courts, Georgia became the nation's primary executioner, carrying out the most executions in the twentieth century before the death penalty was declared unconstitutional in 1972.[46] Between 1924 and 1972, Georgia executed 337 black people and 75 white people.[47]

The death penalty was held unconstitutional in *Furman v. Georgia*[48] because of discrimination and arbitrariness in its infliction.[49] New death penalty statutes were enacted almost immediately by a number of states.[50] Some of those statutes were upheld by the Supreme Court in 1976;[51] however, they have failed to end the influence of racial prejudice in the use of the death penalty.

III. Racial Discrimination after Furman

Most death penalty schemes adopted by the states after *Furman v. Georgia* provide for the death penalty in most first-degree and felony murders. Any murder involving a robbery, arson, burglary, rape, or kidnapping may be prosecuted as a capital case.[52] In addition, death may be imposed for any other "heinous, atrocious or cruel"[53] or "horrible" murders,[54] which of course describe almost all murders. But no crime—no matter how heinous—must be punished by death. In most states, the sentence is determined by the imprecise and wholly subjective consideration of aggravating and mitigating factors. The breadth of the death penalty statutes and the unfettered discretion given to prosecutors and juries provide ample room for racial prejudice to influence whether death is sought or imposed.[55] As a result, "[r]ace plays an especially influential role in capital sentencing decisions."[56]

The criminal courts are the institutions least affected by the civil rights movement that brought changes to many American institutions in the past forty years. Judges and prosecutors are still elected in judicial circuits that are drawn to dilute the voting strength of racial minorities.[57] Thus, even in many areas with substantial minority populations, most of the judges and prosecutors are white.[58] In Georgia, until recently, all of the elected district attorneys have been white.[59] Many states have no or very few African-Americans as prosecutors.[60] Members of racial minorities are often underrepresented in jury pools and excluded in the jury selection process.[61] Often, the only member of a racial minority who participates in the process is the accused. Racial disparities are still apparent in all types of sentencing.[62] The perfunctory capital trial—the legal lynching—is not a thing of the past. Those facing the death penalty still receive token representation by court-appointed lawyers in cases infected by racism.

A. Tolerance of Racial Discrimination in the Criminal Courts

Wilburn Dobbs, an African-American who faced execution in Georgia for the murder of a white man, was referred to at his trial as "colored" and "colored boy" by the judge and defense lawyer and called by his first name by the prosecutor.[63] Two of the jurors who sentenced Dobbs to death for the murder admitted after the trial to using the racial slur "nigger."[64] Dobbs was tried only two weeks after being indicted for murder and four other offenses. His court-appointed lawyer did not know for certain until the day of trial that he was going to represent Dobbs.[65] The lawyer filed only one motion, a demand for a copy of the accusation and a list of witnesses.[66] Counsel sought a continuance on the morning of trial,[67] stating to the trial court that he was "not prepared to go to trial"[68] and was "in a better position to prosecute the case than defend it."[69] Nevertheless, the trial court denied the motion and the case proceeded to trial.[70] The federal district court described the defense lawyer's attitude toward African-Americans as follows:

> Dobbs' trial attorney was outspoken about his views. He said that many blacks are uneducated and would not make good teachers, but do make good basketball players. He opined that blacks are less educated and less intelligent than whites either because of their nature or because "my grand-daddy had slaves." He said that integration has led to deteriorating neighborhoods and schools and referred to the black community in Chattanooga as "black boy jungle." He strongly implied that blacks have inferior morals by relating a story about sex in a classroom. He also said that when he was young, a maid was hired with the understanding that she would steal some items. He said that blacks in Chattanooga are more troublesome than blacks in Walker County [Georgia]. . . .
> The attorney stated that he uses the word "nigger" jokingly.[71]

Dobbs was convicted and sentenced to death in a trial that lasted only three days. During the penalty phase of the trial, when the jury could have heard anything about Dobbs's life, background, and any reasons Dobbs should not have been sentenced to death,[72] the lawyer presented no evidence.[73] For a closing argument, he read part of Justice Brennan's concurring opinion in *Furman v. Georgia*,[74] which expressed the view that the death penalty was unconstitutional and could not be carried out.[75] Thus, rather than emphasizing to the jury the enormously grave decision it had to make about whether Dobbs was going to live or die, the lawyer suggested that because the death penalty would never be carried out, the jury's decision was not important.[76]

The federal courts subsequently determined that the racial prejudice of the judge, prosecutor, defense lawyer, and jurors in the Dobbs case did not require his death sentence to be set aside. The Court of Appeals found that "[a]lthough certain of jurors' statements revealed racial prejudice, no juror stated that [he or she] viewed blacks as more prone to violence than whites," or as morally inferior to whites.[77] Because neither the trial judge nor defense lawyer decided the penalty, the court held that "apart from the trial judge's and defense lawyer's references to Dobbs as 'colored' and 'colored boy,' it cannot be said that the trial judge's or the defense lawyer's racial attitudes affected the jurors' sentencing determination."[78] After a remand from the United States Supreme Court,[79] the district court again held that Wilburn Dobbs did not receive incompetent representation despite his lawyer's racism.[80]

The Dobbs case is only one of many cases that starkly illustrate that racial discrimination not acceptable in any other area of American life today is tolerated in criminal courts. The use of a racial slur may cost a sports announcer his job,[81] but there have been capital cases in which judges, jurors, and defense counsel have called an African-American defendant a "nigger" with no repercussions for anyone except the accused. For example, parents of an African-American defendant were referred to as the "nigger mom and dad" by the judge in a Florida case.[82] The judge did not lose his job; the Florida Supreme Court merely suggested that judges should avoid the "appearance of impropriety" in the future.[83]

Similarly, a death sentence was upheld in a Georgia case in which jurors used racial slurs during their deliberations.[84] The court reasoned that the evidence "shows only that two of the twelve jurors possessed some racial prejudice and does not establish that racial prejudice caused those two jurors to vote to convict [the defendant] and sentence him to die."[85] No state or federal court so much as held a hearing on the racial prejudice that infected the sentencing of Henry Hance before he was executed by Georgia in 1994, even though jurors signed affidavits swearing racial slurs had been used during deliberations.[86] In at least five capital cases in Georgia, the accused were referred to with racial slurs by their own lawyers at some time during the court proceedings.[87]

The publicly announced policy of Ed Peters, the district attorney of Jackson, Mississippi, was to "get rid of as many" black citizens as possible when exercising his peremptory strikes to select a jury.[88] As a result of this "policy" of a government official, Leo Edwards, an African-American, was sentenced to death by an all-white jury, even though he was tried in a community that was 34 percent African-American.[89] The federal courts rejected Edwards's challenge to Peters's discrimination,[90] and Edwards was executed in 1989.[91] In what other area of American life may a public official openly espouse and carry out a policy of "getting rid of" people based upon their race and have it approved by the courts?

The practice of total exclusion from jury service on the basis of race is not limited to the district attorney in Jackson. A prosecutor in Chambers County, Alabama, used twenty-six jury strikes against twenty-six African-Americans who were qualified for jury duty in order to get three all-white juries in a case involving Albert Jefferson, a mentally retarded African-American accused of a crime against a white victim.[92] At the time of Jefferson's trial, marriage records at the courthouse in Chambers County were kept in books engraved "white" and "colored."[93] During state postconviction proceedings, lawyers representing Jefferson discovered lists that had been made by the prosecutor prior to jury selection in which the prosecutor had divided prospective jurors into four categories: "strong," "medium," "weak," and "black."[94] A state circuit judge in Chambers County ruled that no racial discrimination had occurred in the selection of the juries.[95]

Some courts are indifferent to even the most blatant appearances of racial bias. Until recently, African-Americans facing the death penalty in Georgia usually appeared before a white judge sitting in front of the Confederate battle flag. Georgia adopted its state flag in 1956[96] to symbolize its defiance of the Supreme Court's decision in *Brown v. Board of Education*.[97] One federal district judge in Georgia observed that the predominant part of the 1956 flag is the Confederate battle flag, which is historically associated with the Ku Klux Klan. The legislators who voted for the 1956 bill knew that the new flag would be interpreted as a statement of defiance against federal desegregation mandates and an expression of anti-black feelings.[98] The new flag was designed to carry the message that Georgia "intend[s] to uphold what [it] stood for, will stand for, and will fight for" —namely, state-sponsored commitment to black subordination and the denial of equal protection of the laws to Georgia's African-American school children.[99] Although it was well recognized that the flag served as "a visual focal point for racial tensions"[100] and symbolizes defiance of the principle of equal protection under law, it was displayed in most Georgia courtrooms.

B. Discrimination in the Exercise of Discretion

Members of racial minorities have long been excluded from being prosecutors, judges, jurors, and lawyers, and from holding prominent positions in law enforcement. A typical scene in a Georgia courtroom was described as follows:

> Four black men stood before a Cobb County judge recently asking for bond to be set in their cases, all involving drug charges. After reviewing each case, the judge ordered them all held without bond until trial. Virtually everyone else in the courtroom—the judge, two prosecutors, five defense lawyers, law clerks, and bailiff—were white people. "If [my son] had been white, he'd be coming home," said the mother of one defendant. "You saw what happened in there. It resembled some kind of Klan meeting." While the Cobb judge's handling of the case was not unusual, neither was the mother's reaction.[101]

Things are no different in many other courtrooms throughout the nation. The criminal justice system in Jacksonville, Florida, was described as follows:

> Often the only black faces involved in Jacksonville murder cases belong to the victim and the killer.
>
> In a city where most murders are committed by blacks against other blacks, the faces of law and order are overwhelmingly white.
>
> There are:
>
> No black felony judges, the only circuit judges to handle homicides.
>
> No black members of the Public Defender Office homicide team.
>
> Two black prosecutors out of 14 homicide-team members and supervisors at the State Attorney's Office.
>
> Four black homicide detectives and supervisors out of 26 at the Jacksonville's Sheriff's Office.[102]

Thus, members of racial minorities often do not participate in the highly subjective decisions that lead to the imposition of the death penalty. Such decisions are frequently made by persons who are hostile to, or at the very least indifferent or insensitive to, the minority community.

1. DISCRETION EXERCISED BY LAW ENFORCEMENT OFFICIALS
   AND PROSECUTORS

The most important decisions that may determine whether the accused is sentenced to die are those made by the prosecutor. It is the prosecutor who decides whether to seek the death penalty, and whether to resolve the case with a plea bargain for a sentence less than death. In many jurisdictions, these crucial decisions are made by one white man, the elected district attorney, with no input from the community. Even where more than one person decides, there may be no representation for the minority community. For example, in Orange County, the jurisdiction that ranks third in sending people to California's death row, a panel of prosecutors composed exclusively of white males decides whether the death sentence will be sought in a case.[103] Some prosecutors seek the death penalty frequently. Some hardly ever seek it. There are no statewide standards that govern when it is sought. Each local district attorney sets his or her own policy in deciding which cases will be prosecuted as death cases.

In most jurisdictions with the death penalty, all murders accompanied by another felony, as well as all murders considered "heinous, atrocious or cruel" or "outrageously and wantonly vile, horrible and inhuman," may be prosecuted as capital cases.[104] From among the many cases where death could be sought, the local district attorney decides which few will actually be prosecuted as capital cases. For the white men who usually make these decisions in judicial districts all over the country, the crime may seem more heinous or horrible if the victim is a prominent white citizen. As one scholar has observed: "The life-and-death decision is made on trivial grounds, and tends to reflect the community's prejudices."[105]

Race may also influence the decision to seek the death sentence in more subtle ways. Prosecutors make the decision whether to seek it based in part on the strength of the evidence brought to them by law enforcement in each case. Often, the amount of available evidence differs because the local sheriffs and police departments investigate crime in the white community much more aggressively than crime in the black community.[106] Although massive searches involving the police, army units, and even the

Boy Scouts may occur when there is a crime against a white person,[107] nothing more than a missing person report may be completed when a black citizen disappears.[108] This disparity in the investigative treatment of cases results in a disparity of evidence available to prosecute the cases. Thus, racial discrimination against crime victims by police departments results in the prosecutor's having stronger evidence with which to justify seeking the death penalty in white victim cases and not seeking it in cases where the victim is a minority.

As a result of these influences, many cases in which prosecutors decide to seek the death penalty are indistinguishable from hundreds of other murder cases in which the death penalty is not sought. For example, most tragically, there are many convenience-store robberies that result in a loss of life. Only a handful are prosecuted as death cases. A case involving a battered woman with no criminal record who kills her abusive spouse is typically not a death penalty case in most parts of the country. However, the prosecutor in Talladega, Alabama, has obtained death sentences for at least two battered women for their roles in killing their abusers.[109] Of course, there are many other examples of cases that are eligible for the death penalty but are seldom prosecuted as capital cases.

An investigation into why some cases are treated as capital cases when other similar cases are not almost always reveals the influence of race, class, and politics. Often, there is more publicity and greater outrage in the community over an interracial crime than other crimes. Community outrage; the need to avenge a murder because of the prominence of the victim in the community; the insistence of the victim's family on the death penalty; the social and political clout of the family in the community; and the amount of publicity regarding the crime are often far more important in determining whether death is sought than the facts of the crime or the defendant's record and background.

As an example of the foregoing, an investigation of all murder cases prosecuted in Georgia's Chattahoochee Judicial Circuit from 1973 to 1990 revealed that in cases involving the murder of a white person, prosecutors often met with the victim's family and discussed whether to seek the death penalty.[110] In a case involving the murder of the daughter of a prominent white contractor, the prosecutor contacted the contractor and asked him if he wanted to seek the death penalty.[111] When the contractor replied in the affirmative, the prosecutor said that was all he needed to know.[112] He obtained the death penalty at trial.[113] He was rewarded with a campaign contribution of $5,000 from the contractor when he successfully ran for judge in the next election,[114] the largest received by the candidate.[115] There were other cases in which the district attorney issued press releases announcing that he was seeking the death penalty after meeting with the family of a white victim.[116] But prosecutors failed to meet with African-Americans whose family members had been murdered to determine what sentence they wanted. Most were not even notified that the case had been resolved.[117] As a result of these practices, although African-Americans were the victims of 65 percent of the homicides in the Chattahoochee Judicial Circuit, 85 percent of the capital cases in that circuit were white-victim cases.[118]

2. EXCLUSION OF MINORITY PERSONS FROM JURIES

The prosecutor's decision to seek the death penalty may never be reviewed by a member of a racial minority. Many capital cases are tried in white-flight suburban communities in which there are so few minority persons that there is little likelihood a member of a racial minority will serve on the jury. Counties like Baltimore County, Maryland, and Cobb County, Georgia, account for a disproportionately high number of persons sentenced to death in those states.[119] But even in communities where there is a substantial minority population, prosecutors are often successful in preventing or minimizing participation by minorities.

During jury selection for a capital trial, the judge or prosecutor asks potential jurors if they are conscientiously opposed to the death penalty. If they are opposed to the death penalty and cannot put their views aside, the state is entitled to have them removed for cause.[120] Although this process results in a more-conviction-prone jury, it has been upheld by the Supreme Court.[121] This "death-qualification" process often results in the removal of more prospective jurors who are members of minority groups than those who are white. The minority jurors may have reservations about the death penalty because it has been used in a racially discriminatory manner. This is one of many ways in which past discrimination in the application of the penalty perpetuates continued discrimination.

Often the "death-qualification" process reduces the number of minority jurors to so few that those remaining can be eliminated by the prosecutor with peremptory strikes. Even when jurors who express reservations about the death penalty indicate they can put aside their personal views and consider it, the prosecutor may justify his or her strikes with the hesitancy of such jurors to impose the penalty. For example, in *Lingo v. State*,[122] a Georgia prosecutor used all eleven of his jury strikes against African-Americans to obtain an all-white jury in a capital case.[123] In a challenge to those strikes under *Batson v. Kentucky*,[124] the Georgia Supreme Court—over the dissent of its two African-American justices—upheld the strikes based on the "race-neutral" reasons articulated by the prosecutor, many of which had to do with the jurors' answers to the death-qualification questions.[125]

A federal court in Alabama found the "standard operating procedure of the Tuscaloosa County District Attorney's Office" was "to use the peremptory challenges to strike as many blacks as possible from the venires in cases involving serious crimes."[126] The District Court also found that prosecutors

> manipulated the trial docket in their effort to preserve the racial purity of criminal juries. Inasmuch as they actually set the criminal trial dockets until 1982, they implemented a scheme in which juries with fewer black venirepersons would be called for the serious cases.[127]

In Georgia's Chattahoochee Judicial Circuit, which has sent more people to death row than any other circuit in the state,[128] prosecutors used 83 percent of their opportunities to use peremptory jury strikes against African-Americans, even though black people constitute 34 percent of the population in the circuit.[129] As a result, six African-American defendants were tried by all-white juries;[130] two have been executed.[131]

William Henry Hance was the first black defendant tried in a Chattahoochee Circuit capital case after *Furman* to have a member of his race on his jury.[132] During jury selection at Hance's first trial, the prosecutor used nine of his ten peremptory strikes against African-Americans, leaving one black on the jury.[133] The death penalty was imposed. However, it was later set aside because the prosecutor made a lynch-mob-type appeal to the jury for the death penalty in closing argument, which the United States Court of Appeals characterized as a "dramatic appeal to gut emotion" that "has no place in a courtroom."[134] These words from a federal court had no impact on the prosecutor. After the reversal, he called a press conference, insisted that he had done nothing wrong, and announced he would once again seek the death penalty against Hance.[135] At the second trial, he used seven of eight strikes against blacks, again eliminating all but one member of Hance's race from jury service.[136] Hance was again sentenced to death and this death sentence was carried out.[137]

The judicial circuit second only to Chattahoochee in sending people to Georgia's death row is the Ocmulgee Judicial Circuit in middle Georgia.[138]

Joseph Briley tried thirty-three death penalty cases in his tenure as district attorney in the circuit between 1974 and 1994.[139] Of those cases, twenty-four were against African-American defendants.[140] It was discovered that Briley had instructed jury commissioners in one county in the circuit to underrepresent black citizens on the master jury lists from which grand and trial juries were selected.[141] Additionally, the African-Americans who were summoned for jury duty in the circuit were often sent back home after Briley used his peremptory jury strikes against them. In the cases in which the defendants were black and the victims were white, Briley used 94 percent of his jury challenges—96 out of 103—against black citizens.[142]

When a prosecutor uses the overwhelming majority of his jury strikes against a racial minority, that minority is prohibited from participating in the process. A jury does not represent "the conscience of the community on the ultimate question of life or death"[143] when one-fourth or more of the community is not represented on it.[144]

African-Americans and other minorities continue to be excluded from jury service, even after the Supreme Court's decision in *Batson v. Kentucky*,[145] which changed the standard of proof for establishing a prima facie case of discrimination.[146] *Batson* requires trial judges—most of whom are popularly elected—to assess the district attorney's reasons for excluding minority persons in order to determine whether the prosecutor intended to discriminate.[147] Many judges are former prosecutors who may have hired the district attorneys appearing before them. Even if the judge is not personally close to the prosecutor, he or she may be dependent upon the prosecutor's support in the election to remain in office.[148] Thus, in the many jurisdictions where judges are elected, it may be politically impossible and personally difficult for the judge to reject a reason proffered by the prosecutor for striking a minority juror. Courts routinely uphold convictions and death sentences even where a grossly disproportionate number of African-Americans have been excluded from jury service by the prosecutor's peremptory jury strikes.[149]

Racial diversity on juries makes a difference in capital trials. Juries selected through discriminatory practices often bring to the jury box, either consciously or subconsciously, "racial stereotypes and assumptions" that influence them "in the direction of findings of black culpability and white victimization, . . . black immorality and white virtue, . . . blacks as social problems and whites as valued citizens."[150] Experience has taught that the death penalty is much more likely to be imposed in cases tried to all-white juries than in cases tried to more racially diverse juries.[151] Decisions made by all-white juries do not receive the respect of other racial groups that were denied participation. On the other hand, more diverse juries bring to their decision making a broader perspective gained through varied life experiences. An African-American member of the Georgia Supreme Court has observed that "[w]hen it comes to grappling with racial issues in the criminal justice system today, often white Americans find one reality while African-Americans see another."[152] The decisions of representative juries are seen as more legitimate and are accorded greater respect by all segments of the community.

3. THE IMPACT OF RACIAL PREJUDICE OF DEFENSE COUNSEL

In rejecting a challenge to the effectiveness of a defense lawyer who expressed racist sentiments in *Dobbs v. Zant*,[153] both the District Court and the Court of Appeals reasoned that because the defense lawyer did not decide the sentence, the claim should be rejected.[154] But there are numerous other ways in which the racial prejudice of defense counsel may affect a sentencing decision.

A lawyer defending the accused in a capital case has the obligation to investigate the life and background of the client in order to introduce mitigating evidence.[155] To fulfill this constitutional and ethical obligation, a lawyer must be comfortable working with the client, the client's family, and the client's friends. If the appointed lawyer regards the client, his family, or his friends in a demeaning way, the lawyer cannot possibly obtain and present the needed information and fulfill the role of advocate for the client's life. In addition, the defendant who is assigned a lawyer who shares the racial prejudices of the jurors, judge, and prosecutor is left without an advocate to expose and challenge such biases.

For example, a federal district court in Alabama described the representation provided to an African-American woman whose court-appointed lawyers had assumed she would not be sentenced to death for the "shothouse killing" of another black woman:

> Petitioner's counsel did not prepare for the sentencing hearing. . . .
> Roughly one hour after her conviction, petitioner and her counsel appeared before the jury again for the sentencing hearing. [Counsel] testified at the habeas hearing that he told the judge the [capital murder] verdict was so shocking to him that he was not prepared to go forward with sentencing.

Between the time of petitioner's indictment and sentencing, her lawyers did no work on the sentencing aspects of her case. . . .

No social history of petitioner was undertaken prior to either of the sentencing hearings [one before the jury and the second before a judge]. No family members or friends were contacted and informed of either the sentencing hearing before the jury or the trial judge. Therefore, no evidence of mitigation was adduced. . . .

. . . At the onset of petitioner's trial, when they clearly should have challenged the prosecutor's intentional and racially-motivated utilization of peremptory challenge to exclude all blacks from the jury chosen to try their black client, petitioner's counsel inexplicably failed to do so.[156]

One reason for the inadequate representation that Melvin Wade received before being sentenced to death by a California jury may have been the racial attitudes of his attorney. The attorney, who used racial slurs to refer to African-Americans, including Wade, failed to adequately present evidence of Wade's abuse as a child. The attorney also gave harmful closing arguments, including a penalty phase argument that asked the jury to impose the death sentence on his client. Kim Taylor, an associate professor at Stanford University Law School and former director of the Public Defender Service for the District of Columbia, described the relationship between counsel's racial attitudes and his performance as follows:

From the evidence before me, it seems clear that race played a significant and insidious role in Mr. Wade's trial. . . . Mr. Wade was represented by a man who viewed blacks with contempt, and this evidence is supported by the manner in which that attorney conducted himself at trial. Trial counsel failed to take any steps to impeach the state's injection of racial stereotyping and race-based misinformation into the case . . . and counsel comported himself in his argument to the jury in a manner as to convey his raced-based contempt.[157]

Such performances by defense counsel make it impossible for jurors to perform their constitutional obligation to impose a sentence based on "a reasoned moral response to the defendant's background, character, and crime."[158] Nor can courts discharge their responsibility to protect the constitutional rights of the accused, including the right to a trial not infected by racial discrimination, when court-appointed lawyers fail to raise issues of discrimination out of ignorance or indifference.

C. Disparities in Imposition of Death Sentences in the State Courts

Sentencing patterns confirm that racial prejudice plays a role in imposition of the death penalty. Although African-Americans make up only 12 percent of the population of the United States, they have been the victims in about half of the homicides in this country.[159] In some states in the South, where capital punishment is often imposed, African-Americans are the victims of more than 60 percent of the murders, yet 85 percent of the cases in which the death penalty has been carried out have involved white victims.[160]

In Georgia, for example, although African-Americans were the victims of 63.5 percent of the murders between 1976 and 1980, 82 percent of the cases in which death was imposed during that period involved murders of whites.[161] Professor David Baldus and his associates conducted two studies of the influence of race in the application of the death penalty, examining more than 2,000 murder cases that occurred in Georgia during the 1970s.[162] They found that prosecutors are more likely to seek the death penalty where the victim is white and that juries are more likely to impose the death penalty in such cases.[163] Defendants charged with murders of white persons received the death penalty in 11 percent of the cases; defendants charged with murders of blacks received the death penalty in only 1 percent of the cases.[164] Defendants charged with killing white victims were 4.3 times more likely to receive a death sentence than defendants charged with killing blacks.[165]

By July 1, 2005, 972 people had been executed since the Supreme Court's decision in 1976 allowing the resumption of capital punishment.[166] Three hundred and twenty seven were African-Americans.[167] In 80 percent of the cases, the victims were white.[168] Twenty-three of the thirty-six people under federal death sentences in 2005 were black.[169] Half of the thirty-two people executed in Alabama between 1976 and July 1, 2005, were African-American, and twenty-six of the victims in those cases were white.[170] The General Accounting Office summarized its analysis of twenty-eight studies of the death penalty as follows:

> In 82 percent of the studies, race of the victim was found to influence the likelihood of being charged with capital murder or receiving the death

penalty, i.e., those who murdered whites were found to be more likely to be sentenced to death than those who murdered blacks. This finding was remarkably consistent across data sets, states, data collection methods, and analytic techniques.[171]

The United States Supreme Court permitted such racial disparities in the imposition of the death penalty in *McCleskey v. Kemp*.[172] By a 5–4 vote, the Court allowed Georgia to carry out its death penalty law despite racial disparities that would not be officially tolerated in any other area of the law. The Court rejected challenges based on equal protection and the Eighth Amendment's cruel and unusual clause.[173] The Court found that the studies established "at most . . . a discrepancy that appears to correlate with race,"[174] and declined "to assume that that which is unexplained is invidious,"[175] thus holding the disparities insufficient even to raise a prima facie case of racial discrimination. The Court also expressed its concern that "McCleskey's claim, taken to its logical conclusion, throws into serious question the principles that underlie our entire criminal justice system."[176] Justice Brennan, in dissent, characterized this concern as "a fear of too much justice."[177]

The Court's fear of too much justice may result in no justice at all. The decision in *McCleskey* has been employed by lower federal and state courts to avoid dealing with issues of racial discrimination. Its crippling standard of proof (discussed more fully in part IV.C.), is so formidable that many courts have denied even a hearing on gross racial disparities.[178] Such an unwillingness to confront racial issues allows discrimination to go unchecked.

D. Disparities in Federal Death Prosecutions

The federal government, in pursuing death sentences authorized by the Anti-Drug Abuse Act of 1988,[179] has an even worse record of discrimination than the states. The act authorizes the death penalty for murders committed by "kingpins" involved in drug trafficking "enterprises."[180] Federal prosecutors are given wide discretion in deciding whether to seek the death penalty. One congressional committee observed: "The drug trafficking 'enterprise' can consist of as few as five individuals, and even a low-ranking 'foot soldier' in the organization can be charged with the death penalty if involved in a killing."[181]

Although three-fourths of those convicted of participating in a drug enterprise under the general provisions of 21 U.S.C. section 848 are white,[182] the death penalty provisions of the act have been used almost exclusively against minorities. Twenty-three of the thirty-six people on the federal death row in 2005 were members of minority groups.[183] Nevertheless, in 1994, Congress provided the death penalty for more than fifty additional crimes and refused to enact the Racial Justice Act.[184]

Those accused of federal capital crimes are supposedly protected from racial discrimination by the requirements that juries be instructed not to discriminate and that all jurors sign certificates guaranteeing they did not do so.[185] But this provision is hardly a protection against racial discrimination. By the time the jury is selected, racial prejudice may have already influenced the prosecutor's decisions to seek the death penalty, to refuse a plea bargain for a noncapital sentence, and to strike minority jurors. Moreover, the most pernicious racial discrimination that occurs today is that perpetrated by those who have the sophistication not to admit their biases. Persons who live in racially exclusive neighborhoods, are members of racially exclusive social organizations, send their children to segregation academies, and refuse to rent to black citizens may be more than happy to listen to jury instructions and sign the certificate of nondiscrimination before sending some black person off to his death. Of course, many may not even be aware of their unconscious racism.

E. Failure to Pass the Racial Justice Act

Despite the pronounced racial disparities in the infliction of the death penalty in both state and federal capital cases, Congress refused to include the Racial Justice Act as part of the crime bill in 1994, just as it refused to enact the Racial Justice Act in previous years.[186] The Racial Justice Act was a modest proposal that would have required courts to hold hearings on racial disparities in the imposition of the death penalty and look behind the disparities to ascertain whether they were related to race or some other factor.[187]

It is not unreasonable to require publicly elected prosecutors to justify racial disparities in capital prosecutions. If there is an underrepresentation of black citizens in a jury pool, jury commissioners are required to explain the disparity.[188] A prosecutor who strikes a disproportionate number of black citizens in selecting a jury is required to rebut the inference of discrimination by showing race-neutral reasons for his or her strikes.[189] If there are valid, race-neutral explanations for the disparities in capital prosecutions, they should be presented to the courts and the public. Prosecutors, like other public officials, should be accountable for their actions. The bases for critical decisions about whether to seek the death penalty and whether to agree to a sentence less than death in exchange for a guilty plea should not be shrouded in secrecy but should be openly set out, defended, and evaluated.

The likelihood is not that it would be too difficult for prosecutors to rebut the inference of discrimination but that it would be too easy. The task of rebutting an inference of racial discrimination under *Batson* has proven to be remarkably easy for prosecutors, even when they have used all of their jury strikes against minorities.[190] Nevertheless, the Racial Justice Act presented the threat of too much justice to the United States Senate and was defeated.

It is not surprising that Congress failed to pass the Racial Justice Act. Congress steadfastly refused to pass an antilynching law when African-Americans and other minorities were being lynched.[191] Instead, the federal government put much of its law enforcement efforts into pursuing moonshiners. Today, the federal government commits ample resources for questionable and expensive efforts to demonstrate it is "tough on crime": the war on drugs, the pursuit of federal death sentences for many crimes that could be prosecuted in the state courts, and the housing of ever-increasing numbers of people in federal prisons for longer periods of time. But few resources are devoted to the constitutional commitment of equality for racial minorities and the poor.

The United States Department of Justice, which might be expected to be concerned about racial discrimination in the courts and its impact on public confidence in the courts, has been one of the worst offenders in the discriminatory use of the death penalty. There is no large or powerful constituency concerned about racial discrimination in capital cases. Thus, there is no reason to expect solutions or even leadership from the executive or legislative branches of the federal government with regard to the racial discrimination in capital cases.

IV. The Avoidance, Denial, and Tolerance of Racial Discrimination by the Courts

Despite extraordinary competition among politicians to be tough on crime, prosecutors and the judicial system remain remarkably soft on the crime of racial discrimination. Those who discriminate are seldom disciplined or punished. Appellate courts, which normally publish long opinions on minor issues, often do not even mention the extraordinary racial discrimination that comes before them, finding ways to dispose of cases on other grounds. And when racial discrimination is recognized, the remedies are often woefully inadequate.

A. The Crime That Goes Unpunished

Jury officials in Alabama, in an attempt to defeat a challenge to the exclusion of black citizens from jury service in 1933, forged the names of six black citizens on the jury rolls.[192] The local trial judge rejected the assertion of fraud, saying he "would not be authorized to presume that somebody had committed a crime" or had been "unfaithful to their duties and allowed the books to be tampered with."[193] The United States Supreme Court generously observed that "the evidence did not justify that conclusion."[194] Although the case was reversed, no action was taken against those responsible for the forgery.[195]

In 1988, the Supreme Court found that a Georgia prosecutor instructed jury commissioners to underrepresent African-Americans in jury pools in such a way as to avoid detection and defeat a prima facie case of discrimination.[196] No action was taken against the prosecutor, and he remained in office until 1994, when he resigned while under investigation for sexual harassment.[197]

In Columbus, Muscogee County, Georgia, black citizens were excluded for years and then underrepresented in the jury pools. In 1966, the Fifth Circuit Court of Appeals held that this discrimination violated the Constitution.[198] In 1972, the Supreme Court reached the same conclusion in another case from the county, and three Justices even went so far as to point out that the way in which juries were being selected in the county violated 18 U.S.C. section 243, which makes it a criminal offense to exclude persons from jury service on the basis of race.[199]

Despite these court decisions, the unconstitutional, systematic underrepresentation continued throughout the 1970s. It was made possible in part because one lawyer, appointed by white judges in Columbus to represent poor defendants, would not, as a matter of "policy," file challenges to the underrepresentation of blacks in the jury pool for fear of incurring hostility from the community.[200] As a result, at the capital trial of a black man in Columbus, Georgia in 1977—eleven years after the Fifth Circuit decision and five years after the Supreme Court warned that the exclusion of black citizens violated federal criminal statutes—there were only 8 black citizens in a venire of 160 persons.[201] A venire that fairly represented the community would have included 50 black citizens. That case was tried by an all-white jury.[202] The death penalty was imposed.[203]

Some of those who were sentenced to death in Columbus by juries chosen in defiance of the Supreme Court's decision requiring an end to discrimination have been executed. Yet those who defied the federal courts and the Constitution were never prosecuted or disciplined. Some preside as judges in the local courts there.

It simply cannot be said that courts are engaging in "unceasing efforts" to eliminate racial discrimination from the criminal justice system[204] when prosecutors can rig juries on the basis of race with impunity, when decisions from the Supreme Court and the United States Courts of Appeals regarding discrimination in jury selection can be ignored for years with impunity, and a prosecutor may remain in office and death sentences are carried out even though juries are selected pursuant to the prosecutor's practice of striking as many African-Americans as possible. Judicial tolerance of such discrimination sends the unmistakable message that the "war on crime" need not be fought according to the Constitution, and racial discrimination will be tolerated when it is perceived as necessary to obtain convictions and death sentences.

B. Avoiding Issues Involving Race

Despite the racial discrimination that has been a major aspect of the death penalty throughout American history, the Supreme Court and lower federal and state courts have been reluctant to face racial issues presented by capital cases. The courts have been in a state of denial instead of confronting and dealing with the difficult and sensitive issue of race.

After declaring racially discriminatory jury selection practices in one Georgia county unconstitutional in 1953,[205] the United States Supreme Court remanded to the Georgia Supreme Court a capital case in which the jury had been selected by the same illegal means in the same county.[206] However, when the Georgia Supreme Court refused to reconsider its previous holding that the issue had been waived,[207] the United States Supreme Court backed down, denied certiorari, and allowed the execution to be carried out.[208] It appears that the Court, already encountering resistance to its decision in *Brown v. Board of Education*,[209] was anxious to avoid a confrontation with southern state courts over racial discrimination in the criminal courts.[210]

More than ten years later, the United States Supreme Court appeared willing to review the role of racial prejudice in capital cases when it granted certiorari in *Maxwell v. Bishop*,[211] a case in which the Eighth Circuit had rejected a challenge based upon the pronounced disparity in the number of African-Americans sentenced to death for rape in Arkansas and other parts of the South.[212] However, after twice hearing oral argument devoted mostly to the issue of racial discrimination, the Court vacated the death sentence and remanded the case, based upon a jury-qualification issue that had not even been raised in the Court of Appeals.[213]

Although the specter of race discrimination was acknowledged by Justices in both the majority and the dissent in *Furman v. Georgia*,[214] only Justice Marshall discussed racial discrimination at length.[215] Justice Stewart found it unnecessary to decide the issue, while acknowledging that "if any basis can be discerned for the selection of these few to be sentenced to die, it is the constitutionally impermissibly basis of race."[216]

Despite the extraordinary history of discrimination with regard to the infliction of the death penalty upon African- Americans for the rape of white women,[217] the Court did not even mention race in striking down the death penalty for the crime of rape in *Coker v. Georgia*.[218]

It is impossible to know how many courts have avoided the issue of race in deciding capital cases. The Georgia Supreme Court frequently discusses every issue presented to it, even those that need not be addressed for a decision,[219] but in holding that a trial judge should be recused from a case because of his involvement in opposing a motion to disqualify him, the court never mentioned the motion was based on the judge's long history of racial discrimination.[220] Evidence presented in the trial court established that the judge regularly appointed jury commissions that underrepresented African-Americans, tolerated gross underrepresentation of blacks in the grand and trial juries, mistreated black attorneys in court, used racial slurs, and practiced discrimination in his personal life.[221]

The Missouri Supreme Court summarily reversed two capital cases without mentioning evidence that prosecutors in Kansas City used racial slurs to refer to black citizens, systematically excluded black citizens from juries, and refused to plea bargain with African-Americans charged with murders of whites while offering plea bargains in all other potential capital cases, including a case of murderers who killed four generations of African-Americans.[222]

The Alabama Court of Criminal Appeals similarly failed to acknowledge or discuss disturbing evidence of racial discrimination in setting aside a capital conviction and sentence.[223] The court did not mention that the prosecutor had used twenty-six peremptory jury strikes against African-Americans after dividing potential jurors into four lists under the headings "strong," "medium," "weak," and "black" or that the trial court had held there was no discrimination.[224]

Apparently, many courts believe it is best to avoid the sensitive issue of race. Why else did they not denounce these outrageous examples of racial discrimination in the strongest terms? Although the failure of the appellate courts to mention the race issues in these cases may have been coincidence, it is more likely that courts are defensive about the racial discrimination that takes place in what is supposed to be a system of equal justice. Their opinions leave those who read them without any hint that the cases involved racial discrimination and thus provide trial courts with no guidance in considering those issues. In addition, lawyers reading appellate opinions are less likely to realize the importance of race and search out and challenge discrimination. The failure of the courts to discuss and condemn racial discrimination only fosters more discrimination.

C. Unreasonable Burdens of Proof, Impossible Standards, and Inadequate Remedies

In 1965, in the midst of the Warren Court decisions applying the Bill of Rights to state criminal justice systems, the Court upheld a capital conviction in *Swain v. Alabama*,[225] despite evidence that due to peremptory challenges, no black person had ever served on a jury in either a criminal or civil case in Talladega County, Alabama, where African-Americans constituted 26 percent of the population. While reiterating its prior pronouncements that "a State's purposeful or deliberate denial to Negroes on account of race of participation as jurors in the administration of justice violates the Equal Protection Clause,"[226] the Court set an almost impossible burden of proof, holding that to establish discrimination by a prosecutor in the use of peremptory strikes, a defendant must prove the prosecutor engaged in a practice of striking black citizens "in case after case, whatever the circumstances, whatever the crime and whoever the defendant or the victim may be . . . with the result that no Negroes ever serve on petit juries."[227] The decision, disapproving of racial discrimination but allowing it to continue by setting a virtually impossible standard of proof, was subject to "almost universal and often scathing criticism,"[228] but it remained the law for twenty years before the standard was changed in *Batson v. Kentucky.*[229]

The Supreme Court has created an equally difficult barrier to sustaining claims of racial discrimination in the infliction of the death penalty. In *McCleskey v. Kemp,*[230] the Court accepted the racial disparities in the imposition of the death penalty as "an inevitable part of our criminal justice system."[231] The Court held that to prevail under the Equal Protection Clause the defendant must present "exceptionally clear proof"[232] that "the decision makers in his case acted with discriminatory purpose."[233] As in *Swain,* the Court found the evidence insufficient to overcome a presumption of propriety with regard to the exercise of discretion by prosecutors.[234] But while requiring exceptionally clear proof of discrimination, the Court made it almost impossible to obtain proof, concluding that "the policy considerations behind a prosecutor's traditionally 'wide discretion' suggest the impropriety of our requiring prosecutors to defend their decisions to seek death penalties, 'often years after they are made.' "[235]

In rejecting McCleskey's claim under the Eighth Amendment, the Court, while acknowledging the risk of racial prejudice influencing the capital sentencing decision,[236] held that evidence that blacks who kill whites are sentenced to death at nearly twenty-two times the rate of blacks who kill blacks[237] did not "demonstrate a constitutionally significant risk of racial bias affecting the Georgia capital sentencing process."[238] Thus, the Court held the risk of racial discrimination was not "constitutionally unacceptable" under the Eighth Amendment.[239]

This decision is more consistent with the Court's decisions in *Swain, Dred Scott v. Sandford,*[240] and *Plessy v. Ferguson*[241] than its more recent decisions recognizing racial discrimination in other areas of life. The Court could have concluded that racial disparities were "inevitable" or not "constitutionally unacceptable" in education, housing, employment, or so many other areas of life where minorities have experienced racial discrimination. Justice Powell, who authored the majority's opinion in the 5–4 decision in *McCleskey,* expressed his regret, after leaving the Court, at his vote in the case.[242]

Other courts have followed the Supreme Court's head-in-the-sand approach. The Florida Supreme Court, by a 4–3 vote, refused to require a

hearing on racial disparities in the infliction of the death penalty.[243] The
Georgia Supreme Court upheld the denial of a hearing on racial discrimination in a capital prosecution against an African-American accused of
the murder of a white person in Cobb County, a county that has a long
history of racial discrimination.[244] Some criminal defense lawyers in Cobb
County have stated that they have never had the opportunity to accept or
strike an African-American juror due to the regular practice of the district
attorney's office of striking all the African-Americans.[245] To deny even a
hearing on racial discrimination in Cobb County is simply to run from
the truth instead of confronting it.[246]

The willingness of courts to tolerate racial discrimination in order to
carry out the death penalty has a corrupting effect not just on capital cases
but throughout the criminal justice system. For example, the Georgia
Supreme Court, under immense political pressure from Georgia's attorney
general and district attorneys, and from dire warnings that the death
penalty was in danger, did a complete about-face in only thirteen days in a
case regarding gross racial disparities in sentencing for drug offenses.[247]
The Georgia Supreme Court first held by a 4–3 vote that a prima facie case
of racial discrimination was established by evidence that 98.4 percent of
those serving life sentences for certain narcotics offenses were black.[248] All
of the discretion in pursuing life sentences for the offenses was entrusted
to district attorneys.[249] Statistics from the Georgia Department of Corrections established that less than 1 percent of the whites eligible for life sentence for narcotics offenses—just one in 168—received it, while 16.6
percent of African-Americans—202 of 1,219—received it.[250]

The attorney general of Georgia joined by all forty-six district attorneys
in the state—all of whom at the time were white—filed a petition for
rehearing with the court, arguing that the court's decision took a "substantial step toward invalidating" the state's death penalty law and would "par-
alyze the criminal justice system."[251] In response, one member of the court
switched his vote, and the court adopted the position of what had previously been the dissent, that the proper governing standard was *McCleskey
v. Kemp* and, therefore, no prima facie case had been established.[252] The
only way a more compelling showing could have been made would have
been if 100 percent of those serving life sentences for a second narcotics
offense were black, instead of just 98.4 percent. Yet the Georgia Supreme
Court chose to erect an impossible standard of proof based on its interpretation of *McCleskey* in order to avoid even a hearing on the reasons for
the remarkable racial disparities in sentencing for narcotics offenses.

The United States Supreme Court based its decision in *McCleskey* in part on the "safeguards designed to minimize racial bias in the process."[253] Those safeguards include the right to a representative jury, the prohibition of peremptory challenges by prosecutors on the basis of race, and the right in cases involving interracial crimes to question potential jurors about racial bias.[254] But in many cases, such safeguards are either nonexistent or inadequate.

The stages of the process that allow the greatest room for racial prejudice are the prosecutorial decision to seek the death penalty and the plea bargaining process. There are no effective safeguards to prevent discrimination at either of those stages. As previously noted, many courts that rely on *McCleskey* do not even allow hearings on the influence of race at those critical stages. Minorities remain woefully underrepresented in decision-making positions in the criminal justice system. Courts have been increasingly hostile to challenges to the exclusion of minorities from state judicial systems, even when it is apparent that the minority vote has been diluted in order to preserve a primarily white judiciary.[255]

The "safeguards" relied upon by the Court in *McCleskey* are also inadequate because issues of discrimination usually focus on the intent of the decision maker, which is exceptionally difficult to prove, instead of the results of his or her actions. Nor do courts consider unconscious or subtle racial biases of decision makers. As previously discussed, courts allow prosecutors to use even 100 percent of their peremptory jury strikes based on assertions of "race neutral" reasons.[256] The Supreme Court in *McCleskey* found that racial disparities did not sufficiently prove racial discrimination, but the Court failed to examine the role that racial stereotypes and other attitudes may have played in the results.[257]

Although the Supreme Court in *Turner v. Murray*[258] acknowledged the potential impact that the unconscious racism of jurors might have on the capital sentencing decision,[259] *Turner* is limited to interracial crimes.[260] Thus, an accused who is charged with the murder of a member of his own race is not entitled to ask prospective jurors about their racial attitudes. Even in interracial crimes, trial courts may limit voir dire so that it does not disclose subtle racial attitudes that may come into play.[261]

The failure of courts to provide poor defendants with adequate legal representation may leave the accused without any ability to utilize what limited protections are available. Those accused of crimes in Jefferson County, Georgia, were tried for years before patently unconstitutional juries because local lawyers appointed by local judges failed to challenge the severe underrepresentation of African-Americans in the jury pools. It was shown in one capital case in which the accused was represented by pro bono lawyers from outside the judicial circuit that although African-Americans made up 54.5 percent of the population of the county, they made up only 21.6 percent of the jury pool, an underrepresentation of over 50 percent.[262] However, when this evidence was presented in a post-conviction challenge to the conviction and sentence, the federal courts held that the defendant was barred from raising the issue because no challenge had been made by the local court-appointed lawyer prior to trial.[263] The defendant had the misfortune of being represented—over his protests —by a court-appointed lawyer who, when later asked to name the criminal law decisions from any court with which he was familiar, could name only two: *Miranda* and *Dred Scott.*[264]

In Columbus, Georgia, even after the United States Supreme Court declared that jury officials were unconstitutionally and illegally excluding African-Americans from jury service, the practice continued because of the "policy" of the local court-appointed indigent defender of not challenging racial discrimination for fear of incurring hostility from the community.[265] These are not isolated examples regarding a single case. The failure of lawyers to challenge clearly unconstitutional racial discrimination in the composition of jury pools affected every criminal case in these judicial circuits over a span of decades.

In the case of an African-American tried before an all-white jury after the prosecutor struck four black jurors, the United States Court of Appeals for the Eighth Circuit refused to review a prosecutor's emphasis on the difference in race between the "attractive" white victim and "this black man"[266] because no objection had been made at the time of the argument.[267]

The right to question jurors about race in an interracial crime was utilized as follows by defense counsel in an Alabama case tried in 1993:

> *Mr. Nelson* [Defense counsel]: I have just a couple of more questions and I promise I will quit. We are talking about this case and not some fictional case. In this case this is a black man and Mrs. Hargrove's son was a young white man. I will ask you this and it's not—it's like Bob said. I'm not asking you this to embarrass you, but do any of you belong to any organizations such as the Klan or have close family members that belong to the Klan or an organization known as the Skinheads, Na[ ]zi groups or anything like that who believe that a race is inferior or a religion is inferior? Do any of you belong to any of those things? (No response)

Mr. Nelson: Do any of you believe any of that stuff? Is there anybody that believes in that stuff on this jury?

Juror Bartlett: The Klan has a lot of stuff that they stand for that is good.

Mr. Nelson: I'm sorry, Mr. Bartlett?

Juror Bartlett: The Klan has lot of things they stand for that is good. I have read some of their literature.

Mr. Nelson: You believe in some of the doctrine that the Klan has in their literature?

Juror Bartlett: I guess it would be called doctrine. I don't know.

Mr. Nelson: Would you tell me what it is that you believe in that you have read?

Juror Bartlett: Well, there are just certain things about the way things are going, the way the law is going about a lot of this stuff.

Mr. Nelson: Let me ask you this. The fact that this is a black man over here, do you think you could be fair to him even if—

Juror Bartlett: Yeah.

Mr. Nelson: Even if the man that was killed was a young white man?

Juror Bartlett: I would be as fair to him as anybody else.[268]

No further questions were asked of juror Bartlett or any other member of the panel regarding the issue of race.[269] Such a voir dire is hardly adequate to reveal the "[m]ore subtle, less consciously held racial attitudes" that the Supreme Court described in *Turner v. Murray*.[270]

Despite the limitations of *Batson v. Kentucky* and *Turner v. Murray* in preventing racial discrimination, the Court in *McCleskey* indulged in the remarkable presumption that the mere existence of these limited procedural safeguards in jury selection were sufficient to prevent racial discrimination in every capital case. At the same time, the Court discounted evidence that established that in reality the race of the victim and the race of the defendant actually influenced the sentence in *McCleskey* and other cases despite the safeguards.

McCleskey v. Kemp is a manifestation of indifference on the part of the Court to secure justice for racial minorities in cases in which there is a long history of discrimination, and there is every indication that racial prejudice influences the vast discretion exercised in making the highly charged, emotional decisions about who is to die.

V. Conclusion

Many public officials, including judges, continue to peddle the notion that we may ignore more than two centuries of history in race relations as easily as we may ignore yesterday's weather. They readily admit racial discrimination up until 1964, or 1972, or even until yesterday, but argue that it suddenly, magically ended. Unfortunately, this does not square with the reality of race relations in the United States today. As Justice William Brennan observed in his dissent in *McCleskey v. Kemp,*

[I]t has been scarcely a generation since this Court's first decision striking down racial segregation, and barely two decades since the legislative prohibition of racial discrimination in major domains of national life. These have been honorable steps, but we cannot pretend that in three decades we have completely escaped the grip of a historical legacy spanning centuries. . . . [W]e remain imprisoned by the past as long as we deny its influence on the present.[271]

The courts and legislatures have made a tragic mistake by substituting a notion of what criminal justice should be for what it is. Citizens, judges, the bar, and the media would like to believe we have a system that equally and fairly dispenses justice. But neither legal presumptions nor legal fictions will make it so. As Justice Thurgood Marshall said in another context, "[C]onstitutionalizing [the] wishful thinking" that "racial discrimination is largely a phenomenon of the past" does a "grave disservice . . . to those victims of past and present racial discrimination."[272]

The criminal justice systems in many parts of the country have suffered from years of neglect, inadequate funding, and other problems. Often they have been entrusted to persons with neither the ability nor the inclination to carry out their high functions. Members of racial minorities continue to be underrepresented in all positions in the criminal justice system. It should not surprise anyone that the problems of racial exclusion and racial discrimination are greater in that system than in other parts of our society.

The price paid for the denial of racial discrimination by courts, legislatures, and the bar is considerable. Courts cannot deliver justice when they tolerate racial prejudice and racial exclusion. Courts lose respect and credibility when they refuse to acknowledge and remedy racial discrimination that is apparent to everyone else. Advancing the "war on crime" is not justification for ignoring racial discrimination in the court system. Courts of vengeance are not courts of justice.

There is debate over whether racial discrimination in the infliction of the death penalty can be detected and remedied. Some think racial discrimination is inevitable and impossible to prevent; others think the influence of race can be eliminated.[273] This question must be answered, not avoided. If racial discrimination cannot be prevented, the death penalty should not be carried out.[274] If discrimination can be eliminated, then it should be the highest priority of the courts. But to pretend it does not exist, to deny a remedy, to deny even a hearing, is to give up on achieving the goal of equal justice under law. Tragically, that is what the state and federal courts have done.

In *McCleskey v. Kemp*, the Supreme Court asserted that evidence of racial discrimination should be taken to the legislatures.[275] But legislators respond to powerful interests. The poor person accused of a crime has no political action committee, no lobby, and often no effective advocate even in the court where his life is at stake. The crime debate in the United States has become increasingly demagogic and irresponsible, based more on anger than reason. There is little basis for hope in the legislatures.

The constitutional buck of equal protection under law stops with the Supreme Court and with judges on lower courts throughout the land who have taken oaths to uphold the Constitution and the Bill of Rights even against the passions of the moment and the prejudices that have endured for centuries. Decisions tolerating racial discrimination must be assailed until, like *Swain v. Alabama*, they are rejected and replaced with standards that acknowledge and respond to the influence of racial prejudice in the criminal courts in general and in capital cases in particular.[276]

NOTES

1. Death Row U.S.A., NAACP Legal Def. & Educ. Fund, Inc., at 1 (Summer 2005) (reporting that there were 3,415 persons under sentence of death as of July 1, 2005).

2. Id. at 1, 9 (reporting that more than half of those under death sentence are African-American, Latino, Native American, or Asian, and that in 80 percent of the cases in which executions have been carried out, the victims were white).

3. See, e.g., Dorothy Otnow Lewis et al., Psychiatric, Neurological and Psychoeducational Characteristics of 15 Death Row Inmates in the United States, 145

Am. Jur. Psy. 838 (1986). The author has observed the presence of these factors, virtually without exception, in capital cases he has handled and supervised, as well as in cases in which he has consulted other lawyers.

4. Furman v. Georgia, 408 U.S. 238 (1972).

5. Gregg v. Georgia, 428 U.S. 153 (1976); Proffitt v. Florida, 428 U.S. 242 (1976); Jurek v. Texas, 428 U.S. 262 (1976).

6. For a discussion of the impact of poverty on the imposition of the death penalty due to the quality of representation provided by court-appointed counsel, see Stephen B. Bright, Counsel for the Poor: The Death Sentence Not for the Worst Crime but for the Worst Lawyer, 103 Yale L.J. 1835 (1994).

7. Bureau of Justice Statistics, U.S. Dep't of Justice, Sourcebook of Criminal Justice Statistics 1993, at 384, table 3.128 (Kathleen Maguire & Ann L. Pastore eds., 1993).

8. See supra note 2.

9. General Accounting Office, Death Penalty Sentencing: Research Indicates Pattern of Racial Disparities 5 (Feb. 1990).

10. By the start of 2001, 61 persons sentenced to death in Harris County, Texas, had been executed, more than in any state except Texas and Virginia. Harris County accounted for 150 persons on the Texas death row, a larger number than the death rows of most states. Mike Tolson, A Deadly Distinction, Houston Chronicle, Feb. 5, 2001.

11. Bryan Denson, Death Penalty: Equal Justice? Houston Post, Oct. 16, 1994, at A1.

12. Death Row U.S.A., supra note 1, at 29 (stating there are 388 people on Florida's death row).

13. Report and Recommendation of the Florida Supreme Court Racial and Ethnic Bias Study Commission, at xvi (Dec. 11, 1991). See also Michael L. Radelet & Glenn L. Pierce, Choosing Those Who Will Die: Race and the Death Penalty in Florida, 43 U. Fla. L. Rev. 1 (1991); Foster v. State, 614 So. 2d 455 (Fla. 1992) (affirming refusal to hold hearing on claim of racial discrimination where evidence proffered showed prosecutors in Bay County State Attorney's office were four times more likely to charge first-degree murder in cases involving white victims than cases involving black victims; of such cases that went to trial, first degree murder convictions were 26 times more likely in cases with white victims; and even though blacks constituted 40% of the murder victims in Bay County between 1975 and 1987, all 17 death sentences that were imposed were for homicides involving white victims).

14. Staff Report by the Subcommittee on Civil and Constitutional Rights of the Committee of the Judiciary, U.S. House of Representatives, Racial Disparities in Federal Death Penalty Prosecutions 1988–1994, H.R. 458, 103d Cong. 2d Sess. at 2 (Mar. 1994) [hereinafter House Subcommittee, Racial Disparities in Federal Death Penalty Prosecutions].

15. In addition to the studies cited by the General Accounting Office in its report, supra note 9, see David C. Baldus et al., Equal Justice and the Death Penalty (1990); Samuel R. Gross & Robert Mauro, Death and Discrimination: Racial Disparities in Capital Sentencing (1989); Bob Levenson & Debbie Salamore, Prosecutors See Death Penalty in Black and White, Orlando Sentinel, May 24, 1992, at A1 (reporting that "[j]ustice . . . is not colorblind in Central Florida when it comes to the prosecution of first degree murder cases"); Jim Henderson and Jack Taylor, Killers of Dallas Blacks Escape the Death Penalty, Dallas Times Herald, Nov. 17, 1985, at 1 (accompanied by other stories and charts demonstrating the relationship between race and imposition of the death sentence); David Margolick, In the Land of Death Penalty, Accusations of Racial Bias, N.Y. Times, July 10, 1991, at A1 (describing racial disparities in the infliction of the death penalty in Georgia's Chattahoochee Judicial Circuit, which includes the city of Columbus); Paul Pinkham & Robin Lowenthal, The Color of Justice in Jacksonville: Killers of Blacks Get Off Easier than Killers of Whites, Florida Times-Union, Dec. 8, 1991, at D1. Thomas J. Keil & Gennaro F. Vito, Race and the Death Penalty in Kentucky Murder Trials: 1976–1991, paper presented to Academy of Criminal Justice Sciences, Chicago (1994) (finding that blacks accused of killing whites had a higher than average probability of being charged with a capital crime by the prosecutor and being sentenced to death by the jury).

16. There has been a particularly pronounced racial disparity in the infliction of the death penalty for rape of white victims by African-Americans. See Furman v. Georgia, 408 U.S. 238, 364 n.149 (1972) (Marshall, J., concurring); Maxwell v. Bishop, 398 F.2d 138, 145 (8th Cir. 1968), vacated, 398 U.S. 262 (1970).

17. Turner v. Murray, 476 U.S. 28, 35 (1976).

18. Id.

19. Id. See also United States v. Heller, 785 F.2d 1524, 1527 (11th Cir. 1986) (observing that an individual may harbor "certain negative stereotypes which, despite his protestations to the contrary, may well prevent him or her from making decisions solely on the facts and the law that our jury system requires.").

20. Turner, 476 U.S. at 35. The way in which such racial prejudice may come into play in decision making has been described in detail by many scholars. See, e.g., Peggy C. Davis, Law as Microaggression, 98 Yale L.J. 1559, 1571 (1989) (describing the tendency of people to make decisions based on "racial stereotypes and assumptions"); Sheri Lynn Johnson, Black Innocence and the White Jury, 83 Mich. L. Rev. 1611 (1985) (documenting tendency among whites to convict black defendants in instances where white defendants would be acquitted); Samuel H. Pillsbury, Emotional Justice: Moralizing the Passions of Criminal Punishment, 74 Cornell L. Rev. 655, 708 (1989) (describing the psychological tendency of predominantly white decision makers to sympathize more with whites than blacks); Gary Peller, Race Consciousness, 1990 Duke L.J. 758 (1990); Charles R. Lawrence, The ID, the Ego, and Equal Protection: Reckoning with Unconscious Racism, 39 Stan.

L. Rev. 317 (1987); Francis C. Dane & Lawrence S. Wrightsman, Effects of Defendants' and Victims' Characteristics on Jurors' Verdicts, in the Psychology of the Courtroom 104–06 (1982) (reporting that identification with a victim is particularly pronounced and results in the most severe sentences where the victim is of the same race, and the defendant is of a different race from that of the jurors).

21. Turner v. Murray, 476 U.S. 28, 35 (1976).

22. See e.g., Dobbs v. Zant, 720 F. Supp. 1566, 1577 (N.D. Ga. 1989) (describing that a court-appointed defense lawyer, after admitting his belief that blacks are less intelligent than whites and have inferior morals, characterized his client as "arrogant" and "uncooperative"), aff'd, 963 F.2d 1519 (11th Cir. 1991), remanded on other grounds, 113 S. Ct. 835 (1993).

23. See generally Bright, supra note 6.

24. See infra notes 200, 261–64, and accompanying text (describing the failure of court-appointed lawyers to challenge discrimination against African-Americans in composition of jury pools).

25. See Derrick A. Bell, Race, Racism and American Law (3d ed. 1992); A. Leon Higginbotham, In the Matter of Color: Race in the American Legal Process (1978).

26. See infra text accompanying notes 186–191. The Racial Justice Act was passed by the House of Representatives as part of the 1994 Crime Bill, but was rejected in the Senate version of the bill. It was not included in the Violent Crime Control and Law Enforcement Act of 1994, Pub. L. No. 103-322, 108 Stat. 1796 (1994), which was signed into law on September 14, 1994. 55 Crim. L. Rep. (BNA) 2305 (Aug. 31, 1994).

27. See, e.g., McCleskey v. Kemp, 481 U.S. 279, 309, 333 (1987) (describing "unceasing efforts" while finding that racial disparities in capital sentencing do not violate the Eighth or Fourteenth Amendments); Holland v. Illinois, 493 U.S. 474, 504 n.2, 511 (1990) (reiterating the "earnestness" of the Court's "commitment to racial justice" while holding that the prosecutorial use of peremptory strikes against African-Americans did not violate the Sixth Amendment's right to an impartial jury).

28. Stephen Reinhardt, Riots, Racism, and the Courts, quoted in Harper's Magazine, Aug. 1992, at 15, 16.

29. A. Leon Higginbotham, Jr., In the Matter of Color: Race in the American Legal Process 256 (1978).

30. Id.

31. Id. See also *McCleskey*, 481 U.S. at 329–32 (Brennan, J., dissenting).

32. These numbers come from the archives at Tuskegee University, where lynchings have been documented since 1882. Mark Curriden, The Legacy of Lynching, Atlanta J. & Const., Jan. 15, 1995, at M1.

33. Id.

34. Douglas L. Colbert, Challenging the Challenge: Thirteenth Amendment as a Prohibition Against the Racial Use of Peremptory Challenges, 76 Cornell L. Rev.

1, 80 (1990) (quoting Michael Belknap, Federal Law and Southern Order 22–26 (1987)).

35. Dan T. Carter, Scottsboro: A Tragedy of the American South 115 (rev. ed. 1992).

36. Colbert, supra note 34, at 80.

37. 287 U.S. 45 (1932).

38. For excellent accounts of the case of the "Scottsboro boys," see James Goodman, Stories of Scottsboro (1994); and Carter, supra note 35.

39. Carter, supra note 35, at 20–48.

40. Id. at 18–19, 22.

41. Id. at 20–48; Powell, 287 U.S. at 50.

42. Carter, supra note 35 at 104–16; Goodman, supra note 38 at 47–50, 297–98.

43. George C. Wright, Racial Violence in Kentucky, 1865–1940: Lynchings, Mob Rule, and "Legal Lynchings" 252 (1990).

44. Id. at 253. The editorial read as follows: "The fact, however, that Kentucky was saved the mortification of a lynching by an indignant multitude, bent upon avenging the innocent victim of the crime, is a matter for special congratulation." Id.

45. Id. Wright describes other legal lynchings in Kentucky. Id. at 251–305.

46. The Pace of Executions: Since 1976 . . . and Through History, N.Y. Times, Dec. 4, 1994, s 4, at 3. Georgia carried out 673 executions between 1900 and the end of 1994, the most of any state during this period. Id.

47. Prentice Palmer & Jim Galloway, Georgia Electric Chair Spans 5 Decades, Atlanta J., Dec. 15, 1983, at 15A. After adopting electrocution as a means of execution in 1924, Georgia put more people to death than any state and "set national records for executions over a 20-year period in the 1940s and 1950s." Id.

48. 408 U.S. 238 (1972).

49. The five Justices who made up the majority in Furman concluded that the death penalty was being imposed so discriminatorily, id. at 249–52 (Douglas, J., concurring), id. at 310 (Stewart, J., concurring), id. at 364–66 (Marshall, J., concurring), so arbitrarily, id. at 291–95 (Brennan, J., concurring), id. at 306 (Stewart, J., concurring), and so infrequently, id. at 311 (White, J., concurring), that any given death sentence was cruel and unusual. Justice Brennan also concluded that because "the deliberate extinguishment of human life by the State is uniquely degrading to human dignity," it is inconsistent with "the evolving standards of decency that mark the progress of a maturing society." Id. at 291, 270.

50. Gregg v. Georgia, 428 U.S. 153, 179–80 & n.23 (1976) (noting that at least thirty-five states passed death penalty statutes).

51. The Supreme Court upheld the statutes enacted by Florida, Georgia, and Texas: Proffitt v. Florida, 428 U.S. 242 (1976); Gregg v. Georgia, 428 U.S. 153 (1976); Jurek v. Texas, 428 U.S. 262 (1976). The Court struck down the statutes adopted by North Carolina and Louisiana: Woodson v. North Carolina, 428 U.S.

280 (1976); Roberts v. Louisiana, 428 U.S. 325 (1976). The first execution after the Supreme Court allowed the resumption of capital punishment was in 1977, when Gary Gilmore was killed by a firing squad in Utah. Jon Nordheimer, Gilmore Is Executed after Stay Is Upset; 'Let's Do It?' He Said, N.Y. Times, Jan. 18, 1977, at A1.

52. See, e.g., Ga. Code Ann. ss 16-5-1, 17-10-30 (Michie 1994); Fla. Stat. Ann. s 921.141 (West 1985 & Supp. 1994); Ala. Code s 13A-5-40 (1994). For a summary of capital offenses by state, see Bureau of Justice Statistics, Capital Punishment 1993 Table 1, at 5 (Dec. 1994). Under many capital statutes, the death penalty may also be imposed for the murder of a police or correctional officer, contract murders, murders related to drug offenses, and murders committed by persons with a previous conviction for a violent crime. Id.

53. Fla. Stat. Ann. s 921.141(5)(h) (West 1985 & Supp. 1994).

54. Ga. Code Ann. §17-10-30(b)(7) (Michie 1994).

55. The Supreme Court has observed that "[b]ecause of the range of discretion entrusted to a jury in a capital sentencing hearing, there is a unique opportunity for racial prejudice to operate." Turner v. Murray, 476 U.S. 28, 35 (1985). However, as will be discussed in Part IV, infra, the Court has refused to require procedures and remedies adequate to identify and cure the influence of race.

56. Blair v. Armontrout, 916 F.2d 1310, 1351 (8th Cir. 1990) (Heaney, J., concurring and dissenting).

57. Nipper v. Smith, 39 F.3d 1484, 1537–41 (11th Cir. 1994) (en banc); League of United Latin American Citizens, Counsel No. 434 v. Clements, 999 F.2d 831, 904–18 (5th Cir. 1993) (en banc) (King, J., dissenting), cert. denied, 114 S. Ct. 878 (1994). Ruth Marcus, Does Voting Rights Law Cover Judicial Elections? Wash. Post, Apr. 21, 1991, at A4.

58. Lawyers' Committee for Civil Rights Under Law, Answering the Call for a More Diverse Judiciary (2005) at 9 (only 5.9 percent of 11,344 judgeships in the United States); Mark Curriden, Racism Mars Justice in U.S. Panel Reports, Atlanta J. & Const., Aug. 11, 1991, at D1, D3 (observing that only 6 of Georgia's 134 Superior Court judges were African-American, and those 6 were in three judicial circuits); Associated Press, Second Black Alabama Supreme Court Justice Sworn In, Columbus (Ga.) Ledger-Enquirer, Nov. 2, 1993, at B2 (noting that there was only 1 African-American among Alabama's 17 appellate court judges, and only 12 blacks among the state's 255 circuit and district court judges).

59. Mark Curriden, Racism Mars Justice in U.S. Panel Reports, supra note 58, at D3.

60. Jesse Smith & Robert Johns, eds., Statistical Record of Black America 774–75 (3d ed. 1995) (after listing the number of African-Americans as judges, magistrates, and justices of the peace, showing no African-American for "other judicial officials" for Arkansas, Connecticut, Florida, Illinois, Indiana, Michigan, Oklahoma, South Carolina, and Texas).

61. American Bar Association Task Force on Minorities and the Justice System, Achieving Justice in a Diverse America at 15 (1992).

62. See, e.g., State v. Russell, 477 N.W.2d 886 (Minn. 1991) (finding equal protection violation due to more severe sentences imposed for possession of crack cocaine than for powdered cocaine where 96.6% of those charged with possession of crack cocaine are black and 79.6% of those charged with possession of powdered cocaine are white); Stephens v. State, No. S94A1854, 1995 WL 116292 (Ga. S. Ct. Mar. 17, 1995), withdrawn and superseded, Stephens v. State, 456 S.E.2d 560 (Ga. 1995) (stating that of 375 persons serving life sentences for a second conviction for sale or possession with intent to distribute certain narcotics, 98.4% are African-Americans). See, e.g., Samuel Myers, Jr., Racial Disparity in Sentencing: Can Sentencing Reforms Reduce Discrimination in Punishment? 64 U. Colo. L. Rev. 781 (1993); Gary Kleck, Racial Discrimination in Criminal Sentencing, 46 Am. Sociological Rev. 783 (1981); Dennis Cauchon, Sentences for Crack Called Racist, USA Today, May 26, 1993, at 1A; Curriden, supra note 58 at D1; Ruth Marcus, Racial Bias Widely Seen in Criminal Justice System, Wash. Post, May 12, 1992, at A4; Richard A. Berk & Alec Campbell, Preliminary Data on Race and Crack Charging Practices in Los Angeles, 6 Fed. Sent. R. 36 (1993); Douglas C. McDonald & Kenneth E. Carlson, Why Did Racial/Ethnic Sentencing Differences in Federal District Courts Grow Larger Under the Guidelines? 6 Fed. Sent. R. 223 (1994); Charles J. Ogletree, The Significance of Race in Federal Sentencing, 6 Fed. Sent. R. 229 (1994); Rhonda Cook, Sentence Disparities are the Rule in Ga., Atlanta J. & Const., Dec. 3, 1990, at A1; Tracy Thompson, Blacks Sent to Jail More Than Whites for Same Crimes, Atlanta J. & Const., Apr. 30, 1989, at 1A (with related stories and charts); Tracy Thompson, Justice in Toombs Circuit not Colorblind, Some Say, Atlanta J. & Const., Dec. 13, 1987, at 1A (three other articles appeared on the following days).

63. Dobbs v. Zant, 720 F. Supp. 1566, 1578 (N.D. Ga. 1989), aff'd, 963 F.2d 1403 (11th Cir. 1991), rev'd, 113 S. Ct. 835 (1993).

64. Id. at 1576.

65. Trial counsel testified "[t]here was uncertainty all the way up until the trial began as to whether or not I would represent him." Transcript of State Habeas Corpus Hearing of Sept. 28, 1977, at 55, included in Record on Appeal, Dobbs v. Zant, 963 F.2d 1403 (11th Cir. 1991), rev'd and remanded, 113 S. Ct. 835 (1993). Defense counsel testified before the federal court: "As a matter of fact, I didn't know for sure what he was going to be tried for." Transcript of trial at 85, included as part of the Record on Appeal in Dobbs, 963 F.2d 1403.

66. Record on Appeal to Georgia Supreme Court at 24, included in the Record on Appeal in Dobbs, 963 F.2d 1403.

67. Transcript of trial at 2, included in the Record on Appeal in Dobbs, 963 F.2d 1403.

68. Id. at 7.

69. Id. at 5.

70. Id. at 10.

71. Id. at 1577.

72. Any aspect of the life and background of the accused may be considered by the sentencer as a reason to impose a sentence less than death. Penry v. Lynaugh, 492 U.S. 302 (1989); Eddings v. Oklahoma, 455 U.S. 104, 110 (1982); Lockett v. Ohio, 438 U.S. 586, 604 (1978).

73. Transcript of trial at 503–05, included as part of the Record on Appeal in Dobbs, 963 F.2d 1403.

74. 408 U.S. 238, 257–306 (1972).

75. Transcript of Closing Argument, included as part of the Record on Appeal in Dobbs v. Zant, 963 F.2d 1403 (11th Cir. 1991).

76. A prosecutor is not allowed to make an argument that would diminish the jury's sense of responsibility for its life and death decision. See Caldwell v. Mississippi, 472 U.S. 320, 328–30 (1985).

77. Dobbs v. Zant, 963 F.2d 1403, 1407 (11th Cir. 1991), rev'd and remanded, 113 S. Ct. 835 (1993).

78. Id. at 1407–08.

79. Dobbs v. Zant, 113 S. Ct. 835 (1993) (per curiam).

80. Dobbs v. Zant, N.D. Ga. No. 4:80-cv-247-HLM (Order of July 29, 1994).

81. See CBS Drops Commentator, N.Y. Times, Jan. 17, 1988, at A1. See also Richard Harwood, Pressure from the 'Isms,' Wash. Post, Feb. 11, 1990, at C6; Racial Remarks Cost Dodger Official His Job, N.Y. Times, Apr. 9, 1987, at A1.

82. Peek v. Florida, 488 So. 2d 52, 56 (Fla. 1986).

83. Id.

84. Spencer v. State, 398 S.E.2d 179 (Ga. 1990), cert. denied, 500 U.S. 960 (1991).

85. Id. at 185.

86. Hance v. Zant, Super. Ct. of Butts Co., Ga., No. 93-V-172 (affidavits of juror Patricia LeMay & Gayle Lewis Daniels). See also Hance v. Zant, 696 F.2d 940 (11th Cir. 1983), cert. denied, 463 U.S. 1210 (1994) (Blackmun, J., dissenting from denial of certiorari); Bob Herbert, Mr. Hance's 'Perfect Punishment,' N.Y. Times, Mar. 27, 1994, at D17; Bob Herbert, Jury Room Injustice, N.Y. Times, Mar. 30, 1994, at A15.

87. Charlie Young, Curfew Davis, George Dungee, Terry Lee Goodwin, and Eddie Lee Ross were all referred to as "niggers" by their defense lawyers at some point in the trials during which they were sentenced to death. Transcript of Opening and Closing Arguments, Dungee v. Kemp, 778 F.2d 1482 (11th Cir 1985), decided sub nom. Isaacs v. Kemp, 778 F.2d 1482 (11th Cir. 1985), cert. denied, 476 U.S. 1164 (1986); Goodwin v. Balkcom, 684 F.2d 794, 805 n.13 (11th Cir. 1982). See also Ex parte Guzmon, 730 S.W.2d 724, 736 (Tex. Crim. App. 1987) (defense counsel referred to his own client, a Salvadoran man, as a "wetback" in front of all-white jury).

88. Edwards v. Scroggy, 849 F.2d 204, 207 (5th Cir. 1988).

89. Id.

90. Id. at 208.

91. Death Row USA, supra note 1 at 6.

92. Alabama v. Jefferson, Cir. Ct. Chambers County No. CC- 81–77 (Order of Oct. 2, 1992). One jury was for a hearing on Jefferson's mental competence to stand trial; another was for guilt; and the third was for sentencing. Id.

93. Alabama County Still Records Marriages by Race, Atlanta J. & Const., July 21, 1991, at A2.

94. Alabama v. Jefferson, Order of Oct. 2, 1992, supra note 92.

95. Id. The court held there were race-neutral reasons for each of the strikes of African-Americans.

96. Ga. Code Ann. §50-3-1 (Michie 1994).

97. 347 U.S. 483 (1954) (holding that racial segregation in the public schools violates the Equal Protection Clause); Brown v. Board of Education, 349 U.S. 294, 300 (1955) (requiring that desegregation of the public schools proceed "with all deliberate speed").

98. Coleman v. Miller, 885 F. Supp. 1561, 1569 (N.D. Ga. 1995). See also Julius Chambers, Protection of Civil Rights: A Constitutional Mandate for the Federal Government, 87 Mich. L. Rev. 1599, 1601 n.9 (1989).

99. Jim Auchmutey, Unraveling the Flag: A Guide to Rebel Colors, Atlanta J. & Const., Sept. 29, 1991, at M1, M8 (quoting state representative Denmark Groover). Governor Marvin Griffin delivered the same message of defiance during his State of the State address in 1956: "All attempts to mix the races whether they be in the classrooms, on the playgrounds, in public conveyances, [or] in any other area of close contact imperil the mores of the South." Mark Sherman, Pledging Allegiances at Flag Forum, Atlanta J. & Const., Jan. 29, 1993, at G1, G6.

100. Augustus v. School Board of Escambia County, 507 F.2d 152, 155 (5th Cir. 1975). As one court observed:

To some, [the flag] represents the undeniable fact that Georgia was a member of the Confederacy and did secede from the Union. The flag may also represent southern heritage, the old South, or values of independence. Undeniably, to others it represents white supremacy, rebellion, segregation, and discrimination. The court is not prepared to say that any of these perspectives are incorrect. The only thing that is clear is what the flag is not: a symbol of unity for Georgians. (Coleman, supra note 98, at 1569)

101. Curriden, supra note 58, at D1, D3.

102. See generally Paul Pinkham & Robin Lowenthal, Getting More Minorities Involved ... Fosters Respect for the System, Florida Times Union, Dec. 10, 1991, at A1.

103. Rene Lynch, Deciding Life or Death for O.C.'s Worst Murderers, L.A. Times, Feb. 23, 1994, at A1.

104. See supra notes 52–54 and accompanying text.

105. Rick Bragg, Two Crimes, Two Punishments, N.Y. Times, Jan. 22, 1995, at 1

(quoting Franklin Zimring, Director of the Earl Warren Legal Institute at the University of California at Berkeley).

106. Studies and cases documenting discriminatory practices by police against racial minorities are collected and discussed by Charles J. Ogletree, Does Race Matter in Criminal Prosecutions, Champion, July 1991, at 7, 10–12. Even before the notorious Rodney King case and the Mark Fuhrman tapes, there was concern about the racial attitudes of the police department in Los Angeles. See Los Angeles v. Lyons, 461 U.S. 95, 116 n.3 (1983) (Marshall, J., dissenting) (noting that although only 9% of the residents of Los Angeles are black males, they have accounted for 75% of the deaths resulting from chokeholds by police).

107. See, e.g., Carl Cannon, Abducted Girl Found Slain Near Her Columbus Home, Columbus Ga. Ledger-Enquirer, July 17, 1977, at 1 (describing search for missing white victim by police officers, "truckloads of Military Policemen, trained dogs, an Army helicopter, and troops of Boy Scouts").

108. For example, after an African-American youth disappeared in Columbus, Georgia, he was first reported missing. Later, his father was told a body had been found but it could not be identified because it was so badly decomposed. Two weeks later, the police told the father the body was definitely that of his son, who had been stabbed to death. Transcript of hearing held Sept. 1–14, 1991, Sept. 12, 1991, at 176–177, State v. Brooks, Indictment Nos. 3888, 54606, on appeal, 415 S.E.2d 903 (Super. Ct. of Muscogee Co., Ga. 1992) [hereinafter Hearing on Racial Discrimination].

109. Ex parte Haney, 603 So. 2d 412 (Ala. 1992); Walker v. State, 586 So. 2d 49 (Ala. Crim. App. 1991), after remand, 611 So. 2d 1133 (Ala. Crim. App. 1992).

110. Hearing on Racial Discrimination, supra note 108, Transcript of Sept. 12, 1991, at 67–69. The evidence is described in David Margolick, In Land of Death Penalty, Accusations of Racial Bias, N.Y. Times, July 10, 1991, at A1; and Death Penalty Info. Ctr., Chattahoochee Judicial District: The Buckle of the Death Belt 10 (1991).

111. Transcript of Hearing at 38, Davis v. Kemp, Super. Ct. of Butts Co., Ga., (1988) (No. 86-V-865) (testimony of James Isham, father of the victim).

112. Id.

113. Davis v. State, 340 S.E.2d 869, cert. denied, 479 U.S. 871 (1986).

114. Clint Claybrook, Slain Girl's Father Top Campaign Contributor, Columbus Ledger-Enquirer, Aug. 7, 1988, at B1.

115. Id.

116. See, e.g., Phil Gast, District Attorney Criticizes Court for Rejecting Sentence, Columbus Enquirer, Sept. 17, 1983 at A1, A2.

117. Hearing on Racial Discrimination, supra note 108, Transcript of Sept. 12, 1991, at 178, 184–85, 192–93, 197, 199–200.

118. See Defense Exhibit 1A, admitted at Hearing on Racial Discrimination, supra note 108.

119. See Report of the Governor's Commission on the Death Penalty: An Analysis of Capital Punishment in Maryland: 1978 to 1993 (Nov. 1993) at 91, 92, 119 (although Baltimore City has well over ten times as many murders as Baltimore County each year, of forty-one death sentences imposed in Maryland under its current death penalty statute, twenty-two were imposed in Baltimore County; of the fifteen death sentences in effect on June 30, 1993, all but four were from Baltimore County; only five death sentences were imposed in Baltimore City and only two of the sentences in effect on June 30, 1993, were from Baltimore City). The author is aware of seventeen death sentences imposed in Cobb County, Georgia, under the death penalty statute adopted by Georgia in 1973. This is among the highest number of death sentences for a Georgia county.

120. See Wainwright v. Witt, 469 U.S. 412 (1985); Witherspoon v. Illinois, 391 U.S. 510 (1968).

121. Lockhart v. McCree, 476 U.S. 162, 173 (1986).

122. 437 S.E.2d 463 (Ga. 1993).

123. Id. at 465.

124. 476 U.S. 79 (1986).

125. Lingo, 437 S.E.2d at 466–67.

126. Jackson v. Thigpen, 752 F. Supp. 1551, 1554 (N.D. Ala. 1990), rev'd in part and aff'd in part, sub nom. Jackson v. Herring, 42 F.3d 1350 (11th Cir. 1995).

127. Id. at 1555.

128. By the author's count, the death sentence has been imposed twenty-two times in the Chattahoochee Judicial Circuit, more than any other judicial circuit in Georgia. Four of those death sentences have been carried out. Three of the four persons executed were African-Americans.

129. Defense Exhibit 2A, admitted at Hearing on Racial Discrimination, supra note 108.

130. Id.

131. Joseph Mulligan and Jerome Bowden, both sentenced to death by all-white juries, have been executed. Death Row USA, supra note 1, at 5.

132. See Defense Exhibit 1A, admitted in Hearing on Racial Discrimination, supra note 108.

133. Id.

134. Hance v. Zant, 696 F.2d 940, 952 (11th Cir. 1983), cert. denied, 463 U.S. 1210 (1994).

135. Hearing on Racial Discrimination, supra note 108, Transcript of Sept. 12, 1991, at 144–46 (testimony of William J. Smith, the prosecutor in Hance).

136. Defense Exhibit 2A, admitted in Hearing on Racial Discrimination, supra note 108.

137. Hance was executed on March 31, 1994. Death Row USA, supra note 1, at 8.

138. By the author's count, eighteen persons were sentenced to death in the Ocmulgee Judicial Circuit between 1973 and 1995.

139. Charts showing most of the prosecutor's capital trials are included in Horton v. Zant, 941 F.2d 1449, 1468–70 (11th Cir. 1991), cert. denied, 117 L.Ed.2d 652 (1992). Two other capital cases were tried against white defendants before the prosecutor left office. Tharpe v. State, 416 S.E.2d 78 (Ga. 1992); Fugate v. State, 431 S.E.2d 104 (Ga. 1993).

140. Horton, 941 F.2d, at 1468–70.

141. Amadeo v. Zant, 486 U.S. 214 (1988).

142. Horton, 941 F.2d, at 1458.

143. Witherspoon v. Illinois, 391 U.S. 510, 519 (1968).

144. Id.

145. 476 U.S. 79 (1986).

146. Id. After years of criticism about the crippling and virtually impossible burden of proof established in Swain v. Alabama, 380 U.S. 202 (1965), the Supreme Court held that a prima facie case of racial discrimination could be established by disparate strikes against minority jurors in a particular case. Batson v. Kentucky, 476 U.S. 79 (1986). Swain had required the defendant to prove that the prosecutor struck black citizens "in case after case, whatever the circumstances, whatever the crime and whoever the defendant or the victim may be . . . with the result that no Negroes ever serve on petit juries." Swain, 380 U.S. at 223. Swain is discussed further in notes 225–28 and accompanying text.

147. See Batson, 476 U.S., at 98.

148. See, e.g., Mark Ballard, Gunning For A Judge; Houston's Lanford Blames DA's Office for His Downfall, Tex. Law., Apr. 13, 1992, at 1 (describing how Houston District Attorney John B. Holmes, unhappy with rulings by a Republican judge in two murder cases, helped cause the judge's defeat by running one of his assistants against the judge and causing congestion in his docket).

149. See Kenneth B. Nunn, Rights Held Hostage: Race, Ideology and the Peremptory Challenge, 28 Harv. C.R.-C.L. L. Rev. 63 (1993); Michael J. Raphael & Edward J. Ungvarsky, Excuses, Excuses: Neutral Explanations Under Batson v. Kentucky, 27 U. Mich. J.L. Ref. 229 (1993).

150. Peggy C. Davis, Popular Legal Culture: Law as Microaggression, 98 Yale L.J. 1559, 1571 (1989).

151. The psychological tendency of predominantly white decision makers to sympathize more with whites than blacks is described in Samuel H. Pillsbury, Emotional Justice: Moralizing the Passions of Criminal Punishment, 74 Cornell L. Rev. 655, 708 (1989); Francis C. Dane & Laurence S. Wrightsman, Effects of Defendants' and Victims' Characteristics on Jurors' Verdicts, in The Psychology of the Courtroom 104–06 (1982). The effect is particularly pronounced and results in the most severe sentences where the victim is of the same race and the defendant is of a race different from that of the jurors. Id. at 106.

152. Lingo v. State, 437 S.E.2d 463, 468 (Ga. 1993) (Sears-Collins, J., dissenting).

153. See supra notes 63–80 and accompanying text.

154. Dobbs v. Zant, 720 F. Supp. 1566, 1578 (N.D. Ga. 1989), aff'd, 963 F.2d 1403, 1407 (11th Cir. 1991), rev'd and remanded, 113 S. Ct. 835 (1993).

155. Any aspect of the life and background of the accused may be considered by the sentencer as a reason to impose a sentence less than death. See supra note 72. For a discussion of the special demands upon defense counsel in properly preparing for the defense of a capital trial, see Welsh S. White, Effective Assistance of Counsel in Capital Cases: The Evolving Standard of Care, 1993 U. Ill. L. Rev. 323 (1993). See also Gary Goodpaster, The Trial for Life: Effective Assistance of Counsel in Death Penalty Cases, 58 N.Y.U. L. Rev. 299, 303–04 (1983).

156. Jackson v. Thigpen, 752 F. Supp. 1551, 1555, 1556, 1562 (N.D. Ala. 1990), rev'd in part and aff'd in part, sub nom, Jackson v. Herring, 42 F.2d 1350 (11th Cir. 1995).

157. Declaration of Kim Antoinette Taylor, Sept. 30, 1991, filed in Wade v. Calderon, 29 F.3d 1312 (9th Cir. 1994), cert. denied, 130 L. Ed. 2d 802 (1995).

158. Penry v. Lynaugh, 492 U.S. 302, 319 (1989) (quoting California v. Brown, 479 U.S. 538, 545 (1987) (O'Connor, J., concurring)).

159. Erik Eckholm, Studies Find Death Penalty Often Tied to Victim's Race, N.Y. Times, Feb. 24, 1995, at A1; see also Bureau of Justice Statistics, U.S. Dep't of Justice, Sourcebook of Criminal Justice Statistics 1993, at 384, table 3.128 (Kathleen Maguire & Ann L. Pastore eds., 1993).

160. Death Row USA, supra note 1, at 3.

161. Gross & Mauro, supra note 15, at 43–44.

162. The studies are discussed extensively in Baldus et al., supra note 15; and in the Supreme Court's decision in McCleskey v. Kemp, 481 U.S. 279, 286–87 (1987); id. at 325–28 (Brennan, J., dissenting).

163. Baldus et al., supra note 15, at 149–57, 160–78, 311–40; McCleskey, 481 U.S. at 287.

164. Baldus et al., supra note 15, at 314–15; McCleskey, 481 U.S. at 286.

165. Baldus et al., supra note 15, at 316; McCleskey, 481 U.S. at 287.

166. Death Row USA, supra note 1, at 11–29.

167. Id. at 9.

168. Id.

169. Id. at 30.

170. Id. at 10.

171. U.S. General Accounting Office, Death Penalty Sentencing: Research Indicates Pattern of Racial Disparities 5 (Feb. 1990).

172. 481 U.S. 279 (1987).

173. Id. at 306.

174. Id. at 312.

175. Id. at 313.

176. Id. at 314–15.

177. McCleskey v. Kemp, 481 U.S. 279, 339 (1987) (Brennan, J., dissenting).

178. See infra notes 242–51 and accompanying text.

179. 21 U.S.C. s 848 (1988).

180. House Subcommittee, Racial Disparities in Federal Death Penalty Prosecutions, supra note 14, at 2.

181. Id.

182. Id.

183. Death Row USA, supra note 1 at 30.

184. See The Violent Crime Control and Law Enforcement Act of 1994, Pub. L. No. 103-322, 108 Stat. 1796 (1994). There is no reason to expect that the federal government will be more successful in preventing discrimination under the Violent Crime Control Act than it has been with the Anti-Drug Abuse Act.

185. 18 U.S.C. §848(o)(1) (1988).

186. The Racial Justice Act was adopted in a version of the crime bill that passed the House of Representatives in April 1994. See David Cole, Fear of Too Much Justice, Legal Times, May 9, 1994, at 26. However, due to opposition in the Senate, it was not included in the final bill reported by the conference committee and adopted by both the Senate and the House later in the summer.

187. See David Cole, Fear of Too Much Justice, supra note 186.

188. See, e.g., Castaneda v. Partida, 430 U.S. 482 (1977); Gibson v. Zant, 705 F.2d 1543 (11th Cir. 1983). Once it is shown that there is substantial underrepresentation, jury officials must demonstrate that it was not the result of discrimination.

189. Batson v. Kentucky, 476 U.S. 79 (1986).

190. See supra note 149.

191. See W. Fitzhugh Brundage, Lynchings in the New South; Georgia and Virginia, 1880–1930 (1993); see generally George C. Wright, Racial Violence in Kentucky (1990).

192. Norris v. Alabama, 294 U.S. 587, 592 (1935). Expert testimony established that the names of the six black citizens were added by the clerk at the direction of a jury commissioner. Id.

193. Id. at 593.

194. Id.

195. Norris was again sentenced to death. Dan T. Carter, supra note 35, at 370.

196. Amadeo v. Zant, 486 U.S. 214 (1988).

197. The Briley File, Fulton County Daily Rep., Nov. 7, 1994, at 1. The district attorney was not prosecuted for either racial discrimination or sexual harassment and was allowed to retire with a pension after twenty years in office. Id.

198. Vanleeward v. Rutledge, 369 F.2d 584 (5th Cir. 1966).

199. Peters v. Kiff, 407 U.S. 493, 505–07 (1972) (White, J., concurring).

200. Gates v. Zant, 863 F.2d 1492, 1498 (11th Cir.), rehearing denied, 880 F.2d 293, 293–97 (Clark, J., dissenting from denial of rehearing), cert. denied, 493 U.S. 945 (1989).

201. Challenge to the Petit Jury Array filed in State v. Brooks, Indictment No. 3888 (Nov. 1977), on appeal, 261 S.E.2d 379 (1979), vacated and remanded, 446 U.S.

961 (1980), on remand, 271 S.E.2d 172 (Ga. 1980), cert. denied, 451 U.S. 921 (1981), conviction and death sentence vacated sub nom. Brooks v. Kemp, 762 F.2d 1383 (11th Cir. 1985) (en banc), vacated and remanded, 478 U.S. 1016 (1986), decision adhered to on remand, 809 F.2d 700 (11th Cir. 1987) (en banc), cert. denied, 483 U.S. 1010 (1987).

202. Trial Judge's Report to the Georgia Supreme Court in State v. Brooks, supra note 201, at 6, §E(4).

203. Id.

204. See supra note 27.

205. Avery v. Georgia, 345 U.S. 559, 562 (1953).

206. Williams v. Georgia, 349 U.S. 375, 391 (1955).

207. Williams v. State, 88 S.E.2d 376, 377 (Ga. 1955), cert. denied, 350 U.S. 950 (1956).

208. Williams v. Georgia, 350 U.S. 950 (1956).

209. 347 U.S. 483 (1954); Brown v. Board of Education, 349 U.S. 294 (1955). See supra note 97.

210. Del Dickson, State Court Defiance and the Limits of Supreme Court Authority: Williams v. Georgia Revisited, 103 Yale L.J. 1423, 1425–26 (1994).

211. 398 F.2d 138 (8th Cir. 1968), vacated and remanded on other grounds, 398 U.S. 262 (1970).

212. Id. at 147.

213. 398 U.S. 262, 262 (1970). Michael Meltsner, Cruel and Unusual: The Supreme Court and Capital Punishment 163–67, 199–211 (1973).

214. 408 U.S. 238 (1972). See 408 U.S. at 257 (Douglas, J., concurring) (describing the statutes before the Court as "pregnant with discrimination"); id. at 310 (Stewart, J., concurring); id. at 364–65 (Marshall, J., concurring); id. at 389 n.12 (Burger, C.J., dissenting); id. at 449–50 (Powell, J., dissenting).

215. Id. at 364–65 (Stewart, J., concurring).

216. Id. at 310. Justice Douglas concluded there was an unacceptable risk of discrimination. Id. at 257.

217. As Justice Marshall pointed out in Furman, of the 455 persons executed for the crime of rape after the Justice Department began compiling statistics, 405 were African-Americans. Id. at 364.

218. 433 U.S. 584 (1977).

219. See, e.g., Thornton v. State, 449 S.E.2d 98 (Ga. 1994).

220. Isaacs v. State, 355 S.E.2d 644 (Ga. 1987), cert. denied, 497 U.S. 1032 (1990).

221. See id. (transcript of hearing on motion to recuse held Oct. 6–8, 1986).

222. See State v. Taylor, Mo. S. Ct. No. 74220 (Order of June 19, 1993); State v. Nunley, Mo. S. Ct. No. 76104 (Order of June 29, 1993) (both orders vacate the judgments in the two cases and remand for a new penalty hearing without opinion or further elaboration). The evidence of racial discrimination was presented in an evidentiary hearing before the Circuit Court of Jackson County, Missouri, in 1992.

223. Jefferson v. State, 645 So. 2d 313 (Ala. Crim. App. 1994).

224. Id.

225. 380 U.S. 202 (1965).

226. Id. at 203–04.

227. Id. at 223.

228. McCray v. New York, 461 U.S. 961, 964 (1983) (Marshall, J., dissenting from denial of certiorari).

229. 476 U.S. 79 (1986).

230. 481 U.S. 279 (1987).

231. Id. at 312.

232. Id. See supra notes 172–177 and accompanying text.

233. McCleskey, 481 U.S. at 292.

234. Id. at 296.

235. Id.

236. McCleskey v. Kemp, 481 U.S. 279, 308 (1987).

237. Id. at 327 (Brennan, J., dissenting).

238. Id. at 313.

239. Id. at 309.

240. 60 U.S. 393, 407 (1857) (holding that African-Americans were "altogether unfit to associate with the white race, either in social or political relations; and so far inferior, that they had no rights which the white man was bound to respect").

241. 163 U.S. 537, 552 (1896) (holding that "[i]f one race be inferior to the other socially, the Constitution of the United States cannot put them upon the same plane").

242. John C. Jeffries, Jr., Justice Lewis F. Powell, Jr.: A Biography 451 (1994).

243. Foster v. State, 614 So. 2d 455 (Fla. 1992), cert. denied, 114 S. Ct. 398 (1993).

244. Jones v. State, 440 S.E.2d 161 (Ga. 1994).

245. Affidavit of Darrell Green, introduced at hearing, Hill v. Zant, Super. Ct. of Butts Co., Ga., No. CV 85-105(RC), Tr. of Hearing of Dec. 9, 1990 at 39–42, 51–52, of Dec. 9, on appeal, 425 S.E.2d 858 (Ga. 1993), cert. denied, 114 S. Ct. 342 (1993). The extraordinary efforts of officials of Cobb County to keep African-Americans out of their community by refusing to join the Metropolitan Atlanta Rapid Transit Authority and other means is described in the affidavit of Brian Sherman, Ph.D., filed in Hill v. Zant.

246. See also Griffin v. Dugger, 874 F.2d 1397 (11th Cir. 1989), cert. denied, 493 U.S. 1051 (1990) (upholding denial of a hearing on racial discrimination).

247. Stephens v. State, No. S94A1854, 1995 WL 116292 (Ga. S. Ct. Mar. 17, 1995), withdrawn and superseded, Stephens v. State, 456 S.E.2d 560 (Ga. 1995).

248. Id.

249. Id.

250. Id.

251. Stephens v. State, 456 S.E.2d 560 (Ga. 1995); Emily Heller, Second

Thoughts on Second-Offense Law, Fulton County Daily Report, Apr. 3, 1995, at 1, 10.

252. Emily Heller, Racial Test Put to the Test, Fulton County Daily Report, Mar. 30, 1995, at 1, 5.

253. McCleskey v. Kemp, 481 U.S. 279, 309, 313 (1987).

254. Id. at 309 n.30.

255. See, e.g., Nipper v. Smith, 39 F.3d 1494 (11th Cir. 1994) (Mar. 2, 1995); League of United Latin American Citizens v. Clements, 999 F.2d 831 (5th Cir. 1993) (en banc), cert. denied, 114 S. Ct. 878 (1994).

256. See supra notes 92–95,122–129, and 149 and accompanying text.

257. For a discussion of the relationship of unconscious racism to the decisions in McCleskey v. Kemp, Turner v. Murray, and Batson v. Kentucky, see Sheri Lynn Johnson, Comment, Unconscious Racism and the Criminal Law, 73 Cornell L. Rev. 1016 (1988).

258. 476 U.S. 28 (1986).

259. Id. at 35.

260. Id. at 36.

261. The Supreme Court's decision in Turner gives trial judges discretion to limit the form and number of questions and even allows collective questioning of the jurors. Turner, 476 U.S. at 37.

262. Birt v. Montgomery, 725 F.2d 587, 598 n.25 (11th Cir. 1984), cert. denied, 469 U.S. 874 (1984).

263. Id. at 600–01.

264. Transcript of Hearing of Apr. 25–27, 1988, at 231, State v. Birt (Super. Ct. Jefferson Co., Ga. No. 2360, 1988). The lawyer was referring to Miranda v. Arizona, 384 U.S. 436 (1966), and Dred Scott v. Sandford, 60 U.S. 393 (1857). Dred Scott was not a criminal case.

265. See notes 198–203 and accompanying text. See also Barrow v. State, 236 S.E.2d 257, 259 (Ga. 1977) (defense attorney did not challenge underrepresentation of blacks on the jury because "he felt adverse community pressure would inure to him personally" if he did so); Goodwin v. Balkom, 684 F.2d 794, 806 (11th Cir. 1982) (discussing how lawyer's concerns over "community ostracism" not only inhibited his performance at trial, but "every facet of counsel's functions").

266. Blair v. Armontrout, 916 F.2d 1310, 1333, 1351–1352 (8th Cir. 1990) (Heaney, J., concurring in part and dissenting in part).

267. Id. at 1325 n.15.

268. Record at 593–94, State v. Pace, Cir. Court of Morgan County, Decatur, Alabama, No. CC-92-609 (Nov. 9, 1993).

269. Id.

270. 476 U.S. 28, 35 (1976).

271. McCleskey v. Kemp, 481 U.S. 279, 344 (1987) (Brennan, J., dissenting).

272. Richmond v. J. A. Croson Co, 488 U.S. 469, 552–53 (1989) (Marshall, J., dissenting).

273. See David C. Baldus et al., Reflections on the "Inevitability" of Racial Discrimination in Capital Sentencing and the "Impossibility" of Its Prevention, Detection and Correction, 51 Wash. & Lee L. Rev. 359 (1994); McCleskey, 481 U.S. at 367 (Stevens, J., dissenting) (expressing the view that the death penalty could be constitutionally imposed if limited to the upper range of cases where prosecutors consistently seek death and juries consistently impose it).

274. Callins v. Collins, 114 S. Ct. 1127 (1994) (Blackmun, J., dissenting from the denial of certiorari) (expressing the view that the death penalty is unconstitutional because of the racial disparities in its infliction); McCleskey v. Kemp, 481 U.S. 279, 367 (1987) (Stevens, J., dissenting) ("If society were indeed forced to choose between a racially discriminatory death penalty . . . and no death penalty at all, the choice mandated by the Constitution would be plain" since racial disparities influenced by race would flagrantly violate[ ] the Court's prior "insistence that capital punishment be imposed fairly, and with reasonable consistency, or not at all." (quoting Eddings v. Oklahoma, 455 U.S. 104, 112 (1982)); Godfrey v. Georgia, 446 U.S. 420, 442 (1980) (Marshall, J., concurring in judgment) ("the effort to eliminate arbitrariness in the infliction of that ultimate sanction is so plainly doomed to failure that it—and the death penalty—must be abandoned altogether").

275. McCleskey, 481 U.S. at 319.

276. See, e.g., Foster v. State, 614 So. 2d 455, 465–68 (Fla. 1992) (Barkett, J., dissenting) (suggesting a standard for analyzing claims of racial discrimination in the infliction of the death penalty under the equal protection clause of the Florida Constitution); Livingston v. State, 444 S.E.2d 748, 757–61 (Ga. 1994) (Benham, J., dissenting) (asserting that admission of victim impact evidence violates various provisions of the Georgia Constitution).

Chapter 8

The Rhetoric of Race in the "New Abolitionism"

Austin Sarat

It is tempting to pretend that minorities on death row share a fate in no way connected to our own, that our treatment of them sounds no echoes beyond the chambers in which they die. Such an illusion is ultimately corrosive, for the reverberations of injustice are not so easily confined. "The destinies of the two races in this country are indissolubly linked together," and the way in which we choose those who will die reveals the depth of moral commitment among the living.

—Justice William Brennan[1]

Introduction

More than thirty years ago, the United States Supreme Court's *Furman v. Georgia* decision ended one period of abolitionist activity and launched another.[2] It culminated an era in which many opponents of capital punishment seized on traditional abolitionist arguments to mount legal and political challenges to the death penalty.[3] At the same time, it gave birth to the era of what I have elsewhere called "the new abolitionism."[4] In both gestures, *Furman* put race at the center of the legal and political controversy surrounding capital punishment. Yet today the place of race as a factor in the new abolitionist era is in question.

Traditionally, opposition to the death penalty has been expressed in several guises. Some have opposed the death penalty in the name of the sanctity of life.[5] Even the most heinous criminals, so this argument goes, are entitled to be treated with dignity.[6] In this view, there is nothing that anyone can do to forfeit his or her "right to have rights."[7] Others have emphasized the moral horror, the "evil," of the state's willfully taking the lives of any of its citizens.[8] Still others believe that death as a punishment is always cruel and, as such, is incompatible with the Eighth Amendment prohibition of cruel and unusual punishment.[9]

Each of these arguments has been associated with, and is an expression of, humanist liberalism or political radicalism. Each represents a frontal assault on the simple and appealing retributivist rationale for capital punishment.[10] Each puts the opponents of the death penalty on the side of society's most despised and notorious criminals; to be against the death penalty one has had to defend the life of Sirhan Sirhan, John Gacey, or Timothy McVeigh, of cop killers and child murderers. Thus it is not surprising that although traditional abolitionist arguments have been raised repeatedly in philosophical commentary, political debate, and legal cases, none has ever carried the day in the debate about capital punishment in the United States.[11]

Nonetheless, in 1972, when the Supreme Court halted executions, many in the anti-capital-punishment movement saw it as the penultimate step in a long struggle to end state killing.[12] They were confident that the *Furman* opinions of Justices Brennan and Marshall, both of whom gave voice to traditional abolitionist sentiments, pointed the way toward an impending, judicially imposed abolition of capital punishment, and they carefully plotted the steps necessary to bring that result to fruition.[13] As Philip Kurland wrote at the time, "[O]ne role of the Constitution is to help the nation to become 'more civilized.' A society with the aspirations that ours so often asserts can't consistently with its goals, coldly and deliberately take the life of any human being no matter how reprehensible his past behavior. . . . [I]n the *Furman v. Georgia* decision the inevitable came to pass."[14] Jack Greenberg of the NAACP Legal Defense Fund expressed a similar understanding of the significance of *Furman* when he said, "[T]here will no longer be any more capital punishment in the United States."[15]

From the perspective of thirty years later, these predictions look quite naive as well as somewhat forlorn. As is now well known, after *Furman* something unexpected happened. Whereas in other Western nations the abolition of the death penalty was followed by a downturn in public interest and support for capital punishment,[16] in *Furman*'s wake a dramatic pro-capital-punishment backlash occurred. "State legislatures . . . quickly responded to the Court's decision, but instead of conducting a thorough reevaluation of the subject, they enacted whatever statutory revisions they perceived as correcting the constitutional flaws contained in pre-*Furman* capital laws."[17] Public reaction followed a similar pattern, "with a hostile response all over the country."[18] Thus, four years after *Furman*'s limited abolition of capital punishment, the Court, in *Gregg v. Georgia*, found that "it is now evident that a large proportion of American society continues to regard . . . [capital punishment] as an appropriate and necessary criminal sanction."[19] As a result, the Court held that "the punishment of death does not invariably violate the Constitution."[20]

Since the mid-1970s, the political and legal climate for abolition of the death penalty has grown more hostile. Proponents of capital punishment responded to *Furman* with a mean-spirited revisionism.[21] Procedural guarantees once thought minimally necessary to secure fairness and reliability in capital sentencing have been openly and enthusiastically jettisoned. American society has, until very recently, seemed even more impatient with the procedural niceties and delays attendant to what many now see as excessive scrupulousness in the handling of capital cases. What good is having the death penalty, so the refrain goes, if there are so few executions?[22] Blood must be let; lives must be turned into corpses; the charade of repeated appeals prolonging the lives of those on death row must be brought to an end. In response, numerous recent decisions of the Supreme Court have eroded, not enhanced, the procedural integrity of the death sentencing process.[23] Little did abolitionists realize that *Furman* would be the legal and political high-water mark of their efforts and that, more than a quarter century later, they would be still fighting to recapture the terrain that *Furman* opened up.

Even so, *Furman*, particularly the concurring opinions of Justices Douglas and Marshall, pointed the way toward a new strategy for abolitionists, changing the direction of their arguments away from these traditional approaches and toward "the new abolitionism." The plurality in *Furman* was not moved to halt the death penalty in the United States on the basis of a frontal assault on the morality or constitutionality of state killing. Instead, the plurality mobilized arguments grounded in due process and equal protection. They found the death penalty as then administered to be unconstitutional. *Furman* held that the death penalty "may not be imposed under sentencing procedures that create a substantial risk that the punishment will be inflicted in an arbitrary and capricious manner."[24]

Following *Furman,* abolitionists today argue against the death penalty not by claiming that it is immoral or cruel but by pointing out that it has not been, and cannot be, administered in a manner that is compatible with our legal system's fundamental commitments to fair and equal treatment.[25] They seek to provide opponents of capital punishment a position of political respectability while simultaneously allowing them to change the subject from the legitimacy of execution to the imperatives of due process. New abolitionist rhetoric enables those who oppose capital punishment to respond to the overwhelming political consensus in favor of death as a punishment;[26] they no longer have to take on that consensus frontally.

New abolitionists say that the most important issue in the debate about capital punishment is one of fairness, not one of sympathy for murderers. They position themselves as defenders of law itself, as legal conservatives. New abolitionists now concede that one can believe in the retribution- or deterrence-based rationalizations for the death penalty and yet still be against the death penalty; one can be as tough on crime as the next person yet still reject capital punishment. All that is required to generate opposition to execution is a commitment to the view that law's violence should be different from violence outside the law, as well as a belief that that difference could/should be rooted in the fairness and rationality of the violence that law does.

The questions I wish to address in this chapter involve the role of race in the public rhetoric of new abolitionism.[27] When and how do new abolitionists talk about race? How important a factor is race in their critique of capital punishment? Are they sensitive to the constitutive linkage of capital punishment and race, the ways that the use of state killing helps to demonize African-Americans and perpetuate a racial caste system?

Starting with *Furman,* I will examine four moments in the rhetorical development of the new abolitionism for what they reveal about the discourse of race in new abolitionist arguments. In so doing, I want to make several claims. First, arguments about race have been significant in the new abolitionism, though they are often subsumed under, or conjoined with, as they were in *Furman,* more general arguments about arbitrariness.[28] Second, even as evidence about racial discrimination in the application of the death penalty piles up,[29] the rhetorical center of abolitionist argument has come to focus less on race and more on claims of actual innocence.[30] The unreliability of the death penalty's administration, rather than its discriminatory effect, is today the most powerful ammunition in the abolitionist's rhetorical arsenal. Whereas discussion of race divides and polarizes, opposing wrongful conviction universalizes the conversation about capital punishment. One need have no fixed commitments about race to oppose executing the innocent. Thus the place of race in the new abolitionism is, I suggest, no longer certain.

Third, when new abolitionists do talk about race, they do so in a way that takes racial difference as a given, and they assume that the linkage of race and capital punishment is best seen through the lens of discrimination.[31] When race is brought into the discourse of the new abolitionism, it appears in a narrow guise. New abolitionists avoid, or ignore, the role of capital punishment in constituting racial difference itself, in demonizing blacks, and in contributing to the maintenance of a racial caste system.[32] The effect of this discursive tendency is to occlude somewhat the constitutive effects of capital punishment on race in the United States. Yet as Stuart Banner rightly notes,

> When we think about the death penalty, we think, in part, in race-tinged pictures—of black victims lynched by white mobs, of black defendants condemned by white juries, of slave codes and public hangings. For centuries capital punishment was, among other things, a method of racial control, particularly in the South but often in the North as well. These practices have almost entirely disappeared today, but they linger on in our memories, exerting their influence on the instinctive, pre-rational decision-making that drives most of the death penalty debate.[33]

For new abolitionists, the current challenge is twofold: to keep race at the center of their critique of capital punishment and, at the same time, to change the way they talk about the relationship of race and state killing. Criticism of capital punishment should focus on the work it does as a living embodiment of the legacy of lynching[34] and the system of white privilege that it expressed.[35] Abolition politics should, I contend, be linked to a deeper critique of race privilege in the United States.

The Rhetorical Origins of the "New Abolitionism"

If *Furman* was a bridge between traditional and new abolitionism, it was Justices Douglas and Marshall who gave the latter its first public announcement. Douglas used his *Furman* opinion to insist that the issue that the Court had to confront was not what state statutes authorizing capital punishment prescribed but, rather, "what may be done with the law in its application."[36] At the heart of his argument was a conception of cruelty focused not on the method of execution but, rather, on the manner through which the choice of who received the death penalty was made. He claimed that "the basic theme of equal protection is implicit in 'cruel and unusual' punishments."[37] The "desire for equality," Douglas wrote, "was reflected in the ban against 'cruel and unusual punishments' contained in the Eighth Amendment,"[38] and he noted that "a penalty should be considered 'unusually' imposed if it is administered arbitrarily or discriminatorily."[39]

Arbitrary or discriminatory application of the death penalty was, in Douglas's view, made possible by "a system of law and justice that leaves to the uncontrolled discretion of judges and juries the determination whether defendants . . . should die or be imprisoned. Under these laws no standards govern the selection of the penalty. People live or die," he continued, "dependent on the whim of one man or of 12."[40] These laws "enable" the selective application of capital punishment, and it was this selective application that was, for him, most worrisome.[41] Statutes that leave the decision on who lives and who dies to the unfettered discretion of judges or juries are "pregnant with discrimination."[42]

Douglas saw the issue of race and racial discrimination as crucial in determining whether the United States could impose death sentences in a way that did not undermine its basic commitments to fairness and equal treatment. "Prejudice" rather than rational judgment drove the administration of capital punishment.[43] Douglas found ample evidence that the death penalty was being applied "selectively to minorities whose numbers are few, who are outcasts of society, and who are unpopular, but whom society is willing to see suffer though it would not countenance general application of the same penalty across the board."[44]

Yet Douglas takes as a given the question of who is an outcast or how one becomes part of an outcast group. For him, the evil of capital punishment is found not in its contribution to the creation of outcasts on whom society can vent its pent up fears and rage.[45] The evil of capital punishment is its racial application not its racial impact, its disproportionate use against African-Americans not its disproportionate impact on America's racial culture.

Although much of his *Furman* opinion reiterated traditional abolitionist arguments, Justice Marshall emulated Douglas's new abolitionist stance as well as his way of conceptualizing the race–capital punishment linkage. Marshall's embrace of the new abolitionism, the abolitionism that pointed to deficiencies in the administration of capital punishment rather than in its philosophical or legal justifications, came as a strategic response to the fact that a majority of the population supported capital punishment. He argued that the public's support for capital punishment was grounded in ignorance or misinformation and that if people knew the facts about the death penalty they would reject it.[46] Crucial in this regard were three facts that Marshall treated as incontestable, namely, that "capital punishment is imposed discriminatorily against certain identifiable classes of people; that there is evidence that innocent people have been executed before their innocence can be proved; and the death penalty wreaks havoc with our entire criminal justice system."[47] These facts, he said, "would serve to convince even the most hesitant citizens to condemn death as a sanction."[48]

In this threefold critique of the death penalty system, Marshall laid the groundwork for the new abolitionism that would unfold with particular intensity in the 1990s. In his version, race played an important part in the story he thought needed to be told. Yet like Douglas's story, the story that Marshall offered about race in the death penalty was a limited one.

On race, Marshall, like Douglas, focused on disparate treatment of minority groups and on law's existing prohibitions against discrimination. He argued that giving "untrammeled" discretion to juries to decide on the death penalty was "an open invitation to discrimination."[49] Looking at the recent history of capital punishment reveals "that Negroes were executed far more often that whites in proportion to their percentage of the population. Studies indicate that while the higher rate of execution among Negroes is partially due to a higher rate of crime, there is evidence of racial discrimination."[50]

Turning from race to the potential for executing the innocent, Marshall noted that our system of proof in criminal cases is "not foolproof."[51] No matter "how careful courts are, the possibility of perjured testimony, mistaken or dishonest testimony, and human error remain all too real."[52] Finally, Marshall concluded that the death penalty " 'tends to distort the course of the criminal law.' "[53] It does so by sensationalizing trials and bedeviling "the administration of justice all the way down the line."[54] Putting this together with the facts about racial discrimination and the risk of executing the innocent, the "average citizen would . . . find it shocking to his conscience and sense of justice."[55]

After Furman: Race in New Abolitionist Rhetoric

Since Douglas and Marshall, there has been a steady development of new abolitionist rhetoric, but new abolitionists continue to talk about race in a manner that is quite continuous with the agenda set by Douglas and Marshall. Spurred by repeated statistical demonstrations of racial disparities in capital sentencing, by the DNA revolution and the release of large numbers of inmates from death row, and by vivid examples of prejudice, incompetence, and politicization in the death penalty process, new abolitionism has gained some traction.[56] It offers a vehicle through which citizens might give voice to concerns about capital punishment firmly anchored in the American mainstream. It has achieved some success in reversing the rhetorical field in the debate about capital punishment,[57] even though it has yet to make dramatic progress in ending the death penalty.

Harry Blackmun's Refusal to "Tinker with the Machinery of Death"

In February 1994, twenty years after *Furman*, Justice Harry Blackmun announced, "From this day forward I no longer shall tinker with the machinery of death."[58] The announcement marked a major milestone in the development of new abolitionist rhetoric and quickly became a touchstone to which new abolitionists would make regular recourse. His dramatic proclamation capped his own evolution from longtime supporter of the death penalty to tinkerer with various procedural schemes and devices designed to rationalize death sentences to outright abolitionist.

Twenty-two years before his abolitionist announcement, Blackmun dissented in *Furman v. Georgia*, refusing to join the majority of his colleagues in what he labeled the "legislative" act of finding execution, as then administered, cruel and unusual punishment.[59] Four years after *Furman*, he joined the majority in *Gregg v. Georgia*, deciding to reinstate the death penalty in the United States.[60] However, by the time of his abolitionist conversion, Blackmun had left a trail of judicial opinions moving gradually, but inexorably, away from this early embrace of death as a constitutionally legitimate punishment.[61] As a result, the denunciation of capital punishment that he offered in 1994 was as categorical as it was vivid—"I will no longer tinker with the machinery of death." It was most significant as a moment in the transformation of abolitionist politics, as an example of abolition as a kind of legal conservatism, and as an indicator of the anxiety that abolitionists seek to cultivate in the face of the continued popularity of the most dramatic instance of law's violence.

Blackmun's abolitionism was firmly rooted in the mainstream legal values of due process and equal protection. He did not reject the death penalty because of its violence, argue against its appropriateness as a response to heinous criminals, or criticize its futility as a tool in the war against crime. Instead, he shifted the rhetorical grounds.

Harkening back to *Furman*, as if rewriting his opinion in that case, he focused on the procedures through which death sentences were decided.[62] "[D]espite the efforts of the States and the courts," Blackmun noted, "to devise legal formulas and procedural rules . . . , the death penalty remains fraught with arbitrariness, discrimination, caprice, and mistake. . . . Experience has taught us that the constitutional goal of eliminating arbitrariness and discrimination from the administration of death . . . can never be achieved without compromising an equally essential component of fundamental fairness—individualized sentencing."[63]

For Blackmun, the post-*Furman* era was an experiment, an effort to devise ways of reconciling capital punishment and constitutional values. As he put it, "For more than 20 years I have endeavored—indeed, I have struggled—along with a majority of this Court, to develop procedural and substantive rules that would lend more than the mere appearance of fairness to the death penalty endeavor."[64] In *Callins* he announced the results of these efforts. "Rather than continue to coddle the Court's delusion that the desired level of fairness has been achieved and the need for regulation eviscerated, I feel morally and intellectually obligated simply to concede that the death penalty experiment has failed. It is virtually self-evident to me now that no combination of procedural rules or substantive regulations ever can save the death penalty from its inherent constitutional deficiencies."[65]

Two things stand out in Blackmun's argument. First, he acknowledges law's effort to purge death sentences of any taint of procedural irregularity. As he sees it, after *Furman* the death penalty is constitutional only if it *can be* administered in a manner compatible with the guarantees of due process and equal protection. Here Blackmun moves the debate away from the question of whether capital punishment is cruel or whether it can be reconciled with society's evolving standards of decency.

Second, Blackmun identified a Constitutional conundrum in which consistency and individualization—the twin commands of the Supreme

Court's post-*Furman* death penalty jurisprudence—could not be achieved simultaneously. As a result, Blackmun concluded that "the death penalty cannot be administered in accord with our Constitution."[66] Blackmun's language is unequivocal; after more than twenty years of effort, Blackmun said, in essence, "enough is enough."

Like Marshall and Douglas, Blackmun put race front and center in his critique of capital punishment and, like them, he framed the question of race as a question of discrimination, linking racial discrimination to the "arbitrariness inherent in the sentencer's discretion to afford mercy."[67] Two decades after *Furman*, Blackmun observed, echoing the arguments of Douglas and Marshall, "race continues to play a major role in determining who shall live and who shall die."[68] Calling *McCleskey v. Kemp* "a renowned example of racism infecting a capital-sentencing scheme,"[69] Blackmun chided the Supreme Court for turning its back on what he called "staggering evidence of racial prejudice infecting Georgia's capital-sentencing scheme" and suggested that there was no reason to believe that the problem of race prejudice documented in *McCleskey* is "unique to Georgia."[70]

Blackmun argued that under *Gregg*'s guided discretion formula, "the biases and prejudices that infect society . . . influence the determination of who is sentenced to death."[71] He said that "where a morally irrelevant—indeed, a repugnant—consideration plays a major role in the determination of who shall live and who shall die, it suggests that the continued enforcement of the death penalty . . . is deserving of a 'sober second thought.' "[72] The result of such a reconsideration, he suggested, should be recognition of "the fact that the death penalty cannot be administered in accord with our Constitution."[73]

The new abolitionism that Blackmun championed presents itself as a reluctant abolitionism, one rooted in an acknowledgment of the damage that capital punishment does to central legal values and to the legitimacy of the law itself. It finds its home in an embrace, not a critique, of those values. Those who love the law, in Blackmun's view, must hate the death penalty for the damage that it does to the object of that love. Arbitrariness, error, and discrimination could not, in his view, be disentangled. Following Marshall's trilogy, Blackmun concluded that nothing can "save" capital punishment, a conclusion spoken both from within history, as a report of the result of an "experiment," and also from an Archimedean point in which the failure of the death penalty is "self-evident" and permanent.

The American Bar Association: Race in the Call for a
Death Penalty Moratorium

Just three years to the month after Blackmun's dissent in *Callins*, the American Bar Association called for a complete moratorium on executions in the United States.[74] Taking us back to *Furman*'s condemnation of the death penalty as "then administered," the A.B.A. proclaimed that the death penalty as "currently administered" is not compatible with central values of our Constitution. Since *Furman,* the effort to produce a constitutionally acceptable death penalty has, in the view of the A.B.A., been to no avail. Thus the American Bar Association

> calls upon each jurisdiction that imposes capital punishment not to carry out the death penalty until the jurisdiction implements policies and procedures . . . intended to (1) ensure that death penalty cases are administered fairly and impartially, in accordance with due process, and (2) minimize the risk that innocent people may be executed.[75]

The language of the A.B.A. resolution, unlike Blackmun's language in *Callins,* seems conditional and contingent in its condemnation of death as a punishment. Even as it calls for a cessation of executions, it appears to hold out hope for a process of reform in which the death penalty can be brought within constitutionally acceptable norms. As if to leave little doubt of its intention, the A.B.A. resolution concluded by stating that the Association "takes no position on the death penalty."[76]

Yet the A.B.A. recommendation, whatever its explicit refusal to take a position on the ultimate question of the constitutionality of capital punishment, amounted to a call for the abolition, not merely the cessation, of capital punishment. It does the work of Blackmun's new abolition without his overt and categorical renunciation. If one takes seriously the conclusions of the report accompanying the A.B.A.'s recommendation, then the largest association of lawyers in the United States asked Americans to avert further damage to the law by ending the death penalty. In so doing, the A.B.A. provided a striking response to the continuing anxiety that attends law's embrace of the state's ultimate violence.[77] Just as rushing a fresh contingent of troops into a battle going badly may reinvigorate those grown weary even if ultimately it does not stem the tide, so too the A.B.A.'s action provided symbolic capital for the anti-death-penalty community, legitimation to the new abolitionism, and the basis for a nationwide moratorium movement.[78]

The A.B.A. report provides three reasons for its call for a moratorium on executions, each a crucial component of the new abolitionism.[79] First, is the failure of most states to guarantee competent counsel in capital cases. Because most states have no regular public defender systems, indigent capital defendants frequently are assigned a lawyer with no interest, or experience, in capital litigation.[80] The result often is incompetent defense lawyering, lawyering that has become all the more damaging in light of new rules requiring that defenses cannot be raised on appeal or in habeas proceedings if they are not raised, or if they are waived, at trial.[81] The A.B.A. itself calls for the appointment of "two experienced attorneys at each stage of a capital case."[82] Although, in theory, individual states could provide competent counsel in death cases, and although there is ample evidence to suggest the value of skilled lawyers in preventing the imposition of death sentences,[83] the political climate in the United States as it touches on the crime problem suggests that there is, in fact, little prospect for a widespread embrace of the A.B.A.'s call for competent counsel.

The second basis for the A.B.A.'s recommended moratorium is the erosion in postconviction protections for capital defendants. Even though the A.B.A. says that "the federal courts should consider claims that were not properly raised in state court if the reason for the default was counsel's ignorance or neglect and that a prisoner should be permitted to file a second or successive federal petition if it raises a new claim that undermines confidence in his or her guilt or the appropriateness of the death sentence,"[84] the direction of legal change has been, as I already have noted, in the opposite direction. Today courts in the United States are prepared to accept that some innocent people, or some defendants who do not deserve death, will be executed.[85] As Justice Rehnquist observed in *Herrera v. Collins*, " '[D]ue process does not require that every conceivable step be taken, at whatever cost, to eliminate the possibility of convicting an innocent person.' "[86]

And for Rehnquist what is true in the general run of criminal cases is also true in death cases. If a few errors are made, a few innocent lives taken, that is simply the price of a system that is able to execute anyone at all. In Rehnquist's view, finality in capital cases is more important than an extended, and extremely frustrating, quest for justice.[87] For him, and others like him, the apparent impotence of law, its inability to turn death sentences into executions, is more threatening to its legitimacy than a few erroneous, undeserved deaths at the hands of the state. The A.B.A. rejected this position, insisting that the risk of executing the innocent was a major and crippling defect in the system of state killing.

The third reason for the A.B.A.'s call for a moratorium was found in the "longstanding patterns of racial discrimination . . . in courts around the country,"[88] patterns of discrimination that have repeatedly been called to the attention of the judiciary and cited by anti-death-penalty lawyers as reasons that the death penalty violates the Fourteenth Amendment guarantee of equal protection. The A.B.A. report cited research showing that defendants are more likely to receive a death sentence if their victims are white rather than black,[89] and that in some jurisdictions African-Americans tend to receive the death penalty more than do white defendants.[90] The report called for the development of "effective mechanisms" to eliminate racial prejudice in capital cases, yet did not identify what such mechanisms would be.[91] Indeed, it is not clear that there are any such mechanisms.

The pernicious effects of race in capital sentencing are a function of the pervasiveness of racial prejudice throughout the society combined with the wide degree of discretion necessary to afford individualized justice in capital prosecutions and capital trials. Prosecutors with limited resources may be inclined to allocate resources to cases that attract the greatest public attention, which often means cases in which the victim is white and his/her assailant black. Participants in the legal system—whether white or black—demonize young black males, seeing them as more deserving of death as a punishment because of their perceived dangerousness.[92] These cultural effects may not be remediable. As Blackmun noted in *Callins,* "[W]e may not be capable of devising procedural or substantive rules to prevent the more subtle and often unconscious forms of racism from creeping into the system. . . . [D]iscrimination and arbitrariness could not be purged from the administration of capital punishment without sacrificing the equally essential component of fairness-individualized sentencing."[93]

What does all of this say about the meaning and significance of the A.B.A.'s recommendation? In my view, even though it appeared that the A.B.A. was still willing to tinker with the machinery of death, in fact, the A.B.A.'s indictment of the system of capital sentencing was pervasive and damning. No well-intentioned reformism can save that system. Taking its recommendation and report seriously reminds us that the post-*Furman* effort to rationalize death sentences has utterly failed; it has been replaced by a policy that favors execution while trimming away procedural protection for capital defendants. This situation only exacerbates the incompatibility of capital punishment and legality.

Like Douglas, Marshall, and Blackmun, the A.B.A. embraced the new abolitionism, eschewing a direct address to state violence and relying instead on an indirect, though nonetheless devastating, critique. Echoing Marshall's three-part critique, it spoke openly and directly about racial discrimination, advancing it as a bold fact the presence of which undermined the legitimacy of capital punishment. But, like its new abolitionist predecessors, it did not reverse its angle of vision to consider how the death penalty itself perpetuates prejudice, discrimination, and racial subordination.

George Ryan's Clemency

On January 11, 2003, Governor George Ryan of Illinois emptied that state's death row by exercising his clemency powers under the state constitution, first pardoning four condemned inmates and then commuting 167 condemned inmates' sentences in the broadest attack on the death penalty in decades.[94] Ryan's act was the single sharpest blow to capital punishment since the United States Supreme Court declared it unconstitutional in1972 with the result that approximately six hundred death sentences across the nation were reduced to life in prison. It was also a powerful expression of the new abolitionism, drawing its roots from Blackmun's *Callins* opinion.

Although he offered a complex explanation for his decision,[95] Governor Ryan drew particular attention to systemic problems afflicting the administration of the death penalty, what he called "the sorrowful condition of Illinois' death penalty system."[96] Speaking of the relative rarity of capital punishment, he said,

> There were more than 1000 murders last year in Illinois. There is no doubt that all murders are horrific and cruel. Yet, less than 2 percent of those murder defendants will receive the death penalty. Where is the fairness and equality in that? The death penalty in Illinois is not imposed fairly or uniformly because of the absence of standards for the 102 Illinois State Attorneys, who must decide whether to request the death sentence. Should geography be a factor in determining who gets the death sentence? I don't

think so but in Illinois it makes a difference. You are 5 times more likely to get a death sentence for first degree murder in the rural area of Illinois than you are in Cook County. Where is the justice and fairness in that, where is the proportionality?[97]

Where is the justice, fairness, and proportionality? Here Ryan firmly locates his critique of capital punishment in the rhetoric of the new abolitionism. "Our capital system," Ryan said, "is haunted by the demon of error, error in determining guilt, and error in determining who among the guilty deserves to die."[98] This is a stunning, though by now familiar, indictment of a system in which decisions about who gets the death penalty and who does not are made without reference to "objective standards." Ryan finds arbitrariness deeply enfolded in the operations of the death penalty system, pointing to the influence of irrelevant factors like geography and the fact that offenders committing the same acts end up with radically different sentences. Yet the issue that drew his most intense attention, and that marks the recent evolution of the new abolitionism, is the issue of actual innocence.[99]

Talking about the post-*Gregg* history of the death penalty in Illinois, Ryan said, "We had the dubious distinction of exonerating more men than we had executed. 13 men found innocent, 12 executed." He continued,

> As I reported yesterday, there is not a doubt in my mind that the number of innocent men freed from our Death Row (now) stands at 17. . . . That is an absolute embarrassment. 17 exonerated death row inmates is nothing short of a catastrophic failure. But the 13, now 17 men, is just the beginning of our sad arithmetic in prosecuting murder cases. During the time we have had capital punishment in Illinois, there were at least 33 other people wrongly convicted on murder charges and exonerated. Since we reinstated the death penalty there are also 93 people where our criminal justice system imposed the most severe sanction and later rescinded the sentence or even released them from custody because they were innocent. How many more cases of wrongful conviction have to occur before we can all agree that the system is broken?

Today it is the problem of wrongful convictions and the specter of executing the innocent that provides new abolitionists with their most potent rhetorical weapon and a springboard to other issues. Whereas Marshall's new abolitionist sentiments grouped three issues together, in Ryan's rhetoric, wrongful conviction, not race, became the central element. It is from this element that he moved to consider race:

> I started with this issue concerned about innocence, but once I studied, once I pondered what had become of our justice system, I came to care above all about fairness. Fairness is fundamental to the American system of justice and our way of life. . . . If the system was making so many errors in determining whether someone was guilty in the first place, how fairly and accurately was it determining which guilty defendants deserved to live and which deserved to die? What effect was race having? What effect was poverty having?[100]

In fact, Ryan had relatively little to say about race. Unlike Douglas, for whom race was central to the new abolition, or Marshall, Blackmun, and the A.B.A., for whom it was an equal and important part of a complex array of issues speaking to fairness in the administration of capital punishment, for Ryan it was a distinctly subsidiary concern. What he did say linked the concern about racial discrimination in capital punishment to "the great civil rights struggles of our time." And, he noted, "Our own study showed that juries were more likely to sentence to death if the victim were white than if the victim were black—three-and-a-half times more likely to be exact. We are not alone. Just this month Maryland released a study of their death penalty system and racial disparities exist there too."

Ryan's relative disinterest in race is, I believe, symptomatic of the status race in today's new abolitionist arguments. Yet in his rhetorical movement from the individual to the system and in his reference to the effect of race on state killing, Ryan inverts the logic of the Supreme Court's decision in *McCleskey v. Kemp.*[101] Presented with a wholesale challenge to Georgia's death penalty system, the Court refused to inquire into systemic problems that might undermine confidence in decisions at the "heart of the criminal justice system."[102] Unlike the Court, which refused to move from the particular to the general,[103] this is exactly what Ryan's commutation statement insists must be done.

Instead of a system finely geared to assigning punishment on the basis of a careful assessment of the nature of the crime and the blameworthiness of the offender, Ryan, quoting Justice Blackmun, concluded that " 'the death penalty remains fraught with arbitrariness, discrimination, caprice and mistake.' "[104] Staying with Blackmun, Ryan continued,

In 1994, near the end of his distinguished career on the Supreme Court of the United States, Justice Harry Blackmun wrote an influential dissent in the body of law on capital punishment. 20 years earlier he was part of the court that issued the landmark Furman decision. The Court decided that the death penalty statutes in use throughout the country were fraught with severe flaws that rendered them unconstitutional. Quite frankly, they were the same problems we see here in Illinois. . . . Because the Illinois death penalty system is arbitrary and capricious—and therefore immoral—I no longer shall tinker with the machinery of death.

With these words Ryan revisited and reinvigorated Furman's new abolitionism, only this time with race moved to the margins and wrongful conviction occupying pride of place in his distinctive new abolitionist rhetoric.

Conclusion

Over the course of thirty years, from Furman to Governor Ryan's mass commutation, there is both continuity and change in the place of race in new abolitionism's public rhetoric. Continuity comes in the ways race is conceptualized in that discourse. From Furman to Ryan, the problem of race in capital punishment is seen as a problem of discrimination, of failed fairness. This way of talking about race, I have argued, neglects the deeper, constitutive linkages of capital punishment and America's racially organized social system.

Change has been registered in the diminished importance of race in new abolitionist rhetoric. In this sense, Ryan's focus on wrongful conviction at the expense of race is, I suggest, not just a function of the particular history of the death penalty in the post-Gregg era in Illinois. It is symptomatic of a broader evolution in the new abolitionism. The rhetoric of race divides, creating anxieties, conveying accusations of prejudice that makes many uncomfortable. On the other hand, to say that it wrong to execute the innocent speaks, or so it seems, to a practice so repugnant as to transcend the usual political and ideological divides.

Franklin Zimring provides a useful explanation and overview of this change in new abolitionist rhetoric and what he calls "the explosive prominence of wrongful death sentences attained by the late 1990s . . . [and] the rise to centrality of questions of conviction of innocent defendants and the risk of wrongful execution."[105] In his view, "science, scandal, and politics" came together to produce this result. The science was, of course, DNA matching, which seemed to provide an absolutely reliable way of identifying perpetrators of certain crimes. As Zimring says, "[C]areful DNA work was acquiring a reputation as a gold standard for establishing guilt or innocence."[106] The scandals involved dramatic and well-publicized instances in which innocent persons were convicted and sentenced to death in the face of improper police or prosecutorial conduct, tainted testimony, or unreliable eyewitness identification. The cluster of cases of wrongful conviction suggested "that entire systems were malfunctioning."[107] Together, DNA and scandal provided the material out of which public officials could make political capital.

In this context race cannot compete. Racism and racial discrimination in criminal justice is hardly a new or dramatic story. Retelling it offers no immediate political benefit.[108] Moreover, to talk about racial discrimination in the death penalty is as often as not to talk about unfairness in the way we punish the *guilty* rather than the much more galvanizing cases of mistreatment of the *innocent.*

Today, new abolitionists face a twofold challenge. First, they must resist the temptation to further marginalize the discourse of race in their rhetoric and politics. They must do so because no critique of state killing in the United States is, or can be, adequate if it neglects or marginalizes race. And, at the same time, they must change the way they talk when they do talk about race, using the practices of capital punishment to highlight the role that the state has played, and continues to play, in the constitution of race relations.

Here I think Timothy Kaufman-Osborn gets it right when he says, "[A] critique of capital punishment in terms of the workings of prejudice is at best insufficient and at worst productive of a sort of inattentiveness that may simply reinforce the racial polity."[109] As Kaufman-Osborn puts it,

> Implementation of remedies that draw their sense from the fourteenth amendment and, more specifically, the equal protection clause requires a more complete rationalization of the liberal state, for example, through unambiguous demarcation of the law's method of killing from those employed by those whom the law punishes, as well as through unambiguous segregation of the official sphere from its unofficial counterpart. Such triumphs . . . are ambivalent at best insofar as they produce their own forms of blindness and amnesia, which then occlude more subtle ways through

which the racial polity in the United States is produced and sustained. A more promising route must first acknowledge that the administration of capital punishment in the United States, like the practice of lynching, is one of the state practices by means of which the racial polity is reproduced; second, offer a detailed analysis of the specific ways it contributes to this end, for example, by creating spaces for the underlaw to do its work under the cover of law; and, finally, ask how that work . . . is obscured by its . . . thoroughgoing institutionalization of the normative principles articulated by the liberal social contract.[110]

Whether new abolitionists can meet these challenges and do the work Kaufman-Osborn describes remains to be seen. If they cannot, then it may be time for opponents of capital punishment to seek a newer and different public rhetoric through which to make their case. If they can, then opposition to capital punishment may provide a particularly promising way to talk about some of the most profound and troubling injustices that today mark the American condition.

NOTES

1. *McCleskey v. Kemp Georgia,* 481 U.S. 279, 312.

2. *Furman v. Georgia,* 408 U.S. 405 (1972).

3. See Michael Meltsner, *Cruel and Unusual: The Supreme Court and Capital Punishment.* New York: Random House, 1973. Also Eric L. Muller, The Legal Defense Fund's Capital Punishment Campaign: The Distorting Influence of Death, 4 *Yale Law & Policy Review* (1985), 158.

4. Austin Sarat, *When the State Kills: Capital Punishment and the American Condition.* Princeton: Princeton University Press, 2001, chapter 9.

5. See Albert Camus and Arthur Koestler, *Reflections on the Guillotine.* Paris: Calman-Levy, 1958.

6. Hugo Adam Bedau, *Death Is Different: Studies in the Morality, Law, and Politics of Capital Punishment.* Boston: Northeastern University Press, 1987.

7. See *Furman,* 257, Justice Brennan concurring.

8. George Kateb, *The Inner Ocean: Individualism and Democratic Culture.* Ithaca: Cornell University Press, 1992, 191–192.

9. Bedau, *Death Is Different.*

10. For one example of the retributivist rationale, see Walter Berns, *For Capital Punishment: Crime and the Morality of the Death Penalty.* New York: Basic Books, 1979.

11. Franklin Zimring and Gordon Hawkins, *Capital Punishment and the American Agenda*. Cambridge: Cambridge University Press, 1986.

12. See, for example, Hugo Adam Bedau, "Challenging the Death Penalty," 9 *Harvard Civil Rights-Civil Liberties Law Review* (1974).

13. Stuart Banner, *The Death Penalty: An American History*. Cambridge: Harvard University Press, 2002, chapter 9.

14. Philip Kurland, "1971 Term: The Year of the Stewart-White Court," 1972 *Supreme Court Review* (1972), 296–297.

15. Quoted in Meltsner, *Cruel and Unusual*, 291.

16. Zimring and Hawkins, *Capital Punishment and the American Agenda*, chapters 1 and 2.

17. *Id.*, 41.

18. *Id.*, 42.

19. See *Gregg v. Georgia* 428 U.S. 153, 179 (1976).

20. *Id.*, 169.

21. See Lewis Powell, "Commentary: Capital Punishment," 102 *Harvard Law Review* (1989), 1035, 1038. For an illuminating discussion of this mean spirited revisionism, see Anthony Amsterdam, "Selling a Quick Fix for Boot Hill: The Myth of Justice Delayed in Death Cases," in *The Killing State: Capital Punishment in Law, Politics, and Culture*, Austin Sarat, ed., New York: Oxford University Press, 1998.

22. For an interesting argument about the execution rate, see Samuel Gross, "The Romance of Revenge: Capital Punishment in America," 13 *Studies in Law, Politics, and Society* (1993), 71.

23. For example, *Teague v. Lane*, 489 U.S. 288 (1989) and *Penry v. Lynaugh*, 492 U.S. 302 (1989).

24. Godfrey v. Georgia, 446 U.S. (1980), 420, 427.

25. See Austin Sarat, "Recapturing the Spirit of *Furman*: The American Bar Association and the New Abolitionist Politics," 61 *Law and Contemporary Problems* (1998), 5.

26. Phoebe Ellsworth and Samuel Gross, "Hardening of Attitudes; Americans' Views on the Death Penalty," 50 *Journal of Social Issues* (1994), 48. Also see Samuel R. Gross, Update: American Public Opinion on the Death Penalty—It's Getting Personal, 83 *Cornell Law. Review* (1998) 1448, and Jeffrey M. Jones, "Support for the Death Penalty Remains High at 74%: Slight Majority Prefers Death Penalty to Life Imprisonment as Punishment for Murder," *The Gallup Organization* (May 19, 2003), http://www.deathpenaltyinfo.org/article.php?scid=23&did=592.

27. According to Stuart Banner, "The emphasis on racial disparity is often more a rhetorical tactic than a substantive criticism. But it is a rhetorical tactic that plays very well, probably better than the straightforward moral argument against capital punishment, because it can draw on our collective memory of three

and a half centuries of American history." See Stuart Banner, "Traces of Slavery: Race and the Death Penalty in Historical Perspective," in Charles J. Ogletree, Jr., and Austin Sarat, eds., *From Lynch Mobs to the Killing State*, chapter 3, 107

28. As Banner notes, "[I]t was race that lurked beneath the Court's 1972 opinion in *Furman v. Georgia*, finding capital punishment unconstitutional." *Id.*, 108.

29. For example, David C. Baldus, George Woodworth, Catherine M. Grosso, and Aaron M. Christ, "Arbitrariness and Discrimination in the Administration of the Death Penalty: A Legal and Empirical Analysis of the Nebraska Experience (1973–1999)," 81 *Nebraska Law Review* (2002), 486; Glenn Pierce and Michael Radelet, "Race, Region, and Death Sentencing in Illinois, 1988–1997," 81 *Oregon Law Review* (2002), 39; and Raymond Paternoster et al., "An Empirical Analysis of Maryland's Death Sentencing System with Respect to the Influence of Race and Legal Jurisdiction" (January 2003), http://www.urhome.umd.edu/newsdesk/pdf/finalrep.pdf.

30. See Jim Dwyer, Peter Neufeld, and Barry Scheck, *Actual Innocence: Five Days to Execution and Other Dispatches from the Wrongly Convicted*. New York: Doubleday, 2000.

31. For an important critique of the antidiscrimination paradigm in the context of race, see Kimberlé Crenshaw, "Race, Reform, and Retrenchment: Transformation and Legitimation in Antidiscrimination Law," 101 *Harvard Law Review* (1988), 1331. Also Kimberlé Crenshaw, "Colorblind Dreams and Racial Nightmares: Reconfiguring Racism in the Post–Civil Rights Era," in Toni Morrison and Claudia Lacour, eds., *Birth of a Nationhood: Gaze, Script, and Spectacle in the O. J. Simpson Case*. New York: Random House, 1997.

32. For a analysis of the role of imprisonment in maintaining the racial caste system, see Loic Wacquant, "Deadly Symbiosis: Rethinking Race and Imprisonment in Twenty-First-Century America," *Boston Review* (April/May 2002) http://bostonreview.net/BR27.2/wacquant.html.

33. Banner, "Traces of Slavery," 97.

34. "The death penalty," declares Stephen Bright, director of the Southern Center for Human Rights, "is a direct descendant of lynching and other forms of racial violence and racial oppression in America." See Stephen Bright, "Discrimination, Death, and Denial: The Tolerance of Racial Discrimination in Infliction of the Death Penalty," *Santa Clara Law Review* 35 (1995), 439. For a different view of the relationship of lynching and capital punishment, see Timothy Kaufman-Osborn, "Capital Punishment as Legal Lynching," in Charles J. Ogletree, Jr., and Austin Sarat, eds., *From Lynch Mobs to the Killing State*. As Kaufman-Osborn argues, "[C]onflation of these two practices draws attention away from the ways that capital punishment, as now conducted in the United States, occludes what lynching accomplished all too well, i.e., its production of the color-coded bodies that are a crucial ingredient of the reproduction of racial subordination. The analogy to lynching, in other words, deflects inquiry from the means by which

the contemporary practice of capital punishment contributes to much the same end, but without provoking the outrage once incited by its extra-legal counterpart" (p. 23).

35. On white privilege, see Cheryl Harris, "Whiteness as Property," 106 *Harvard Law Review* (1993), 1707. As Benjamin Steiner says, "In other words, possessing white skin color (and thus disproportionately possessing middle or upper class status) has become a ubiquitous part of public understandings of and expectations for what, for example, it means to be hardworking, law-abiding, and or trustworthy. In short, as markers of white suburban privilege, one's skin color and material or social capital (e.g., cars, clothing, education) are in effect, prerequisite for dominant group membership." See Benjamin Steiner, "Death in 'Whiteface': Modern Race Minstrels, Death Penalty Judgments, and the Culture of American Apartheid,' in Charles J. Ogletree, Jr., and Austin Sarat, eds., *From Lynch Mobs to the Killing State*, 152.

36. See *Furman v. Georgia*, 242.

37. *Id.*, 249.

38. *Id.*, 255.

39. *Id.*, 249.

40. *Id.*, 253.

41. *Id.*, 255.

42. *Id.*, 259.

43. *Furman*, 249.

44. *Id.*, 245.

45. See William Connolly, "The Desire to Punish," in *The Ethos of Pluralization.* Minneapolis: University of Minnesota Press, 1995. See also George H. Mead, "The Psychology of Punitive Justice," 23 *American Journal of Sociology* (1917), 577, and Joseph E. Kennedy, "Monstrous Offenders and the Search for Solidarity Through Modern Punishment," 51 *Hastings Law Journal* (2000), 829.

46. *Id.*, 363. For a discussion and test of Marshall's hypothesis, see Austin Sarat and Neil Vidmar, "The Public and the Death Penalty: Testing the Marshall Hypothesis," 1976 *Wisconsin Law Review* (1976), 145.

47. *Id.*, 364.

48. *Furman*, 363–364.

49. *Id.*, 365.

50. *Id.*, 364.

51. *Id.*, 366.

52. *Id.*, 367.

53. *Id.*, 368.

54. *Id.*

55. *Id.*, 369.

56. Alan W. Clarke et al., "Executing the Innocent: The Next Step in the Marshall Hypothesis," 26 *N.Y.U. Review of Law & Social Change* (2001), 309.

57. As Wayne Logan notes, "For opponents of capital punishment, these would appear promising times. Not since 1972, when the Supreme Court invalidated the death penalty as then administered, has there been such palpable concern over its use." See Wayne Logan, "Casting New Light on an Old Subject: Death Penalty Abolitionism for a New Millennium," 100 *Michigan Law Review* (2002), 1336.

58. See *Callins v. Collins*, 510 US 1141 (1994).

59. *Furman*, Justice Blackmun dissenting.

60. *Gregg v. Georgia*, 428 U.S. 153 (1976).

61. See Jeffrey King, "Now Turn to the Left: The Changing Ideology of Justice Harry A. Blackmun," 33 *Houston Law Review* (1996), 297, 296. Also Randall Coyne, "Marking the Progress of a Humane Justice: Harry Blackmun's Death Penalty Epiphany," 43 *University of Kansas Law Review* (1995), 367.

62. See Carol Steiker and Jordan Steiker, "Sober Second Thoughts: Reflections on Two decades of Constitutional Regulation of Capital Punishment," 109 *Harvard Law Review* (1995), 355.

63. *Callins*, 1141.

64. *Id.*, 1130.

65. *Id.*

66. *Id.*, 1143.

67. *Id.*, 1153.

68. *Id.*

69. *Id.*, 1153.

70. *Id.*, 1154.

71. *Id.*, 1153.

72. *Id.*, 1156.

73. *Id.*

74. Recommendation 107, A.B.A. House of Delegates, February 3, 1997. The argument in this section is taken from Sarat, "Recapturing the Spirit of *Furman*."

75. Recommendation 107.

76. *Id.*

77. This anxiety arises because that violence, as both a linguistic and physical phenomenon, as fact and metaphor, is integral to the constitution of the modern state. See Austin Sarat and Thomas R. Kearns, "A Journey Through Forgetting: Toward a Jurisprudence of Violence," in *The Fate of Law*, Austin Sarat and Thomas R. Kearns, eds. Ann Arbor: University of Michigan Press, 1991. That state is built on representations of aggression, force, and disruption lurking just beyond its boundaries. In large measure, the state seeks to authorize and legitimate its bloodletting as a lesser or necessary evil and as a response to our inability to live a truly free life without external discipline and restraint. Yet the proximity of the modern state to, and its dependence on, violence raises a nagging question and a persistent doubt about whether it can ever be more than violence or whether the violence law condones, is truly different from, and superior to, what lurks beyond its

boundaries. Jacques Derrida, "The Force of Law: The 'Mystical Foundation of Authority,'" 11 *Cardozo Law Review* (1990), 921.

78. Jeffrey L. Kirchmeier, "Another Place Beyond Here: The Death Penalty Moratorium Movement in the United States," 73 *University of Colorado Law Review* (2002), 1.

79. The report and recommendation also called for a permanent halt to the execution of juveniles and the mentally retarded.

80. Stephen Bright, "Counsel for the Poor: The Death Sentence Not for the Worst Crime, But for the Worst Lawyer," 103 *Yale Law Journal* (1994), 1835.

81. Charlotte Holdman, "Is There Any *Habeas* Left in this *Corpus*?" 27 *Loyola University of Chicago Law Journal* (1996), 524.

82. *Report of the A.B.A. Submitted with Recommendations* 107, 5.

83. See Austin Sarat, "Speaking of Death: Narratives of Violence in Capital Trials," 27 *Law & Society Review* (1993), 19.

84. *Report*, 11.

85. See Michael Radelet et al., *In Spite of Innocence: Erroneous Convictions in Capital Cases*. Boston: Northeastern University Press, 1992.

86. See *Herrera v. Collins*, 113 S. Ct. 860 (1993).

87. *Id.*, 869.

88. *Report*, 13.

89. David Baldus, George Woodworth, and Charles Pulaski, *Equal Justice and the Death Penalty: A Legal and Empirical Analysis*. Boston: Northeastern University Press, 1990.

90. See Samuel Gross and Robert Mauro, *Death and Discrimination: Racial Disparities in Capital Sentences*. Boston: Northeastern University Press, 1989.

91. *Report*, 14.

92. Judith Butler, "Endangered/ Endangering: Schematic Racism and White Paranoia," in *Reading Rodney King/Reading Urban Uprising*, Robert Gooding-Williams, ed. New York: Routledge, 1993. Also Jerome G. Miller, *Search and Destroy: African-American Males in the Criminal Justice System*. Cambridge: Cambridge University Press, 1997.

93. *Callins*, 3549.

94. Ryan commuted 164 death sentences to life without parole. The previous day he pardoned four death row inmates. Another three inmates had their sentences shortened to forty-year terms.

95. See Austin Sarat and Nasser Hussain, "On Lawful Lawlessness: George Ryan, Executive Clemency, and the Rhetoric of Sparing Life," 56 *Stanford Law Review* (2004), 1307.

96. See Governor George Ryan, "I Must Act," January 11, 2003, 2. Speech at the Northwestern University College of Law. Found at http://www.deathpenaltyinfo.org/article.php?scid=13&did=551.

97. Ryan, "I Must Act," 6, 10.

98. *Id.*

99. See Richard A. Rosen, "Innocence and Death," 82 North Carolina Law Review (2003), 61.

100. Ryan, "I Must Act," 6.

101. *McCleskey v. Kemp,* 481 U.S. 279 (1987).

102. *Id.,* 281.

103. For a useful analysis of the implications of this refusal for our understanding of narrative and rhetoric, see Patricia Ewick and Susan Silbey, "Subversive Stories, Hegemonic Tales: Toward a Sociology of Narrative," 29 *Law & Society Review* (1995), 197, 215–216.

104. Ryan, "I Must Act," 3.

105. Franklin Zimring, *The Contradictions of American Capital Punishment.* New York: Oxford University Press, 2003, 159.

106. *Id.*

107. *Id.,* 160.

108. A poll conducted in 1997 reported that 49% of Americans believe blacks are more likely than whites to receive the death penalty for the same crime. Yet this fact did not appear to be significant as a factor in explaining why people support or oppose capital punishment. http://www.deathpenaltyinfo.org/article .php?scid=23&did=210#Time97.

In contrast, according to a recent Harris poll, "The replies to another question suggest that continuing news coverage of the convictions of apparently innocent defendants could well reduce support for the death penalty even more, but probably not reverse it. The majority in favor of capital punishment falls to 53% when people are asked what their position would be 'if you believed that a substantial number of innocent people are convicted of murder.' " http://www.harrisinterac-tive.com/harris_poll/index.asp?PID=101.

109. Kaufman-Osborn, "Capital Punishment as Legal Lynching," 30.

110. *Id.*

Contributors

Stuart Banner is Professor of Law at the University of California at Los Angeles, and author of *The Death Penalty: An American History* (Harvard University Press).

Stephen B. Bright is Director of the Southern Center for Human Rights in Atlanta. He has represented people facing the death penalty at trials, on appeal, and in postconviction review. He has taught courses on the death penalty and criminal law at the Harvard, Yale, and other law schools.

Benjamin Fleury-Steiner is Associate Professor of Sociology and Criminal Justice at the University of Delaware. He is author of *Jurors' Stories of Death: How America's Death Penalty Invests in Inequality* (University of Michigan Press).

Timothy V. Kaufman-Osborn is the Baker Ferguson Professor of Politics and Leadership at Whitman College. He is the author of *From Noose to Needle: Capital Punishment and the Late Liberal State* (University of Michigan Press) as well as other publications on the death penalty.

Mona Lynch is Associate Professor of Justice Studies at San José State University. She is currently writing a book-length manuscript that examines the relationship between Arizona's penal practices and the state's recent social, cultural, and political history.

Charles J. Ogletree, Jr., is the Jesse Climenko Professor of Law at Harvard Law School, and the Founding and Executive Director of the Charles Hamilton Houston Institute for Race and Justice. Professor Ogletree's publications include *All Deliberate Speed: Reflections on the First Half-Century of Brown v. Board of Education* (Norton) and, with Deborah Rhode, *Brown at 50: The Unfinished Legacy* (American Bar Association).

Glenn Pierce is Acting Director of the Institute for Security and Public Policy and Principal Research Scientist for the College of Criminal Justice at Northeastern University. His research on gun control, delivery in mental health services, status of children and families, domestic violence and violence protection, as well as other public policy topics has been published in several journals, including the *American Journal of Public Health, The Annals, Criminology,* and *American Journal of Psychiatry.*

Michael L. Radelet is Professor and Chair of the Department of Sociology at the University of Colorado. He is the author or coauthor of six books relating to capital punishment, including *Executing the Mentally Ill* (Sage) and *In Spite of Innocence* (Northeastern University Press).

Austin Sarat is the William Nelson Cromwell Professor of Jurisprudence and Political Science at Amherst College and Five College Fortieth Anniversary Professor. His publications include *When the State Kills: Capital Punishment and the American Condition* (Princeton University Press) and *Mercy on Trial: What It Means to Stop an Execution* (Princeton University Press).

Index

natory patterns, 55–56; Federal Death
Penalty Act (1994), 69–70; Fourteenth
Amendment, 2, 67; *Furman v. Georgia*,
62; Illinois, 118, 120–121, 137–138, 139,
140–142, 143; Kentucky, 3; lack of high-
quality data, 143–144; Marshall on, 62;
Maxwell v. Bishop, 2, 62; *McCleskey v.
Kemp*, 2, 6, 56, 63–64, 66, 87n92, 182,
236; new abolitionism, 272; Pennsylvania, 3; race-of-defendant disparities,
121; race-of-victim disparities, 56, 121;
Racial Justice Act (RJA), 4, 65–68,
89n108, 148n12; rape, 2; rejection of, 6;
relevancy of, 88n99; statistical significance, 147n7; Supreme Court, 2; validity of, 88n99, 88n100; "war of the
experts," 89n105
Steiner, Benjamin, 154, 281n35
Stereotypes. *See* Racial stereotypes
Stevens, John Paul: abolition of the death
penalty, 174; Amnesty International,
78; in *Atkins v. Virginia*, 174, 177n14; on
burdens of proof of discriminatory
intent, 76; on executing mentally
retarded defendants, 78; international
law, 78, 177n14; in *Johnson v. California*, 76; in *McCleskey v. Kemp*,
259n274; in *Thompson v. Oklahoma*, 78
Stewart, Potter, in *Furman v. Georgia*, 108,
234, 246n49
Storey, Tonnie, 42
Strain of Violence (Brown), 31
Strayhorn, Ivan, case of, 163–164
Stroud, George, 99
Subconscious racism: death sentencing,
11; Equal Protection, 90n120; *Turner v.
Murray*, 92n126
Subpersons, 24–25, 26, 28, 43
Sullivan, Thomas, 118
Super-capital punishment, 103–105
Supplemental Homicide Reports (SHR),
122, 127, 128, 147n8
Support for capital punishment: among
blacks, 52n39; among whites, 52n39;
deterrence, 2, 263; DNA testing,
177n15; domestic support in U.S.,

72–74, 262, 263; geographical disparities in, 52n39; *Gregg v. Georgia*, 262;
international support, 74–75; jettison-
ing of procedural safeguards, 262;
legitimacy of execution, 2–3; prejudice, 52n39, 188; pro-capital backlash
against *Furman v. Georgia*, 12–13,
261–262; race-of-defendant disparities
in death sentencing, 284n108; racial
stereotypes, 52n39; retribution, 2, 263;
the South, 52n39; in South Africa, 174
Supreme Court: death penalty jurisprudence, 80; Fifth Circuit Court of
Appeals, 6; first African-American
lawyers to plead a case, 59; international law, 5, 80; jury selection, 6; limitations on applying capital
punishment, 4–5; statistical evidence
of racial discrimination in death sentencing, 2; Texas Court of Criminal
Appeals, 5–6, 16n33
Swain v. Alabama: discriminatory intent,
253n146; *McCleskey v. Kemp*, 236; pre-
emptory challenges/strikes, 235; rejection of, 242

Tabbarok, Alexander, 177n15
Taney, Roger, on blacks, 57
Tarring and feathering, 27
Taylor, Kim, 227
Templeton, Jean M., 119–120
Tennessee: jury discretion, 100; lynching,
34, 83n23; public execution, 39; rape,
59, 101; Shelby Avengers, 34
Texas: adoption of electric chair, 212;
adoption of electrocution, 53n40;
black defendants/white victims, 6;
blacks executed for murder, 107; death
row inmates, 212, 243n10; exclusion of
blacks from juries, 6; execution,
176n10, 212, 243n10; hanging, 106;
Harris County, 212, 243n10; jurors'
stories, 176n10; Latino defendants,
176n10; legal lynching, 106; lynching,
29, 32, 35–36, 51n27, 58; number executed, 52n39; "Old Sparky," 212;

Printed in the United States
60641LVS00003B/88-99